Cruise Sh...

WILLIAM MA...

Overview
PRESS

Published by Overview Press Ltd
**MAYES HOUSE, VANSITTART ESTATE, ARTHUR ROAD,
WINDSOR, BERKS, ENGLAND, SL4 1SE**
TEL: +44 (0) 1753 620237 FAX: +44 (0) 1753 832430

the **leading** *guide to the cruise industry*

contents

Overview PRESS

ISBN: 0 954 7206 1 X
First published 2005

Front cover picture: QUEEN ELIZABETH 2 *(William Mayes)*

Frontispiece: The NORWAY on her long tow to the Far East *(FotoFlite)*

Back cover picture: ORIANA at Palma, Majorca *(William Mayes)*

Design by Miles Cowsill and Lily Publications Limited
        PO Box 33, Ramsey, Isle of Man, British Isles, IM99 4LP

Printed by Kristianstads Boktryckeri AB, Kristianstad, Sweden

Disclaimer: The publishers, the author and the shipping companies referred to herein accept no liability for any loss or damage caused by error or inaccuracy in the information published in this edition of Cruise Ships

the **leading** *guide to the cruise industry*
introduction

This is the first edition of what is intended to become a regular publication, detailing the cruise and passenger ship fleets of the world. Although future editions will give increased coverage as fresh information comes to hand, it is apparent that the coverage and detail included here by far surpasses the amount of information available from any other single source.

The idea for this book was first discussed aboard a ferry in the Irish Sea in June 2001. Little did we then know of the effect on the cruise industry of the events that were to take place just three months later on the other side of the Atlantic Ocean. Even now, almost four years later, the industry has still not fully recovered from the fallout, and prices are generally still below those immediately before 9/11. The cruise industry has undergone radical changes in the past few years and an astonishing number of older ships have gone for scrap.

In this book I have included all known ocean-going cruise ships (including as far as possible those laid-up), together with significant day cruise and coastal vessels with overnight accommodation serving Europe and North America. I have set a minimum standard of thirty passengers to be included for cargo operations that also carry passengers, but nowadays most of those ships carry fewer than twelve. That makes a total of more than 550 ships. As this book moves to future editions it is intended that the content will evolve to include coverage of other coastal ships, significant river and lake operations, and other freighters that take passengers.

A bibliography, showing information sources is included towards the back of this book, but special mention should be made of Sea-Web, the on-line ship register from Lloyds Register-Fairplay, without which this book might not have been completed, and would certainly have been significantly less comprehensive.

Grateful thanks are also due to Jonathan Boonzaier, shipping journalist, of Singapore, who filled many gaps in the information on ships and companies in the Far East and wrote several completely new entries about operators in that area, of whom I had been unaware.

Some of my good friends have been kind enough to allow the use of their pictures, enabling me to include a good mix of photographs, almost all previously unpublished. Several of the names credited in the photo captions will be familiar to the reader as notable maritime authors. In this way, it has been possible to include ships from many operators and almost all of the spheres of operation.

The text is as correct as it was possible to get it as at July 31, 2005.

William Mayes
Mayes House
Windsor
England
SL4 1SE

william.mayes@overviewpress.co.uk

the **leading** *guide to the cruise industry*

a guide to using this book

Criteria for Inclusion In compiling this book I have attempted to include all sea-going passenger ships listed as having overnight accommodation for more than 30 passengers. All roll-on roll-off vessels, regardless of their passenger capacity, have been excluded unless, at the time of compilation, the ship was in use exclusively as a cruise ship. Overnight passenger vessels that previously provided cabin accommodation, but which in their current roles (day cruise or gambling ships, generally) no longer do so are included within the ships in other roles section. A few of the more important river and canal operations are included, and this coverage will be expanded in future editions.

Order The companies and groups of companies are listed in alphabetical order in all sections. Note that the definite article and words meaning company do not count. Companies are listed under their popularly known names where these differ from their official names, although the official name is shown in the text. Where ships have numbers expressed as words forming part of their names, they are listed in numerical order. For example R TWO comes before R THREE.

Where companies are part of a larger grouping they are listed under the parent company, so Holland America Line appears under Carnival Corporation. There is a company index in addition to current and former ship name indices.

Company Information Some general company information and a little historical background are given here. Some of the smaller companies may only have some basic information in this section, but as this work progresses through new editions the detail will be expanded.

Address This is the location of the company's administrative headquarters.

Contact Details The telephone and fax numbers given are the contact numbers for the administration offices. These numbers are expressed in the form + (access code for international calls) followed by the country code and then the telephone number within the country, normally with the first digit omitted. So to call the British telephone number 01867 890900 from abroad the following would be dialled + 44 1867 890900. Any good travel agent should be able to contact the reservations department of any of these companies. With increasing use of the Internet and e-mail many companies now have these facilities. A good guess at a web-site address is often as fast as using a search engine. Most companies can be e-mailed through their websites so separate e-mail addresses are not given.

Areas Operated The areas of operation have been listed here. It is not always possible to tie particular ships to any one area, but where practical the area has been shown at the end of each ship history. In view of the recent upheavals in the travel industry, it is quite possible that further changes will have occurred after this edition closed for press.

Place Names All countries, cities and towns have been given the English version of their name most commonly used, unless the local version is now generally used by English speakers. Thus Antwerpen in Belgium is shown as Antwerp, but Livorno in Italy is referred to as such, not the English – Leghorn.

List of Vessels The layout is as follows:

Name	Gross Tons	Year Built	Service Speed (knots)	Prop. method Screws	Passenger Normal	Capacity Maximum	Crew Number	Length	Beam All in Metres	Draft	Flag

Gross Tonnage is now mainly listed under the 1969 convention, and is a measure of the volume of the ship. The tonnages used are generally those given by Lloyds Register, unless the author has reason to doubt those figures, in which case other sources have been used. In theory, all vessels laid down or significantly altered since 1982 should be measured under the 1969 convention, but this is not always the case. Where a tonnage figure is given which is not is accordance with the 1969 convention the entry is marked with a ‡.

Service Speed is generally that quoted by the company, and may be significantly less than the ship's top speed.

To convert to Feet from Metres
deviide . 3048

Celebrity Cruises' *Zenith* sailing from New York *(Theodore W Scull)*

Machinery and Screws Machinery types are shown as follows with the number of screws after the type code.

Gas Turbine	GT	Steam Reciprocating	SR
Gas Turbine with Electric Drive	GE	Diesel	D
Steam Turbine	ST	Diesel with Electric Drive	DE
Steam Turbine with Electric Drive	SE	Sail with Diesel Assistance	SD

A recent phenomenon has been the use of pod propulsion systems. These feature rotateable pods incorporating the propellers, and cut down on the need for separate directional thrusters. Pod technology is relatively new and ships incorporating this drive system have not been without technical difficulties. Ships with pods are indicated with a P.

Normal Passenger Capacity, **Maximum Passenger Capacity** and **Crew Numbers** are again those quoted by the company, where possible, or from other authoritative sources if these are considered more reliable.

Dimensions are given in metres to one decimal place. Length is overall length. Beam is moulded breadth, which may be less than the width of the ship above the hull. Draught is full load draught.

Flag (and country codes) used throughout this book are as follows.

AA	Aland Islands	GN	Grenada	NZ	New Zealand
AU	Australia	GR	Greece	NO	Norway
BA	Bahamas	GY	Germany	PA	Panama
BB	Barbados	HD	Honduras	PH	Philippines
BD	Bermuda	HK	Hong Kong	PL	Poland
BE	Belgium	IC	Iceland	PO	Portugal
BR	Brazil	ID	India	RU	Russia
BZ	Belize	IN	Indonesia	SA	South Africa
CA	Canada	IS	Israel	SI	Singapore
CH	China	IT	Italy	SK	South Korea
CI	Cayman Islands	JP	Japan	SP	Spain
CL	Chile	KE	Kerguelen Islands	SV	St Vincent &
CO	Cook Islands	LB	Liberia		Grenadines
CR	Croatia	LX	Luxembourg	SW	Sweden
CY	Cyprus	MA	Malta	TH	Thailand
DK	Denmark	MI	Marshall Islands	TR	Trinidad & Tobago
EC	Ecuador	MU	Mauritius	TU	Turkey
EG	Egypt	MV	Maldives	TV	Tuvalu
FA	Faroes	MX	Mexico	UK	United Kingdom
FI	Finland	MY	Malaysia	UR	Ukraine
FJ	Fiji	NA	Netherlands	US	United States
FP	French Polynesia		Antilles	VZ	Venezuela
FR	France	NI	Norwegian	WF	Wallis & Futuna
GE	Georgia		International		
GI	Gibraltar	NK	North Korea		
GL	Greenland	NL	Netherlands		

Ownership of many vessels is complicated. Some ships are owned by their operator or one of its associated companies, while others are chartered in and some are owned by banks and finance companies. Within this book ships are only listed as chartered if they are chartered from a company that is not part of the same group, as many ships are owned by one-ship companies within a group but operated by other group companies.

There are occasions when a ship appears more than once, under different operators. Examples of reasons why this happens are where a ship is to be transferred or sold part way through the currency of this book and, where the sale is already known about before the book closed for press or in a situation where a ship is chartered to different operators at different times of the year. Many ships are chartered f operator. I have tried to list these ships under the operator with whom they spend most time. One area where it has been particularly difficult to decide how to list the ships is the Arctic and Antarctic expedition ships, especially those owned by Russian companies, but marketed throughout the world by a number of tour operators. In all cases I have tried to present the information in the most logical and accessible way, but suggestions for future improvement will be welcomed.

Names of ships are shown in capitals throughout this book. Ship name derivations are given where known and relevant either to the sphere of operation or to the owner. Some of these derivations are continuations of earlier themes and are perhaps less relevant today than formerly, but serve to link the current operation with earlier history of the owner.

Acknowledgements

I would like to thank the following individuals without whose help this would have been a less good book.

Jonathan Boonzaier, Tony Cooke, Miles Cowsill, Egidio Ferrighi, Clive Harvey, John Hendy, Roger Hurford, Andy Kilk, Bill and Doreen Lawes, Willem van der Leek, David Littlejohn, Ben Lyons, Chris Mason, Paul Mason, John May, Brenda Mayes, Richard Mayes, Phil Neumann, Alan Ryszka-Onions, Bruce Peter, Gillian Ridgway, Richard Seville, Ted Scull, Philip Simons, Lizette van Tonder, David Trevor-Jones, Nick Widdows and John Wiseman.

American West's **Empress of the North** (*American West Steamboat Company*)

Princess Cruises' *Golden Princess* arriving in Southampton for the first time *(William Mayes)*

the **leading** *guide to the cruise industry*

a brief review of the cruise industry

Until the events of 11th September 2001, it would be fair to say that the cruise industry, although still on the rise, was facing a slowdown in the rate of growth, as evidenced by a number of major operators trying to delay future deliveries. It was apparent that in the short term it would be difficult to fill the number of beds coming online; but passenger shipping is not a short term industry as it has long lead times prior to delivery of new ships, and the vessels themselves have long working lives. The liners of the past have often lasted for 40 or more years as their roles have changed and they have been converted for cruising. It is not likely that many of the new ships of today will survive that long, but each of them should serve for at least 30 years.

Since 11th September 2001 there has been a significant change in the industry, and it is very difficult to predict for how long the effects will continue. The initial inability of passengers to travel by air to join ships was replaced by a reluctance to travel. This had a disastrous effect on some airlines and the first casualties in the cruising world were the companies that were already financially vulnerable. Renaissance Cruises was the first victim, filing for chapter 11 bankruptcy a few days after the attack on the World Trade Centre. The Renaissance fleet, in better times, would have had no trouble in finding buyers for the series of eight nearly new ships, but the bulk of the fleet, arrested at various locations worldwide, was bought by an investment group connected with the shipyard that had built them and put into lay-up to await better times. Fortunately all of these ships have now found work. There was an initial major knock-on effect at Alstom, the builder of these ships, as it emerged that it may have guaranteed various loans in connection with the Renaissance building programme.

The second casualty was American Classic Voyages, operators of the Delta Queen Steamboat Company, American Hawaii Cruises, United States Lines and American Classic Cruises. This company, too, had been reported to be in a weak financial condition, and with insurers starting to refuse passenger insurance cover for operator default (first with American Classic Voyages and later extended by some insurers to other operators) the end was pretty well inevitable. The company ceased to trade in mid-October 2001. A much-slimmed down phoenix has risen from these ashes, but even now some of the ships from this group, including two brand-new vessels remain in lay-up.

Owners of old liners and cruise ships, some of which had been laid up for many years finally realised that their ships were not going to be able to sail again, and sent them for scrap. A surprisingly large number of these never made it to the breakers torch, sinking en-route. Initially the scrappings were unconnected with the terrorism problem, but later withdrawals were accelerated as a result of it. But for these events, the COSTA RIVIERA may have seen another season with Costa and may then have been sold for a further period of service elsewhere. In the event, she was withdrawn at the end of the 2001 Mediterranean season and was sold for scrap soon afterwards. Other ships scrapped, although for other reasons, include Royal Olympic's ORPHEUS, through age, and Mediterranean Shipping Company owned (but not operated by them at the time) OCEAN GLORY 1, in disgrace following detention by the United Kingdom's Maritime and Coastguard Agency.

The trend towards new ships being bigger continues with the entry into service of further vessels in Royal Caribbean's Project Eagle class of 140,000 ton cruise ships, Princess' Grand class of 110,000 tonners and the similarly sized Destiny class for Carnival. Cunard, itself part of the Carnival empire, introduced the first new ocean liner to be built for more than 30 years, the 148,000 ton QUEEN MARY 2, at the time of writing the largest passenger ship ever built. However in 2006 she will be eclipsed in terms of size by the first of the new 'Ultra Voyager' class of ships currently under construction for Royal Caribbean. Star Cruises, the other member of the big three at the top of the cruise industry also has large ships on order, but currently nothing over 100,000 tons.

The three largest groups, Carnival, Royal Caribbean and Star Cruises control between them more than 125 mostly large cruise ships (including those on order). With the exception of Disney's two ships and two vessels under construction for MSC, they own the world's entire passenger fleet of ships over 75,000 tons. The latter company is reported to be close to ordering a pair of ships in excess of 100,000 tons, but this was still unconfirmed as this edition closed for press. Within the industry now we have fairly clear dividing lines between the various operators. At the top are the 'big three', catering generally for the mass-market in both standard and premium sectors, and to a small extent the luxury and expedition sectors. Then come the more exclusive operators such as Crystal Cruises, with small fleets of luxury ships, the small fleets of premium and upper standard ships, the lower end mass-market companies including Thompson and MSC, and finally the specialised operators of smaller expedition type ships and discovery cruises. It is difficult to see that in the future any of the companies outside the big three will either want or be able to operate big three cruise ships as they come to the end of their initial careers, so we are likely to be entering a period now in which large cruise ships will stay within their original owner-group until being retired and scrapped. This means that there will no longer be a natural source of suitable second-hand tonnage for most of the smaller operators, and the difficult decision will have to be made between buying new ships (a trend already under-way in some companies, but many others of them will not be able to afford to follow this path) or moving out of the cruise business altogether.

The *Jewel of the Seas* off St Peter Port, Guernsey *(William Mayes)*

A Mediterranean sunset aboard the **Oriana** *(William Mayes)*

Winter lay-up in Piraeus *(William Mayes)*

Fortunately, as there are still a few ships cascading from the major fleets, we are some time away from this situation, but it is likely that it will happen eventually.

Older ships have been much in the news recently. The UNITED STATES, the proud former flagship of a previous United States Lines and the fastest liner ever built, continues to deteriorate in a backwater. As time passes it becomes, sadly, very much less likely that anything constructive will ever happen to this ship, despite the recent purchase of this vessel by Norwegian Cruise Line. The operators of the QUEEN MARY in long Beach, California have recently filed for bankruptcy protection, putting the future operation of the ship in some doubt. The owners of the ROTTERDAM, the elegant former flagship of Holland America Line have also failed recently. That ship, currently undergoing asbestos removal in Gibraltar, has been saved as a new consortium has come forward to operate her in Rotterdam as an accommodation and exhibition ship. The WINDSOR CASTLE finally left Eleusis Bay, near Athens, after many years of lay-up in spring 2005, bound for Indian ship-breakers. Finally, the first ORIANA may not have recovered from her partial sinking as reports suggest that she is heading for Chinese breakers.

The demise of Royal Olympic Cruises was less of a surprise within the industry than was the total collapse of Festival Cruises and forced sale of its 6 ships. The fleets of both operators were quickly dispersed and most ships are already working for new owners in the Mediterranean. Mediterranean Shipping Cruises acquired both of Festival's new large ships, near sisters of some of MSC's own vessels. The void in Greek cruising created by the failure of ROC has now been partially filled by Louis Cruise Lines of Cyprus in the shape of its new subsidiary Louis Hellenic Cruises.

Consolidation continues, with the merger of the Carnival and P&O Princess companies to form the massive dual-listed Carnival Inc and Carnival plc. It is unlikely that any more major operators will find their way into this group, but there is always the chance of a smaller niche operator being acquired (or, indeed, disposed of).

In Europe cruise fares fell sharply in the wake of the September 11 attacks, but more recently have been firming up again. Industry estimates indicate that the fares are expected to regain early 2001 levels by the end of 2005. However, it is increasingly difficult to ascertain exactly what is the real price of most cruises within Europe, due to the astonishingly complicated discounting regime embraced by most operators. With opening discounts of 50% or more, it is clear that brochure prices are artificially inflated and in most cases totally unachievable.

All of the established markets are experiencing impressive growth in passenger numbers and many new areas of operation have come on stream in the past few years, notably dedicated ships for the markets of Spain and Brazil. The German market in particular has seen impressive growth with the establishment of new operators and the massive expansion of established company's such as Carnival's Aida Cruises.

The airliner, once the enemy of the passenger ship, is now its friend as it carries passengers to far flung destinations for cruising in distant waters, enabling itineraries during the off-peak season to become more adventurous, particularly for European based ships, which now venture to the Far East and South America quite separately from the series of World Cruises. There are now more large passenger ships around the world than there have ever been, and this number is increasing as the major operators start to order new ships again for this still fast-growing leisure market. We've still not seen the end of the race for the world's largest passenger ship as Carnival and Royal Caribbean continue to leapfrog over one another. The next few years should be very interesting.

Abercrombie & Kent's **Explorer II** at Calshot as the **Saga Pearl** *(William Mayes)*

Abou Merhi's **Orient Queen** laid up at Gibraltar as the **Bolero** *(William Mayes)*

the **leading** *guide to the cruise industry*

section I

ABERCROMBIE & KENT

The Company Abercrombie & Kent is a British tour operator specialising in luxury tours to exotic destinations, which was founded in 1962. The company also owns and operates the Nile cruise ships SUN BOAT III and SUN BOAT IV, and offers European river cruises in association with Travel Renaissance.

Chairman and Chief Executive Officer Geoffrey Kent **Managing Director** Redmond Walsh

Address St George's House, Ambrose Street, Cheltenham, Gloucestershire GL50 3LG England

Telephone +44 845 0700610 **Fax** +44 845 0700607

Website www.abercrombiekent.co.uk

Area operated Antarctica (also markets ships in the Galapagos Islands and Tahiti)

EXPLORER II	12231t	1996	16.0k	D2	362p	394p	157c	133.0m	20.0m	5.1m	BA

EXPLORER II was partially constructed by the Sudostroitelnyy Zavod Okean Shipyard (yard number 1) at Nikolaev in the Ukraine as the research vessel OKEAN. Her keel was laid in 1987 and she was launched in 1989 but not completed. She was purchased by V-Ships and towed to the Mariotti shipyard in Genoa for completion as a passenger ship. On completion in 1996 she was chartered to the Peninsular and Oriental Steam Navigation Company for use by Swan Hellenic Cruises, as a replacement for the smaller ORPHEUS, and given the name MINERVA. At the end of her charter in 2003, she was returned to V-Ships, who succeeded in setting two new charters for her. For the summer of 2003 she became the SAGA PEARL for the 'over 50' tour operator, Saga Holidays, and in the winter she took the name EXPLORER II for Abercrombie & Kent's expedition cruises. For summer 2004 she was operated by Saga again, reverting to her Saga name. In November 2004 she took up employment with Abercrombie & Kent, but for the summer of 2005 she will operate for Phoenix Reisen (q.v.) as the ALEXANDER VON HUMBOLDT on South American cruises.

ABOU MERHI LINES

The Company Abou Merhi Lines is a Lebanese registered ship owner operating a small fleet of vehicle carriers within Europe.

Address 3rd Floor, Atrium Building, Weygand & Maarad Streets, Beirut, Lebanon

Telephone +961 1 999 612 **Fax** +961 1 999 612

Website www.aboumerhilines.com

Area operated Eastern Mediterranean from Beirut

ORIENT QUEEN	15781t	1968	20.0k	D2	656p	928p	315c	160.1m	22.8m	6.7m	PA

ORIENT QUEEN was built by AG Weser Werk Seebeck (yard number 935) at Bremerhaven, Germany as the STARWARD for Kloster's Norwegian Caribbean Cruise Line. She spent the bulk of her career with NCCL cruising in the Caribbean. In 1995 she became the BOLERO following her sale to Festival Cruises. For Festival she initially cruised in the Mediterranean but was later chartered out to other operators, including Britain's First Choice in 2000 and the now defunct Spanish Cruise Line in 2001. Following the collapse of Festival Cruises in early 2004 she was laid up at Gibraltar. She was registered under the ownership of Cruise Elenora in February 2004 and renamed as the ORIENT QUEEN in November 2004 She commenced service in the Eastern Mediterranean in the summer of 2005 for Abou Merhi Lines.

ADVENTURE LIFE

The Company Adventure Life is a US based specialist travel operator whose principal destinations are Central and South America and Antarctica. The ships listed here all operate in Antarctica, but the company also markets yacht cruises in the Galapagos Islands, although those vessels are considered to be too small to qualify for inclusion in this book. The ships listed here are not all exclusive to Adventure Life and some are marketed by other tour operators around the world. The 'Professors' of Quark Expeditions (q.v.) and the 'Akademiks' of Peregrine Adventures (q.v.) are also marketed by Adventure Life.

President Brian Morgan

Address 1655 South 3rd West, Suite 1, Missoula, Montana, MT 59806, United States of America

Telephone +1 800 344 6118 **Fax** +1 406 541 2676

Website www.adventure-life.com

Area operated Antarctica, generally from Argentina between November and March

AKADEMIK SHOKALSKIY	1764t	1982	11.0k	D2	46p	46p	c	71.6m	12.8m	4.5m	RU
POLYARNYY PIONER	1764t	1985	11.0k	D2	54p	54p	c	71.6m	12.8m	4.5m	RU

AKADEMIK SHOKALSKIY was built by Oy Laivateollisuus Ab (yard number 343) at Turku, Finland for the Russian Hydrometeorological Institute. She was transferred to the Far Eastern Research Institute in 1994.

POLYARNYY PIONER is marketed by Adventure Life as the POLAR PIONEER. She was built by Oy Laivateollisuus Ab (yard number 342) at Turku, Finland as the AKADEMIK SHULEYKIN for the Russian Hydrometeorological Institute. She was transferred to the Arctic and Antarctic Research Institute in 1994 and to the Russian Government controlled Marine Service in 1997. In 2001 she was refitted as a polar expedition ship and renamed POLYARNYY PIONER.

AFRICAN SAFARI CLUB (STAR LINE CRUISES)

The Company African Safari Club is a long-established Swiss-owned travel company specialising in holidays in East Africa and cruises in the Indian Ocean.

Address Imperial House, 21-25 North Street, Bromley, Kent, England

Telephone UK only 0845 345 0014 **Fax** +44 208 466 0020

Website www.africansafariclub.com

Area operated East Africa and the Indian Ocean

ROYAL STAR	5067t	1956	15.5k	D2	248p	276p	125c	112.0m	15.5m	5.6m	BA

ROYAL STAR was built for the Italian liner and ferry operator Adriatica as the SAN GIORGIO by Cantieri Riunite dell'Adriatico (yard number 1813) at Trieste, Italy and was used on Mediterranean Sea passenger/cargo services from Venice and Trieste to Istanbul, Izmir and Piraeus. Sometimes these voyages were extended to call at Alexandria and other Eastern Mediterranean ports. In 1976 this elegant little ship was sold to the Greek Kavounides Group and converted for pure cruising in and around the Aegean Sea. She was rebuilt and renamed as the CITY OF ANDROS and operated under the Cycladic Cruises banner. In 1984 she passed to Ocean Cruise Lines, becoming the high-quality OCEAN ISLANDER. She then cruised in Europe in summer and in the Caribbean Sea in winter. Ocean Cruise Lines was sold to Paquet, the French cruise operator in 1990, but the OCEAN ISLANDER was sold to the African Safari Club, renamed ROYAL STAR and put to work in the Indian Ocean.

AMERICAN CANADIAN CARIBBEAN LINE

The Company American Canadian Caribbean Line was founded in 1966 by Captain Luther Blount to serve the demand for small ship cruising in American coastal waters. The ships are all shallow draft, have retractable wheelhouses to allow access to rivers that would otherwise be inaccessible, and are fitted with a bow ramp to allow direct disembarkation onto secluded beaches.

Management President Nancy Blount **Chairman and Chief Executive Officer** Luther H Blount

Address 461 Water Street, PO Box 368, Warren, Rhode Island, RI 02885, United States of America

Telephone +1 401 247 0955 **Fax** +1 401 247 2350

Website www.accl-smallships.com

Area operated Caribbean and Central America (winter), East Coast USA and Canada (summer)

GRANDE CARIBE	761t	1997	10.0k	D2	100p	100p	17c	55.6m	11.9m	2.0m	US
GRANDE MARINER	829t	1998	10.0k	D2	100p	100p	17c	56.0m	11.9m	1.9m	US
NIAGARA PRINCE	667t	1994	10.0k	D2	84p	94p	17c	53.0m	12.2m	2.0m	US

All three ships were built for the company by Blount Industries, Warren, Rhode Island, USA

Adventure Life's **Akademik Shokalskiy** *(William Mayes Collection)*

American Canadian Caribbean Line's **Niagara Prince** *(William Mayes Collection)*

AMERICAN CRUISE LINES

The Company American Cruise Lines was established in 2000.

Address 741 Boston Post Road, Suite 200, Guildford, Connecticut, CT 06437 United States of America

Telephone +1 203 453 6800

Website www.americancruiselines.com

Area operated East Coast USA from New England to Florida

AMERICAN EAGLE	1148t	2000	12.5k	D2	49p	49p	22c	51.2m	13.1m	2.0m		US
AMERICAN GLORY	1148t	2002	12.5k	D2	49p	49p	22c	51.2m	13.1m	2.0m		US
AMERICAN SPIRIT	c1200t	2004	k	D1	93p	93p		c	65.2m	13.9m		US

All three ships were built for the company by Chesapeake Shipbuilding, Salisbury, Maryland, USA.

AMERICAN WEST STEAMBOAT COMPANY

The Company American West Steamboat Company was established in 1995, with the new QUEEN OF THE WEST reintroducing sternwheeler cruising to the Columbia, Willamette and Snake Rivers after an absence of almost 80 years. The 2,000-mile long Columbia River is the second longest river in the USA and saw its first sternwheeler, the JENNIE CLARK, in 1855. The company is owned by Oregon Rail Holdings of Portland, Oregon.

Address 2101 Fourth Avenue, Suite 1150, Seattle, Washington, WA98121 United States of America

Telephone +1 206 292 9606 **Fax** +1 206 340 0975

Website www.columbiarivercruise.com

Area operated Columbia, Willamette and Snake Rivers and Alaska's Inside Passage

EMPRESS OF THE NORTH	3388t	2003	14.0k	DE2	235p	p		c	109.7m	16.4m	3.8m	US
QUEEN OF THE WEST	2115t	1994	11.0k	DE1	163p	p		c	67.5m	15.2m	2.1m	US

EMPRESS OF THE NORTH and **QUEEN OF THE WEST** were built at the Nichols Brothers Boat Builders Yard (yard numbers S142 and S110) at Freeland Washington State, USA.

ANEDIN LINE

The Company Rederi AB Allandia (Anedin Linjen), is a Swedish private sector company operating a single overnight cruise ship between Stockholm and Mariehamn on the Finnish Aland Islands. The company, whose trading name is thought to be a Swedish version of Onedin Line – the title of a popular British television drama series of the 1970's about a 19th century ship owner – had begun running this service in that decade using the chartered ACHILLEUS. Ownership of the company passed through a number of hands over the years, including Sally Line and Effjohn International.

Address Vasagatan 6, 11181 Stockholm, Sweden

Telephone +46 8 456 2200

Website www.anedinlinjen.com

Area operated 24 hour cruises from Stockholm, Sweden

BIRGER JARL	3564t	1953	15.0k	D1	300p	369p		c	99.7m	14.2m	4.9m	SW

BIRGER JARL was built under that name by Finnboda Varf (yard number 351) in Stockholm, Sweden as a steam powered ferry for Stockholms Rederi AB Svea for service on the routes from Stockholm to Helsinki and Turku. By 1973, when she was sold to Bore Line subsidiary Jakob Lines, she had been wearing the corporate livery of the Silja Line consortium for a number of years. Her new owner set her to work in the north of the Gulf of Bothnia and renamed her as the BORE NORD. In the following summer she operated cruises for Bore Line between Turku and Visby, Gotland. She later served as an accommodation ship at Stavanger, Norway. Her next move was to Mini Carriers, in 1977, for use on a new Baltic Sea service as the MINISEA; this service never materialised. In 1978 she was sold to the perhaps inappropriately named Caribbean Shipping Company of Panama as a replacement for the ACHILLEUS, referred to above. She began her new career under the name BALTIC STAR and a little later was re-engined with diesels. She has proved to be a very popular ship, despite the impressive tonnage against which she competes. In 2002, she reverted to her original name. Birger Jarl is said to have been the founder of what we now know as the city of Stockholm, in about 1250.

American Cruise Lines' **American Eagle** (American Cruise Lines)

American West's **Empress of the North** (American West Steamboat Company)

Anedin Line's **Birger Jarl** seen off Kapellskar as the **Baltic Star** (*William Mayes*)

Blue Dream's **TDI Karadeniz** in Istanbul while in service with TML (*Theodore W Scull*)

ANTARCTIC SHIPPING CORPORATION

The Company Antarctic Shipping Corporation is a Chilean company founded in 2003.

Address Office 904, Avenida Vitacura 2771, Santiago, Chile

Telephone +562 236 5360 **Fax** +562 236 5360

Website www.antarctic.cl

Area operated Antarctica and Patagonia

ANTARCTIC DREAM	1685t	1959	10.0k	D3	84p	84p	40c	82.0m	11.9m	4.6m	PA

ANTARCTIC DREAM was built by Haarlemsche Scheepsbouw (yard number 552) at Haarlem in the Netherlands as the PILOTO PARDO for the Chilean Navy. In 1998 she was sold to Paoa Naviera and renamed as the HOTU MATUA. She joined her current owner, Dreamright Investment in 2003 and adopted the name ANTARCTIC DREAM for her new cruise services.

ARCTIC UMIAQ LINE

The Company Arctic Umiaq Line is a Greenland Government owned company, which was founded in 1774 as the (in English) Royal Arctic Line and first started operating ships on its own account in 1797. In addition to the ships shown here, the company operates a number of passenger day ferries. The company operated under the rather long name of Government of the Kingdom of Denmark (Den Kongelige Gronlandske Handel Trafikkavdelingen) until 1986 and then became Greenland Trading (Gronlands Handel).

Administration Director Soren Andersen

Address PO Box 608, 3900 Nuuk, Greenland

Telephone +299 349900 **Fax** +299 349949

Website www.aul.gl

Area operated Cruises and passenger services on the west coast of Greenland

DISKO II	1211t	1992	13.0k	D1	58p	58p	15c	49.6m	11.0m	3.4m	GL
SARFAQ ITTUK	2118t	1992	13.0k	D1	104p	246p	21c	72.8m	11.3m	3.3m	GL
SARPIK ITTUK	2118t	1992	13.0k	D1	104p	246p	21c	72.8m	11.3m	3.3m	GL

DISKO II was built as the SAGGIT ITTUK for the local services of Royal Arctic Line (later restyled as Arctic Umiaq Line) within Greenland by the Orskov Shipyard (yard number 157) at Frederikshavn, Denmark. She was renamed as DISKO II in 2003.

SARFAQ ITTUK and **SARPIK ITTUK** were built by the Orskov Shipyard (yard numbers 156 and 159) in Frederikshavn, Denmark for the company. In 1999/2000 the ships were lengthened and modernised.

BIRKA CRUISES

The Company Birka Line is a Finnish (Aland Island) owner of ro-ro freighters that also operates two cruise ships on 22 hour duty free and party cruises from Stockholm. For a while the company owned the BIRKA QUEEN, built as the ROYAL VIKING SKY, but her operation was not totally successful and she was chartered to Princess Cruises as the GOLDEN PRINCESS before being sold to Star Cruises.

Address PO Box 175, Mariehamn, Aland Islands, AX 22101, Finland

Telephone +358 182 7027 **Fax** +358 181 5118

Website www.birka.se

Area operated 24 hour cruises from Stockholm, Sweden plus some longer Baltic Sea cruises

BIRKA PARADISE	34728t	2004	21.0k	D2	1468p	1800p	180c	176.9m	28.0m	6.6m	AA
BIRKA PRINCESS	22712t	1986	17.0k	D2	1118p	1537p	150c	142.9m	24.7m	6.0m	AA

BIRKA PARADISE was built by Aker Finnyards (yard number 442) at Rauma, Finland for Birka Line. She has been designed to attract a younger clientele than that usually associated with her fleet mate.

BIRKA PRINCESS was built by Valmet (yard number 321) at Helsinki, Finland for Birka Line. As built she had a garage for about 20 cars, but this was removed during her major refit in 1998.

Bora Bora Cruises' *Tu Moana* (Bora Bora Cruises)

BLUE DREAM SHIPPING

The Company Blue Dream Shipping is a Turkish-owned Maltese registered company founded in 2005 to acquire the TDI KARADENIZ from Turkish Maritime Lines as part of the Turkish Government privatisation scheme.

Area operated The Mediterranean coast of Turkey, the Black Sea and the Eastern Mediterranean

TDI KARADENIZ	4326t	1997	16.8k	D2	180p	180p	62c	93.0m	15.8m	3.9m	MA

TDI KARADENIZ was built by the Halic Shipyard (yard number 303) in Istanbul, Turkey as an overnight passenger vessel and cruise ship for Turkish Maritime Lines. Latterly she has operated summer cruising seasons in the Eastern Mediterranean. As part of the Turkish Government's privatisation policy, the ship was sold to her current owner in early 2005 and may be renamed in due course.

BLUE LAGOON CRUISES

The Company Blue Lagoon Cruises was founded in 1950 by New Zealander, Captain Trevor Withers, initially as a tuna boat charter business.

Management Chief Executive Officer Gerrard Harvet

Address PO Box 130, Lautoka, Fiji Islands

Telephone +679 666 1622 **Fax** +679 666 4098

Website www.bluelagooncruises.com

Area operated Fiji

FIJI PRINCESS	1258t	1998	15.0k	D2	68p	76p	20c	55.5m	15.0m	2.1m	FJ
LYCIANDA	‡385t	1984	12.0k	D2	42p	60p	16c	39.5m	7.8m	1.8m	FJ
MYSTIQUE PRINCESS	1533t	1996	11.5k	D2	72p	108p	24c	55.3m	12.5m	2.8m	FJ
NANUYA PRINCESS	394t	1988	11.0k	D2	50p	75p	18c	42.6m	8.5m	2.0m	FJ
YASAWA PRINCESS	917t	1985	11.0k	D2	64p	96p	20c	55.0m	11.0m	m	FJ

FIJI PRINCESS was built by Chantiers Navale (yard number B234) at Marseilles, France as the RIVAGE MARTINIQUE for Rivages Croisieres. She was renamed PEARL OF SEYCHELLES in 2001 and joined the fleet of her present owner in 2004 as the FIJI PRINCESS.

LYCIANDA was built for Blue Lagoon Cruises by Industrial & Marine Engineering (yard number 31) at Suva, Fiji.

MYSTIQUE PRINCESS was built by Astilleros Servicios Navales (yard number 111) at Valdivia, Chile for Blue Lagoon Cruises.

NANUYA PRINCESS and **YASAWA PRINCESS** were built by the Fiji Marine Shipyard & Slipways (yard numbers 84 and 81) at Suva, Fiji for the company.

BORA BORA CRUISES

The Company Bora Bora Cruises is a privately owned Tahitian company, founded in 2002 and operating two luxury yachts in the islands of French Polynesia.

Address PO Box 40186, Fare Tony-Vaiete, 98713 Papeete, Tahiti, French Polynesia

Telephone +689 544505 **Fax** +689 451065

Website www.boraboracruises.com

Area operated Tahiti and the Leeward Islands

TI'A MOANA	1697t	2003	14.0k	D2	60p	60p	37c	69.1m	13.8m	2.1m	FP
TU MOANA	1697t	2003	14.0k	D2	60p	60p	37c	69.1m	13.8m	2.1m	FP

TI'A MOANA and **TU MOANA** were built by Austal Ships (yard numbers 173 and 172) at Fremantle, Western Australia for the company. The names both mean 'to stand upright in the sea' and come from the Polynesian dialect of Tahiti.

Captain Cook's Explorer in Sydney Harbour *(Jonathan Boonzaier)*

Canodros' ***Galapagos Explorer II*** *(Ben Lyons)*

CANODROS

The Company Canodros SA is an Ecuador registered company operating a single ship within the Galapagos Islands.

Management General Manager Marco Pino Palacios

Address Urnabizacion Santa Leonor, Manzana 5, Solar No 10, Guayaquil, Ecuador

Telephone +593 4 228 5711 **Fax** +593 4 228 7561

Website www.canodros.com

Area operated Galapagos Islands

| GALAPAGOS EXPLORER II | 4077t | 1990 | 15.0k | D2 | 100p | 100p | 70c | 88.3m | 15.3m | 3.4m | EC |

GALAPAGOS EXPLORER II was built by Cantieri Navali Ferrari (yard number 45) at La Spezia, Italy as the RENAISSANCE THREE for Renaissance Cruises. She was purchased by her current owner in 1997, as a replacement for the GALAPAGOS EXPLORER.

CAPTAIN COOK CRUISES

The Company Captain Cook Cruises is an Australian family-owned business, established in the 1970's.

Management Chief Executive Officer Trevor Haworth

Address No 6 Jetty, Circular Quay, Sydney, New South Wales 2000, Australia

Telephone +61 2 9206 1122 **Fax** +61 2 9251 4725

Website www.captaincook.com.au

Area operated Great Barrier Reef, Murray River, Fiji and Sydney Harbour

CAPTAIN COOK'S EXPLORER	t		k		118p	118p	c	m	m	m	AU
MURRAY PRINCESS	c1500t	1986	6.0k	D1	120p	120p	c	67.0m	15.0m	1.2m	AU
REEF ENDEAVOUR	3125t	1996	11.5k	D2	150p	150p	c	73.6m	14.0m	3.7m	AU
REEF ESCAPE	1815t	1987	9.0k	D2	120p	120p	c	69.7m	13.5m	1.5m	AU

CAPTAIN COOK'S EXPLORER was built as the MURRAY EXPLORER. She operates occasional overnight and weekend cruises from Sydney.

MURRAY PRINCESS was built at Goolwa, Australia as a river cruise ship, and is currently operating in the Murray River.

REEF ENDEAVOUR was built at the Fiji Marine Shipyard & Slipways (yard number 920) at Suva, Fiji. She operates cruises to the Great Barrier Reef.

REEF ESCAPE was built by Carrington Slipways (yard number 182) at Newcastle, New South Wales, Australia and cruises in the Fiji Islands.

The company also operates the day sailing vessel SPIRIT OF THE PACIFIC in the Fiji Islands, and a fleet of nine day boats around Sydney Harbour.

CARNIVAL CORPORATION and CARNIVAL plc

The Company In 1972, entrepreneur Mr. Ted Arison purchased the 1960 built Canadian Pacific Steamships' transatlantic liner EMPRESS OF CANADA, renamed her MARDI GRAS, and began operating her on cruises from Miami. Arison had been involved in Norwegian Caribbean Lines, so was no stranger to the Caribbean cruise trade. Who, in 1972, could have foreseen that from these modest beginnings Carnival would, by the end of the century, have become the largest cruise-ship owning group in the world. This transformation has come about not only by building new ships, but also by means of an ambitious acquisition programme. Commencing with the purchase of Holland America Line in 1989, Seabourn in 1992, a 50% stake in Costa Crociere (Airtours had the other 50% and Carnival acquired just under 30% of Airtours) in 1997, Cunard in 1998 and finishing (to date) with the acquisition of the remaining 50% share in Costa Crociere in 2001. There was also the hard fought merger with P&O Princess Cruises in 2003 to form a dual listed company (on the London and New York stock exchanges). P&O Princess itself was a relatively new company, albeit with a long and impressive pedigree, having been formed as recently as the autumn of 2000 when P&O (The Peninsular and Oriental Steam Navigation Company) de-merged its cruising businesses. The operational name Carnival Corporation came into use in 1993. Where not operating for an international clientele the marketing area of each subsidiary is shown after the company name. The operating companies within the group are shown in alphabetical order, but the section headed 'structure' may be useful for viewing how this conglomerate developed.

Aida Cruises' **Aidacara** at Malaga (*William Mayes*)

Aida Cruises' **Aidavita** in Istanbul *(William Mayes)*

Chairman and Chief Executive Officer Micky Arison **Vice-Chairman and Chief Operating Officer** Howard Frank

Address Carnival Place, 3655 N.W. 87th Avenue, MIAMI, FL 33178 United States of America and Mountbatten House, Grosvenor Square, Southampton, SO15 2BF, England

Website www.carnivalplc.com or www.carnivalcorp.com

Structure: Holding Company Carnival Corporation Inc/ Carnival plc

Carnival Division		
	Carnival Cruise Lines	C
Holland America Division		
	Holland America Line	C
	Wind Star Cruises	C
Princess Division		
	Cunard Line	C
	Ocean Village	P
	P&O Cruises	P
	P&O Cruises Australia	P
	Princess Cruises	P
	Seabourn Cruise Line	C
	Swan Hellenic	P
Costa Division		
	Aida Cruises	P
	A'Rosa Cruises*	P
	Costa Crociere	C

C = Formerly part of Carnival Corporation P = Formerly part of P&O Princess Cruises

* A'Rosa Cruises ceased operating ocean cruise ships in 2004 and the river cruise operation was sold.

AIDA CRUISES (GERMANY)

The Company At the end of September 1999 it was announced that P&O and the German cruise operator Arkona Touristik had agreed to form a new company, Aida Cruises, to develop the German cruise market. The marketing of Aida Cruises, now part of the Costa reporting line, is aimed squarely at the younger, active German passenger who would normally have taken a premium quality, resort style holiday. With the demise of A'Rosa Cruises that organisation's single ocean cruise ship was transferred to Aida. Previously it had been intended that the A'Rosa brand would also operate the REGAL PRINCESS, but that ship has remained with Princess Cruises. On the transfer of control of Aida cruises from P&O Princess to Costa, the ships were re-registered to Italy. Germany is the world's third largest market for cruise passengers, justifying the recent order for a further trio of ships.

President Michael Thamm **Senior Vice President Operations** Michael Ungerer

Address Am Strande 3d, 18055 Rostock, Germany

Telephone +49 381 4440 **Fax** +49 381 444 8888

Website www.aida.de

Areas operated Mediterranean, Atlantic Isles, Scandinavia and the Caribbean

AIDAAURA	42289t	2003	19.4k	DE2	1262p	1582p	418c	203.2m	28.1m	6.2m	IT
AIDABLU	70210t	1990	19.5k	DE2	1664p	1792p	671c	245.1m	32.3m	7.9m	IT
AIDACARA	38531t	1996	21.0k	D2	1186p	1250p	370c	193.3m	27.6m	6.2m	IT
AIDAVITA	42289t	2002	19.4k	DE2	1262p	1582p	418c	203.2m	28.1m	6.2m	IT

AIDAAURA was built by the Aker MTW Yard (yard number 4) in Wismar, Germany for Aida Cruises. For the winter 2004/2005 she was based at Montego Bay, Jamaica and in the summer of 2005 she operated in the Mediterranean Sea, from Heraklion, Crete and Venice, Italy.

AIDABLU is one of the last pair of ships ordered by Sitmar Line in 1988 prior to that company being acquired by P&O. Built by Fincantieri (yard number 5839) at Monfalcone, Italy, she was delivered to Princess Cruises in 1990 as the CROWN PRINCESS. Princess employed her on a variety of itineraries including European cruises until the summer of 2002, when she was transferred within the Group to the newly formed A'Rosa Cruises of Germany, taking the name A'ROSA BLU. On the sale of A'Rosa's river cruise business in 2004, she was transferred to Aida Cruises and renamed as the AIDABLU. She operates in the Canary Islands, based at Tenerife in the winter months, and to Norway from Kiel in summer 2005.

AIDACARA was built by Kvaerner Masa Yards (yard number 1337) at Turku, Finland for Arkona Touristik of Germany as the AIDA. As a result of the financial difficulties of her owners, she was sold to Norwegian Cruise

Carnival Cruise Lines' **Carnival Glory** at St Thomas *(Andrew Kilk)*

Carnival Cruise Lines' **Fascination** at Southampton *(Alan Ryszka-Onions)*

Carnival Cruise Lines' **Carnival Legend** on her maiden voyage *(William Mayes)*

Carnival Cruise Lines' **Carnival Spirit** at Vancouver *(Andrew Kilk)*

Line in 1997, but chartered back. She was re-purchased by Arkona Touristik in 1999, and the operating company was restyled as Aida Cruises. The AIDA was renamed AIDACARA in 2001 in anticipation of the delivery of the first of the pair of ships under construction in Germany. Her summer 2005 Mediterranean cruises were based on Palma, Majorca, and those to the Baltic at Warnemunde, Germany.

AIDAVITA was built at Wismar in Germany by Aker MTW (yard number 3) for Aida Cruises. She was based in the Dominican Republic for winter 2004/2005 Caribbean cruises, and at Palma, Majorca for the summer of 2005.

Cruise ships on order

NEWBUILDING 1	68500t	2007	21.0k	DE2	2030p		p	c	249.0m	32.2m	7.3m	IT
NEWBUILDING 2	68500t	2008	21.0k	DE2	2030p		p	c	249.0m	32.2m	7.3m	IT
NEWBUILDING 3	68500t	2009	21.0k	DE2	2030p		p	c	249.0m	32.2m	7.3m	IT

NEWBUILDINGS 1, 2 and 3 were ordered from the Meyer Werft yard at Papenburg, Germany in 2004 and 2005.

CARNIVAL CRUISE LINES

The Company Carnival Cruise Lines began operations in 1972 with the MARDI GRAS (formerly the EMPRESS OF CANADA), an inauspicious start as she ran aground on her maiden voyage. Her former running mate on Canadian Pacific's transatlantic service, the EMPRESS OF BRITAIN, suitably renamed CARNIVALE, joined her at the end of 1975. A third ship, the S A VAAL of the South African Marine Corporation (earlier the TRANSVAAL CASTLE of the Union Castle Mail Steamship Company), renamed FESTIVALE, joined the fleet in 1977 following her closing the joint Union Castle/Safmarine service between Southampton and South Africa. The first new ship was ordered shortly afterwards, and entered service in January 1982 as the TROPICALE. All of these ships have now left the Carnival Cruise Lines fleet. The delivery of the TROPICALE, however, signalled the start of what has proved to be the most expansive passenger shipbuilding programme of the past 50 years, and by 1987 Carnival Cruise Lines was carrying more passengers than any other cruise line.

President Bob Dickinson

Address Carnival Place, 3655 N.W. 87th Avenue, Miami, FL 33178 United States of America

Telephone +1 305 5992600   **Fax** +1 305 4064779

Website www.carnival.com

Areas operated Caribbean, Mexico, Alaska, East Coast USA, Mediterranean

CARNIVAL CONQUEST	110239t	2002	22.5k	DE2	2974p	3783p	1170c	290.0m	35.5m	8.2m	PA
CARNIVAL DESTINY	101353t	1996	19.0k	DE2	2642p	3360p	1040c	272.2m	35.5m	8.2m	BA
CARNIVAL GLORY	110239t	2003	22.5k	DE2	2974p	3783p	1170c	290.0m	35.5m	8.2m	PA
CARNIVAL LEGEND	85942t	2002	22.0k	DEP2	2124p	2667p	930c	292.5m	32.2m	7.8m	PA
CARNIVAL LIBERTY	110239t	2005	22.5k	DE2	2974p	3783p	1170c	290.0m	35.5m	8.2m	PA
CARNIVAL MIRACLE	85942t	2003	22.0k	DEP2	2124p	2680p	930c	292.5m	32.2m	8.0m	PA
CARNIVAL PRIDE	85920t	2001	22.0k	DEP2	2124p	2680p	930c	292.5m	32.2m	7.8m	PA
CARNIVAL SPIRIT	85920t	2001	22.0k	DEP2	2124p	2680p	930c	292.5m	32.2m	7.8m	PA
CARNIVAL TRIUMPH	101509t	1999	19.0k	DE2	2758p	3360p	1040c	272.2m	35.5m	8.2m	BA
CARNIVAL VALOR	110239t	2004	22.5k	DE2	2974p	3783p	1170c	290.0m	35.5m	8.2m	PA
CARNIVAL VICTORY	101509t	2000	19.0k	DE2	2758p	3360p	1040c	272.2m	35.5m	8.2m	PA
CELEBRATION	47262t	1987	21.5k	D2	1486p	1896p	670c	223.3m	28.0m	7.6m	PA
ECSTASY	70367t	1991	19.5k	DE2	2040p	2634p	920c	260.8m	31.5m	7.8m	PA
ELATION	70390t	1998	19.5k	DEP2	2040p	2634p	920c	260.8m	31.5m	7.8m	PA
FANTASY	70367t	1990	19.5k	DE2	2040p	2634p	920c	260.8m	31.5m	8.0m	PA
FASCINATION	70367t	1994	19.5k	DE2	2040p	2594p	920c	260.8m	31.5m	7.8m	BA
HOLIDAY	46052t	1985	21.5k	D2	1452p	1800p	660c	221.6m	28.0m	7.5m	BA
IMAGINATION	70367t	1995	19.5k	DE2	2040p	2634p	920c	260.8m	31.5m	7.8m	BA
INSPIRATION	70367t	1996	19.5k	DE2	2040p	2634p	920c	260.8m	31.5m	7.8m	BA
PARADISE	70390t	1998	19.5k	DEP2	2040p	2594p	920c	260.8m	31.5m	7.8m	PA
SENSATION	70367t	1993	19.5k	DE2	2040p	2634p	920c	260.8m	31.5m	7.8m	BA

CARNIVAL CONQUEST was built by Fincantieri (yard number 6057) at Monfalcone, Italy. She sails year-round on a 7-day Western Caribbean itinerary, based on New Orleans.

CARNIVAL DESTINY was Carnival Cruise Lines' first 100,000+ gross ton cruise ship. At the time of her delivery by Fincantieri's Monfalcone, Italy yard (yard number 5941) in 1996 she was the largest passenger ship ever built. She operates 7-day Southern Caribbean cruises from Aruba, Barbados and San Juan, Puerto Rico. She also operates shorter cruises in the same area ranging from 2 to 5 days.

Carnival Cruise Lines' **Holiday** *(Andrew Kilk)*

Costa Cruises' **Costa Atlantica** in Venice *(Egidio Ferrighi)*

CARNIVAL GLORY is another product of the Monfalcone, Italy shipyard of Fincantieri (yard number 6059). She undertakes alternate 7-day Eastern and Western Caribbean itineraries from Port Canaveral, Florida.

CARNIVAL LEGEND was delivered in 2002 by Kvaerner Masa Yards (yard number 501) at Helsinki, Finland, as the third of the 'Spirit' class for Caribbean cruising. She was the first Carnival ship to cruise in Europe as she undertook a number of voyages from Harwich, England prior to heading for New York. Her itinerary then became 8-day Southern or Western Caribbean cruises from Miami, Florida. She now operates 8-day Eastern Caribbean from New York and 8-day Southern Caribbean from Fort Lauderdale.

CARNIVAL LIBERTY was built by Fincantieri (yard number 6111) at Monfalcone, Italy. She starts the summer of 2005 in the Mediterranean, based at Civitavecchia, Italy, and later transfers to Fort Lauderdale for a variety of Eastern and Western Caribbean itineraries. She returns to Europe in 2006.

CARNIVAL MIRACLE currently operates 7-day Western Caribbean cruises from Tampa, Florida. She was built by Kvaerner Masa Yards (yard number 503) in Helsinki, Finland.

CARNIVAL PRIDE is the second of the 'Spirit' class ships and was delivered by the Helsinki, Finland shipyard of Kvaerner Masa Yards (yard number 500) at the end of 2001 for alternate 7-day Eastern and Western Caribbean cruising based at Port Canaveral, Florida. She now operates on an itinerary to the Mexican Riviera from Los Angeles.

CARNIVAL SPIRIT is the name-ship of the 'Spirit' class. When delivered by Kvaerner Masa Yards (yard number 499) of Helsinki, Finland in 2001, she became Carnival Cruise Lines' first ship to serve the Alaska and Hawaii markets. She also cruises the Mexican Riviera from San Diego.

CARNIVAL TRIUMPH was built by Fincantieri (yard number 5979) at Monfalcone, Italy and delivered in 1999, as the second ship in the 'Destiny' class. She operates 7-day Eastern and Western Caribbean cruises from Miami and Canadian itineraries from New York.

CARNIVAL VALOR was built by Fincantieri (yard number 6082) at Monfalcone, Italy. She operates on 7-day Eastern and Western Caribbean cruises from Miami.

CARNIVAL VICTORY is the third member of the 'Destiny' class, built by Fincantieri (yard number 6045) at Monfalcone, Italy and was delivered in 2000. She cruises alternate 7-day Eastern and Western itineraries based in Miami.

CELEBRATION was built by Kockums (yard number 597), at their Malmo, Sweden shipyard. She was delivered in 1987 for her owners' Caribbean cruising operation. In 1989 the CELEBRATION collided with, and sank, the Cuban vessel CAPITAN SAN LOUIS but sustained only minor damage herself. Now one of the two oldest units in the fleet she could be earmarked for early disposal. Her time is spent on 4- and 5-day Bahamas cruises from Jacksonville, Florida.

ECSTASY was built by the Helsinki, Finland shipyard of Masa Yards (yard number 480) and delivered in 1991 as the second of the 'Fantasy' class. Following her naming ceremony in New York, she began cruising from Miami in June 1991. Now based in Galveston, Texas, she operates 4- and 5-day cruises to the Western Caribbean.

ELATION is the seventh ship in the 'Fantasy' class and was delivered in 1998 by Kvaerner Masa Yards (yard number 491), Helsinki, Finland. She was the first Carnival ship to be deployed on the West Coast of the USA, and now spends all of her time on the 7-day Western Caribbean itinerary, based in Galveston, Texas.

FANTASY is the first ship in an eight ship series ordered from Wartsila and its successors in Finland. She was delivered by Masa Yard's Helsinki shipyard (yard number 479) in 1990, following the failure of Wartsila Marine Industries, and was immediately employed on cruises from Miami. She now operates 3- and 4-day Bahamas cruises from Port Canaveral, Florida.

FASCINATION is the fourth of the 'Fantasy' class (yard number 487), delivered by Masa Yards, Helsinki, Finland and entering service in 1994. FASCINATION now operates 3-day Bahamas and 4-day Western Caribbean cruises from Miami.

HOLIDAY is the second new ship ordered by Carnival Cruise Lines, being delivered from the Aalborg Vaerft shipyard (yard number 246) at Aalborg, Denmark in June 1985. Her current employment is on 4- and 5-day Western Caribbean itineraries from Mobile, Alabama.

IMAGINATION is the fifth member of the 'Fantasy' class (yard number 488) and was delivered by Masa Yards, Helsinki, Finland in 1995. IMAGINATION now undertakes 4- and 5-day Western Caribbean cruises from Miami, Florida.

INSPIRATION entered service with Carnival in 1996. She is the sixth ship to be constructed by Masa Yards, Helsinki, Finland in the 'Fantasy' class (yard number 489). Her current employment includes 4- and 5-day Western Caribbean cruises from Tampa, Florida.

PARADISE is the final member of the eight ship 'Fantasy' class (yard number 494), and when delivered to Carnival Cruise Lines in 1998 became the world's first totally smoking-free ship (funnel excepted, we assume).

Costa Cruises' **Costa Classica** against the backdrop of Messina *(William Mayes)*

Costa Cruises' **Costa Europa** at Genoa *(Egidio Ferrighi)*

Costa Cruises' **Costa Marina** at Dover *(William Mayes)*

She later quietly dropped her non-smoking status and is employed on 3- and 4-day Mexican cruises from Los Angeles.

SENSATION is the third member of the 'Fantasy' class. Following the failure of Wartsila Marine Industries in November 1989, the order was cancelled. The contract was renewed with Masa Yards, Helsinki, Finland (yard number 484) in 1991 and the ship joined Carnival's growing Caribbean fleet in 1993. She now operates on the 4- and 5-day Western Caribbean itineraries from New Orleans.

Cruise ship on order

CARNIVAL FREEDOM	c110000t	2007	22.5k	DE2	2974p	3540p	1118c	290.0m	35.5m	8.2m	PA

CARNIVAL FREEDOM was ordered in 2004 from Fincantieri, and will be built in the Sestri yard at Genoa, Italy.

COSTA CRUISES

The Company The origins of the Costa Line date from 1924 when the brothers Federico, Eugenio and Enrico Costa bought their first cargo ship. It was not until after the Second World War that the business entered passenger shipping. In 1948 the ANNA C and ANDREA C were the first passenger ships for what had now become known as Linea C. The company was initially involved in the post-war migrant trades, but subsequently built up a route network linking South America with Mediterranean ports. In 1959 the FRANCA C (built in 1914 and still sailing as the mission ship DOULOS) became the first Costa Line ship to be exclusively allocated to American cruising. This major Italian passenger line was re-styled Costa Armatori S.p.A. in 1967 and in the following year the company introduced Caribbean fly-cruises based on San Juan. In 1986, in response to changed markets, the company was renamed Costa Crociere S.p.A. and thereafter was involved solely in cruise operations. In 1993 the French Croisieres Paquet became part of Costa, and two years later the company began cruises to Havana. In December 1996 the shareholders accepted a joint bid by Airtours of the United Kingdom and Carnival Corporation, and so the last major Italian passenger ship operator ceased to be independent. In spring 2001 Carnival Corporation acquired the Airtours holding in Costa, and the latter company then became a full subsidiary.

Chief Executive Officer Pierluigi Foschi

Address Via de Marini 60, 16149 Genoa, Italy

Telephone +34 010 54831 **Fax** +34 010 5483290

Website www.costacruises.co.uk www.costacruise.com

Areas operated Mediterranean, Scandinavia, South America and the Caribbean

COSTA ALLEGRA	28430t	1969	20.0k	D2	800p	1030p	418c	187.7m	25.8m	8.2m	IT
COSTA ATLANTICA	85619t	2000	22.0k	DEP2	2112p	2680p	902c	292.5m	32.2m	8.0m	IT
COSTA CLASSICA	52926t	1991	19.8k	D2	1308p	1783p	650c	220.6m	28.0m	7.3m	IT
COSTA EUROPA	53872t	1986	22.5k	D2	1494p	1773p	642c	243.2m	29.7m	6.5m	IT
COSTA FORTUNA	102587t	2003	20.0k	DE2	2718p	3470p	1068c	272.2m	35.5m	8.2m	IT
COSTA MAGICA	c102600t	2004	20.0k	DE2	2718p	3470p	1068c	272.2m	35.5m	8.2m	IT
COSTA MARINA	25558t	1969	20.0k	D2	763p	1025p	391c	174.2m	25.8m	8.2m	IT
COSTA MEDITERRANEA	85619t	2003	22.0k	DEP2	2114p	2680p	920c	292.5m	32.2m	8.0m	IT
COSTA ROMANTICA	53049t	1993	19.8k	D2	1356p	1787p	650c	220.6m	28.0m	7.3m	IT
COSTA VICTORIA	75166t	1996	23.0k	D2	1928p	2394p	792c	251.0m	32.3m	7.8m	IT

COSTA ALLEGRA was built by Wartsila (yard number 1170) at Turku in Finland as one of a class of five container ships for the Johnson Line of Sweden in 1969. As the ANNIE JOHNSON she served Johnson Line's North American service to Northern Europe until 1985, when she was sold to Peleus Marine Company of Cyprus (a company owned by Greek ship-owner Antonis Lelakis) who planned to convert her and two sisters into cruise-ships. She was renamed the REGENT MOON, but these plans eventually fell through, and in 1988 she was sold to the Swiss-based Mediterranean Shipping Company and renamed the ALEXANDRA. In 1990, following the successful conversion of the COSTA MARINA, Costa approached MSC and bought the ship, which was sent to the Mariotti shipyard in Genoa for conversion. In addition to the conversion the ship was lengthened by 13.5 metres and equipped with new engines, being re-delivered to Costa Crociere in September 1992 as the COSTA ALLEGRA. She currently operates in the Caribbean and Mediterranean Seas and in Northern Europe.

COSTA ATLANTICA is the first example within Carnival Corporation of similar designs being used for ships built for more than one operator. The COSTA ATLANTICA is a sister to the CARNIVAL SPIRIT class of ships and was delivered to the company by Kvaerner Masa Yards (yard number 498), Helsinki, Finland in June 2000. Her sister ship, the COSTA MEDITERRANEA, was delivered during 2003. The COSTA ATLANTICA operates cruises in Northern Europe, the Mediterranean and Caribbean Seas.

COSTA CLASSICA, ordered in July 1987, was the first new passenger ship to be built for Costa Line since the elegant EUGENIO C of 1966. Built by Fincantieri (yard number 5877) at Venice, Italy, she was floated out of her building dock in February 1991 and delivered at the end of that year. She has operated in both the

Cunard Line's **Queen Elizabeth 2** off Calshot *(William Mayes)*

Cunard Line's **Queen Mary 2** sailing from Southampton *(William Mayes)*

Mediterranean and Caribbean markets. In 2000 she was due to have been lengthened by Cammell Laird at Birkenhead, England, but while the ship was on her way to the shipyard a dispute arose and the lengthening didn't take place, despite the shipyard having constructed the new centre section. Her current areas of operation include the Mediterranean Sea in summer and the Caribbean Islands in winter.

COSTA EUROPA was built for Home Lines by Jos.L.Meyer (yard number 610) at Papenburg, Germany and delivered in 1986 as the HOMERIC. She operated for Home Lines on their summer service between New York and Hamilton, Bermuda, but spent her winters cruising in the Caribbean. Home Lines was acquired by Holland America Line in 1988 and on 2 November the HOMERIC was renamed WESTERDAM. Her duties were now split between the Caribbean (winter) and Alaska cruises from Vancouver (summer). In October 1989 the ship was returned to her builders to have a 39.6 metre mid section inserted, resuming service in March 1990 and subsequently being re-registered to the Dutch flag in 1996. She was transferred to Costa Crociere during 2002 and renamed COSTA EUROPA. In 2005 she operates throughout Europe and the Atlantic Isles.

COSTA FORTUNA was built by Fincantieri at the Sestri yard (yard number 6086) in Genoa, Italy. She is currently operating Mediterranean Sea and Atlantic Isles cruises.

COSTA MAGICA was built by Fincantieri at the Sestri yard (yard number 6087) in Genoa, Italy. For 2005 the COSTA MAGICA operates exclusively in the Mediterranean Sea.

COSTA MARINA was the first in a series of five container ships built by Wartsila (yard number 1169) at Turku, Finland for Johnson Line of Sweden; a sister to the ANNIE JOHNSON, she was named the AXEL JOHNSON. In 1985 she was sold to Lelakis-owned company Universal Glow Inc. and renamed the REGENT SUN. The plan to convert the ship for cruising was abandoned in 1986 and she was sold and renamed ITALIA. Two years later she was sold to Costa company Mediterranean Cruise Lines and renamed the COSTA MARINA. A further two years elapsed before the new cruise ship emerged from the Mariotti shipyard at Genoa. She has subsequently operated in the Caribbean, Europe, Scandinavia and South America. From spring 2002 the COSTA MARINA became the first Carnival group ship to be dedicated to the growing German cruise market, offering cruises in the Mediterranean and Baltic Seas.

COSTA MEDITERRANEA was built by Kvaerner Masa Yards (yard number 502) at Helsinki, Finland. The COSTA MEDITERRANEA currently operates in the Caribbean Sea in winter and the Mediterranean Sea in summer.

COSTA ROMANTICA is a near sister to the COSTA CLASSICA and was delivered to the company by the Venice shipyard of Fincantieri (yard number 5899) in September 1993. She, too, alternates between the Mediterranean Sea in summer and the Caribbean Sea in winter.

COSTA VICTORIA is one of a pair of ships ordered from Bremer Vulkan at Bremen, Germany (yard number 107) at the end of 1993. Her keel was laid in November 1994 and she was floated out of her building dock less than ten months later. She was delivered in July 1996. The second ship of this pair (to have been named COSTA OLYMPIA) was not delivered due to the bankruptcy of the shipyard, but was later bought and completed for Norwegian Cruise Line as the NORWEGIAN SKY (now PRIDE OF ALOHA). The COSTA VICTORIA currently operates in South America during the winter and in the Mediterranean Sea in summer.

Cruise ships on order

COSTA CONCORDIA	c112000t	2006	k	DE2	3000p	3800p	c	290.2m	35.5m	8.3m	IT
NEWBUILDING 2	c112000t	2007	k	DE2	3000p	3800p	c	290.2m	35.5m	8.3m	IT

COSTA CONCORDIA and her sister were ordered in 2004 from Fincantieri, and will be built in the Sestri yard at Genoa, Italy.

The company also operates the COSTA TROPICALE until the autumn of 2005 on a variety of Mediterranean Sea itineraries. She then transfers to P&O Cruises (Australia) as the PACIFIC STAR (q.v.).

CUNARD LINE

The Company In 1840 Samuel Cunard's British and North American Royal Mail Steam Packet Company inaugurated the first North Atlantic steamship mail service under a contract with the Admiralty for which the latter would pay the sum of £55,000 per annum. This company soon became known as the Cunard Line. The 1,135-ton wooden paddle steamer BRITANNIA took the first sailing on 4th July 1840 between Liverpool, Halifax and Boston. By 1848 Cunard Line was operating a weekly transatlantic service using nine steamers. During the 1850's Mediterranean services were established and by the time of Samuel Cunard's death in 1865 the company had built up an impressive route network served by modern ships. To raise capital for new ships, the company, along with its associated companies, was merged into the new Cunard Steam Ship Company Limited in 1878, and two years later the public were invited to subscribe for £800,000 of the issued capital of £2,000,000. The next 50 years was a period of growth, spurred on to a great extent by the rivalry between the many emerging European and American shipping companies. In 1881, Cunard's SERVIA was the first ship to be lit by electric light, and twelve years later the CAMPANIA was the company's first twin-screw vessel. Steam turbines began to power the fleet in 1905, with the arrival of the CARMANIA. In 1907, the company's largest and most prestigious ships to date, the 31,000 gross ton sisters LUSITANIA and MAURETANIA entered service, taking the 'Blue Riband' for Cunard. With the arrival in 1914 of the 45,000-ton AQUITANIA the company could maintain the weekly New York service with just these three ships. After the end of the First World War, Cunard acquired the former German owned 52,000 ton IMPERATOR and renamed her BERENGARIA. During the depression of the early 1930's it became necessary for Cunard Line to merge with the White Star Line to form Cunard-White Star Limited in order to secure British Government finance to pay for the building of the 81,000 ton QUEEN MARY. In order to maintain the New York service with just two ships a second 'Queen' was ordered in 1936, but due to the outbreak of war the QUEEN ELIZABETH did not enter Cunard service until 1946. The company's first ship designed with cruising in mind was the 1949 built CARONIA; painted in three shades of green, she served the lucrative American market. The QUEEN MARY made her last transatlantic voyage in 1967 and was sold eventually for use as a hotel and museum at Long Beach, California. The last voyage of the QUEEN ELIZABETH took place the following year, and in early 1969 the QUEEN ELIZABETH 2 made her debut on the North Atlantic. Trafalgar House Investments Limited acquired Cunard in 1971, and in the same year the first of Cunard's new generation of cruise ships, the 14,000-ton sisters CUNARD ADVENTURER and CUNARD AMBASSADOR began sailing in the Caribbean. The former was sold to Klosters (the forerunner of Norwegian Cruise Line) in 1976 and the latter was converted for use as a livestock carrier following a fire in 1974. The CUNARD PRINCESS (launched as the CUNARD CONQUEST) and the CUNARD COUNTESS, both 18,000 tons, were the next cruise ships to join the fleet and were again used in the Caribbean. These were sold to other operators in 1995/96. Norwegian America Cruises, together with the elegant near-sisters SAGAFJORD and VISTAFJORD was acquired in 1983, and retained as a separate brand for a number of years. Trafalgar House Investments was taken over towards the end of 1996 by the Norwegian construction and engineering group Kvaerner, and thus Cunard became Norwegian owned. Cunard didn't fit well into the Kvaerner group, so was sold to a consortium led by Carnival in May 1998. That company subsequently acquired the remaining shares from the other members of the consortium. Cunard's first new vessel subsequent to the acquisition, the QUEEN MARY 2 entered service in January 2004, thus ending almost a quarter of a century of no investment in new ships. The previously announced QUEEN VICTORIA, due for delivery in 2005 has now been transferred to P&O Cruises as the ARCADIA, and a new QUEEN VICTORIA has been ordered from Fincantieri. It is widely expected that she will be the replacement for the QUEEN ELIZABETH 2. The CARONIA (formerly VISTAFJORD) left the Cunard fleet in the autumn of 2004 when she began a new career with Saga Cruises, leaving this most famous of all the Atlantic lines with just the two 'Queens'.

Chief Executive Officer Peter Ratcliffe

Address   **USA** 24303 Town Centre Drive, Suite 200, Valencia CA 91355

           UK Mountbatten House, Grosvenor Square, Southampton SO15 2BF

Telephone USA +1 305 463 3000   **Fax** +1 305 463 3010

            UK +44 845 071 0300 **Fax** +44 02380 225843

Website www.cunard.com or www.cunard.co.uk

Areas operated Europe and World Cruises (QUEEN ELIZABETH 2); Europe, Caribbean, North America and Transatlantic (QUEEN MARY 2)

QUEEN ELIZABETH 2	70327t	1969	28.5k	DE2	1778p	1778p	921c	293.5m	32.0m	9.9m	UK
QUEEN MARY 2	148528t	2003	29.3k	DE2	2620p	3090p	1253c	345.0m	41.0m	10.0m	UK

QUEEN ELIZABETH 2 is named as the second ship to bear the name QUEEN ELIZABETH, and not as might be expected in honour of Her Majesty Queen Elizabeth II. The ship's builders, Upper Clyde Shipbuilders (yard number 736), delivered her in December 1968, but a number of problems caused the curtailment of her inaugural cruise and the ship was returned to the shipyard. She eventually commenced her maiden voyage in May 1969, sporting a revolutionary single thin black funnel with white casing. In 1982 she served as a British troopship during the Falklands War and following her refit she emerged with a light grey hull and traditional Cunard funnel colours. This hull colour lasted for only a short time and she soon reverted to a traditional black hull. In October 1986 she was sent to the Lloyd Werft shipyard at Bremerhaven, Germany for a six-month refit that included the replacement of her sometimes-troublesome steam turbines with a new diesel-electric propulsion system. When she was re-delivered in April 1987 she had a much more substantial funnel. During her 35 years of service with Cunard she has provided the traveller with a regular transatlantic service, has undertaken numerous cruises in Europe and from the United States of America, and has completed many round-the-world cruises. From 2004 she is UK based, but still undertakes world cruises. It is very likely that she will be retired when the new QUEEN VICTORIA enters service towards the end of 2007.

QUEEN MARY 2 was built by Chantiers de l'Atlantique (yard number G32) at St Nazaire in France in 2003 as the first traditionally hulled liner for more than a quarter of a century. She was delivered at the end of the year and made a triumphant entrance to the Port of Southampton for the first time on 26 December 2003. Following her maiden voyage to Fort Lauderdale on 12 January 2004 she spent the spring in the Caribbean before undertaking a varied programme of cruises from both Southampton and New York, interspersed with Atlantic crossings. Her 2005 programme re-affirms her position as an Atlantic liner with 26 scheduled crossings. She is currently the largest passenger ship ever built, but will shortly be overtaken by the 'Freedom' class being built for Royal Caribbean International.

Holland America Line's **Oosterdam** at San Francisco *(Andrew Kilk)*

Holland America Line's **Veendam** at Vancouver *(William Mayes Collection)*

Cruise ship on order

QUEEN VICTORIA	c88500t	2007	22.0k	GDE2	1848p	1968p	c	289.8m	32.2m	8.0m	UK

QUEEN VICTORIA was ordered as a replacement for the previous ship intended to carry this name, now P&O Cruises' ARCADIA, from Fincantieri (yard number 6127) at Monfalcone, Italy.

HOLLAND AMERICA LINE

The Company The Nederlandsch Amerikaansche Stoomvaart Maatschappij (Netherlands American Steamship Company) came into being on 18 April 1873 to operate transatlantic liner services in competition with the other already well-established European steamship lines. The company gradually built up its services, fleet and reputation, and in 1898 adopted the yellow, green and white funnel colours which were to identify its ships for more than 70 years. The company was officially established as De Holland Amerika Lijn N.V. (The Holland America Line Ltd.) in 1896, a name by which it had been known unofficially for many years. The company was able to operate during most of the First World War as The Netherlands was a neutral country, but that didn't stop the loss of a number of ships to mines and later to submarine and surface attack. After the war, the Depression began to set in and the operations of the company started to be scaled back at the end of the 1920's. However, Holland America's passenger shipping was less severely affected than that of some other liner companies and by 1934 the STATENDAM was in need of a running mate on the New York service. That running mate was to be the NIEUW AMSTERDAM of 1938, Holland America's most elegant ship and certainly one of the best looking passenger liners ever built.

At the beginning of the Second World War the company moved its headquarters from Rotterdam to Willemstad, Curacao even though The Netherlands attempted to remain neutral. In 1940 Germany overran its small neighbour and in the accompanying air raids the Holland America office was destroyed. After the end of the war the first new passenger ships were the predominantly tourist class ships RYNDAM (1951) and MAASDAM (1952), for the North Atlantic service. The company then began to think more positively about using ships for cruising in the off-season. Although the NIEUW AMSTERDAM had already proved successful in this role, the newer ships were not really suitable. The next delivery, however, had been built with an eye to cruising and entered service in 1956 as the STATENDAM. A running mate was now required for the NIEUW AMSTERDAM, and thus the ROTTERDAM with her revolutionary profile and thin uptakes in place of a funnel arrived in 1959. During the 1960's and 1970's cruising gained in importance to the company's revenues and a pair of former Moore McCormack liners were acquired for this purpose. As if to add emphasis to the change in direction a new house flag, hull colour and an orange and blue funnel marking were introduced. The grand old NIEUW AMSTERDAM made the last scheduled transatlantic crossing for the Holland America Line in 1971, bringing to an end almost 100 years of the Rotterdam to New York passenger service. She remained in a cruising role for a further two years before being sold to Taiwanese breakers at the end of 1973. That year also saw the entry into service of the first new passenger ship for almost a quarter of a century, the 9,000-ton PRINSENDAM. Sadly she was to have a very short life as she was lost on 11th October 1980 following an engine room fire in the Gulf of Alaska. However, she had established the popularity of Alaskan cruising and in the following year both the ROTTERDAM and the STATENDAM served this market. In 1983, just before the delivery of the new NOORDAM and NIEUW AMSTERDAM, the company merged fully with its recently acquired subsidiary, Westours Inc., to form Holland America Westours Inc. In 1985 this name was further changed to Holland America Line – Westours Inc. July 1987 saw the new holding company Holland America Line N.V. take a 50% stake in Windstar Cruises Inc. and in the following year the company acquired Home Lines Inc. with its two ships, the ATLANTIC (not operated by Holland America and later sold to Premier Cruise Lines) and the HOMERIC, renamed the WESTERDAM. Later in 1988 Holland America purchased the remaining 50% of Windstar.

In November 1988 agreement was reached for Carnival Holdings Ltd to acquire the businesses of the Holland America group for $625 million. The first major effect of the takeover was the ordering of three (later increased to four) new ships from Fincantieri, beginning with the STATENDAM, delivered in 1993. The 1959-built ROTTERDAM was retired in September 1997; her replacement, delivered shortly afterwards was the sixth ship to bear that name. The WESTERDAM left the fleet in 2002 and joined fellow Carnival subsidiary Costa in Europe. Thereafter a steady stream of new-buildings joined the premier brand fleet of Holland America.

President and CEO Stein Kruse **Senior Vice-President** Richard D Meadows

Address 300 Elliott Avenue West, Seattle, WA 98119, United States of America

Telephone +1 206 281 3535 **Fax** +1 206 281 7110

Website www.hollandamerica.com

Areas operated North, Central and South America, Caribbean, Europe, Scandinavia, Africa and world cruises

AMSTERDAM	60874t	2000	24.5k	DEP2	1380p	1738p	642c	237.8m	32.2m	7.8m	NL
MAASDAM	55451t	1993	20.3k	DE2	1266p	1625p	588c	219.3m	30.8m	7.5m	NL
OOSTERDAM	81769t	2003	22.0k	GDEP2	1848p	1968p	842c	289.8m	32.2m	7.8m	NL
PRINSENDAM	37845t	1988	21.8k	D2	794p	837p	443c	204.0m	28.9m	7.1m	NL
ROTTERDAM	59652t	1997	22.5k	DE2	1316p	1668p	644c	234.0m	30.8m	7.5m	NL

Holland America Line's **Rotterdam** at Warnemunde *(William Mayes)*

Holland America Line's **Prinsendam** at San Francisco *(Andrew Kilk)*

RYNDAM	55451t	1994	20.3k	DE2	1266p	1625p	588c	219.3m	30.8m	7.5m	NL
STATENDAM	55451t	1993	20.3k	DE2	1266p	1625p	588c	219.3m	30.8m	7.5m	NL
VEENDAM	55451t	1996	20.3k	DE2	1266p	1627p	588c	219.3m	30.8m	7.5m	BA
VOLENDAM	60906t	1999	20.2k	DE2	1440p	1824p	647c	238.0m	32.3m	7.8m	NL
WESTERDAM	81811t	2004	22.0k	GDEP2	1848p	1968p	843c	289.8m	32.2m	7.8m	NL
ZAANDAM	60906t	2000	20.2k	DE2	1440p	1824p	647c	238.0m	32.3m	7.8m	NL
ZUIDERDAM	81769t	2002	22.0k	GDEP2	1848p	1968p	842c	289.8m	32.2m	7.8m	NL

AMSTERDAM, named in honour of the capital city of The Netherlands, was delivered to Holland America by Fincantieri (yard number 6052), Venice, Italy during 2000. Following her 2002 world cruise she was deployed on cruises to Alaska and the Caribbean Sea. In 2005 she operates in South America, Alaska, the Far East and Hawaii.

MAASDAM is the second of three ships ordered from Fincantieri (yard number 5882) at Monfalcone, Italy on November 25, 1989. The ship entered service under the Bahamas flag in December 1993 and was transferred to the Dutch flag in 1996. Her current itineraries include the Caribbean Sea, Canada and New England. Maasdam is a village situated to the south of Rotterdam.

OOSTERDAM was built by Fincantieri (yard number 6076) in Italy as the second ship in what has emerged as a four ship series (with a fifth similar ship becoming P&O Cruises' ARCADIA). Her name is derived from the easterly point of the compass. She is employed on Caribbean Sea, Mexico and Alaska cruises in 2005.

PRINSENDAM was built by Wartsila Marine Industries (yard number 1296) at their Turku, Finland yard, for Kloster's Royal Viking Line of Oslo as the ROYAL VIKING SUN. She was to be the penultimate ship built for this company, which had been owned since 1984 by Norwegian Caribbean Line. In 1994 she was sold to Cunard Line but retained her name. Following the partial amalgamation of Cunard and Seabourn, she was transferred to the Seabourn fleet and renamed the SEABOURN SUN. Considered to be unsuitable as a fleet-mate for the trio of yacht-like ships in the Seabourn fleet, she was transferred to fellow Carnival subsidiary Holland America Line as the PRINSENDAM. She operates cruises based in Europe and South America, in addition to a grand world voyage.

ROTTERDAM was ordered in January 1995 from the Marghera, Venice yard of Fincantieri in Italy (yard number 5980) as a larger and faster version of the STATENDAM class, but particularly as a replacement for the much-loved 1959-built ROTTERDAM. This is the sixth Holland America ship to bear the name of the second largest city and busiest seaport in The Netherlands. Her 2005 programme includes the Panama Canal, Europe and South America.

RYNDAM is the final member of the trio of cruise ships ordered from the Monfalcone, Italy yard of Fincantieri (yard number 5883) on November 25, 1989. She began her commercial career under the Bahamas flag with a ten day Caribbean cruise on October 20, 1994. She was re-flagged to the Netherlands in 1996, and currently operates Holland America's Mexico and Alaska programmes.

STATENDAM is the lead ship in a series of three sisters ordered from Fincantieri (yard number 5881) at Monfalcone, Italy on November 25, 1989. She was the first ship to be ordered for Holland America Line following the takeover by Carnival and entered service on January 25, 1993. She was originally registered under the ownership of Windsurf Ltd of Nassau, Bahamas but was transferred to the Dutch flag under Holland America Line ownership in 1996. She currently cruises Mexico and Alaska.

VEENDAM became the fourth member of the STATENDAM class when ordered from Fincantieri's Marghera shipyard (yard number 5954) in Venice, Italy on December 3, 1993. She was delivered in May 1996 and, after being named by the actress Debbie Reynolds, entered commercial service at the end of that month. She had a large complement of British deck and engineering officers due to a shortage of suitable Dutch personnel. She retains her Bahamas registry. The VEENDAM is named in honour of a town in the eastern part of The Netherlands, close to Groningen. She operates in the Caribbean Sea and Alaska in 2005.

VOLENDAM, named after a small town on the coast of the inland sea, Ijssel-Meer, and delivered by the Venice, Italy yard of Fincantieri (yard number 6035) in 1999 . She is yet another of this company's fleet that moves from the Caribbean Sea in winter to Alaska in summer.

WESTERDAM was built by Fincantieri (yard number 6077) in Italy as the third ship in a series of four. Her name is derived from the western point of the compass. She is programmed to sail in the Caribbean Sea and Europe during 2005.

ZAANDAM takes her name from a town that now forms part of the northern suburbs of Amsterdam. Delivered by the Venice yard of Fincantieri, (yard number 6036). She operates in the Caribbean Sea and in Alaska.

ZUIDERDAM has a name incorporating the southern compass point together with the traditional Holland America 'Dam' ending. This ship is the first of a series of five vessels (then six – one of which was cancelled and one of which is P&O Cruises' ARCADIA) ordered from Fincantieri (yard number 6075) in Italy. ZUIDERDAM is employed year-round in the Caribbean Sea.

Cruise ship on order

NOORDAM	c82000t	2006	22.0k	GDEP2	1848p	1968p	842c	289.8m	32.2m	7.8m	NL

NOORDAM has a name incorporating the northerly compass point together with the traditional Holland America 'Dam' ending. She is the last in a series of four vessels built for the company by Fincantieri (yard number 6079) in Italy.

Holland America line also owns the THOMSON CELEBRATION, chartered to Thomson Cruises and the THOMSON SPIRIT, chartered to Louis Cruise Lines and sub-chartered to Thomson Cruises (q.v.).

OCEAN VILLAGE (UK)

The Company Ocean Village is undoubtedly one of the newest operators to feature in this book, having commenced operation in the spring of 2003 as a company providing, bizarrely, 'cruises for people who don't do cruises'. In a fairly radical departure from the accepted cruise concept, Ocean Village is seeking to adopt a resort style in order to attract a younger and more active type of passenger, and includes self-service meals and a vast range of sporting and other active pursuits. The concept appears to have been successful, as the REGAL PRINCESS is now due to join the Ocean Village fleet in November 2006. Ocean Village is a division within P&O Cruises.

Managing Director Peter Shanks

Address Richmond House, Terminus Terrace, Southampton SO14 3PN, England

Telephone +44 845 358 5000 **Fax** +44 2380 523720

Website www.oceanvillageholidays.co.uk

Areas operated Mediterranean and Caribbean

OCEAN VILLAGE	63524t	1989	19.5k	DE2	1620p	1692p	514c	245.6m	32.2m	7.7m	UK

OCEAN VILLAGE was laid down in May 1988 as the SITMAR FAIRMAJESTY by Chantiers de l'Atlantique (yard number B29) at St Nazaire, France for the Sitmar Line. That company passed into the ownership of the P&O Group in September 1988, and the ship was subsequently delivered as the STAR PRINCESS in the spring of 1989 for service within P&O's Princess Cruises division. In late 1997 the ship was transferred to P&O Cruises for operation within the UK passenger fleet and renamed ARCADIA, thus reviving a traditional P&O name. She cruised from the UK in the summer and in the Caribbean during the winter until the spring of 2003, when she was transferred to Ocean Village. She is now based in the Mediterranean in summer and the Caribbean in winter.

P&O CRUISES (UK)

The Company As the ownership of this company changes over the years since its de-merger from the Peninsular and Oriental Steam Navigation Company, it is easy to forget that this is the descendant of the company that invented cruising. Its history of passenger services goes back to 1837 and the formation of the Peninsular Steam Navigation Company (the peninsula being Iberia), which later became The Peninsular and Oriental Steam Navigation Company, or P&O as it was both universally and affectionately known. The company was founded as the Peninsular Steam Navigation Company to fulfil the new British Admiralty-controlled mail contract serving Vigo, Oporto, Lisbon, Cadiz and Gibraltar from Falmouth. The first mail steamer, the DON JUAN, was lost on the homeward leg of her maiden mail voyage, but the reputation of the company was little damaged as all of the passengers, crew, mail and cargo were saved. In 1839 the company won the tender for the mail contract from Falmouth to Alexandria, via Gibraltar and Malta, but had insufficient capital for new ships. The answer came in the form of a merger with the Trans-Atlantic Steamship Company of Liverpool, bringing two large ships to the fleet. In 1840, a new company was set up with liability limited by Royal Charter; the Peninsular and Oriental Steam Navigation Company had been born. P&O invented cruising in 1844 when it advertised a 'Grand Tour' by sea from Southampton to Gibraltar, Malta, Athens, Smyrna, Jaffa and Alexandria utilising three ships, the LADY MARY WOOD, the TAGUS and the IBERIA. This voyage was recorded in William Makepeace Thackeray's 'Notes of a Journey from Cornhill to Grand Cairo'. Subsequently round trips from Southampton to destinations such as Constantinople and Alexandria were recorded.

Throughout the second half of the nineteenth century the ships of the P&O became larger and more luxurious as the company increased its routes to cover the far-flung corners of the British Empire. Australia, the Indian Sub-Continent and the Far East became the most important routes for the company, and it was on these that the newest and largest ships served. The company was also an important supplier of vessels for use as troopships, both for overseas campaigns and on long-term contract.

Innovation continued apace with the RAVENNA of 1880 being the first passenger ship to be built with a full steel superstructure, and four years later the VALETTA was the first of the company's ships to use electric light.

In 1904 the company advertised its first proper cruise on a ship refitted specifically for that purpose. The 6000-ton VECTIS had been adapted to carry just 150 first-class passengers. Ten years later, after the company had

Ocean Village at Tortola *(Chris Mason)*

P&O Cruises' ***Arcadia*** sailing from Southampton *(William Mayes)*

P&O Cruises' *Aurora* anchored in the Solent *(William Mayes)*

P&O Cruises' *Oceana* off Calshot *(William Mayes)*

P&O Cruises' **Oriana** at Kusadasi *(William Mayes)*

P&O Cruises (Australia)'s **Pacific Sun** *(Jonathan Boonzaier)*

merged with the British India Steam Navigation Company, its fleet totalled 197 ships. That year also saw the company relieved of almost two-thirds of its fleet for war service as hospital ships, troop transports and armed merchant cruisers. P&O lost 17 ships during the First World War, but subsidiary companies lost a further 68.

In December 1918 one of the most significant acquisitions took place when P&O purchased 51% of the share capital of the Orient Steam Navigation Company. The Orient Line had been a joint operator with P&O on the Australian Mail Contract for some time. By 1921 the company had reintroduced its long haul services to India (weekly), China (fortnightly) and Australia (four-weekly). In the 1920's P&O and Orient Line between them took delivery of more than twenty new passenger liners, most of which were used on the Australia service. Cruising began again in 1925 when the RANCHI undertook a cruise to Norway as her maiden voyage. For the 1929 season, P&O offered a total of 15 cruises, including some aboard the new VICEROY OF INDIA, the first turbo-electric ship for the company.

The combined fleets of the companies within the P&O Group peaked in the mid 1920's, when more than 500 ships ranging from the excursion vessels and coasters of the General Steam Navigation Company, to the modern refrigerated cargo ships of New Zealand Shipping Company and Federal Steam Navigation, and the state of the art passenger liners of P&O and Orient Line were owned.

The Second World War took its toll on the P&O Group with the loss of 156, ships including such passenger liners as the VICEROY OF INDIA, RAWALPINDI, CATHAY, STRATHALLAN, ORONSAY and ORCADES. By the late 1940's commercial aviation was beginning to take a hold, so the passenger fleet renewal programme concentrated on fewer but larger and faster ships. When these ships came on stream between 1947 and 1954 they cut the sailing time to Australia from five to four weeks.

In 1955 both P&O and Orient Line ordered what were to be their last passenger liners, the CANBERRA and the ORIANA. These were fast ships and shaved another week off the Australian run; ORIANA recorded a speed of 30.64 knots on trials. These two ships came under full common ownership in 1961 when P&O acquired the remaining minority interests in Orient Line and restyled its passenger operations as P&O-Orient Lines. The 1960's saw a general downturn in line voyages and a reduction in the number of ships operated, a trend that was to continue into the 1970's when cruising became a vital employment for ships between line voyages.

In 1971 the company underwent a massive reorganisation when the activities of more than 100 subsidiaries operating 239 ships were structured into a number of operating divisions. The Passenger Division, the forerunner of P&O Cruises, commenced with 13, including the last two large ships of British India, NEVASA and UGANDA. During the early 1970's times were really bad for the passenger liner with relatively young ships being sent for scrap becoming a regular occurrence. Princess Cruises was acquired in 1974 and the almost new SPIRIT OF LONDON was transferred to that company. By the late 1970's the CANBERRA and ORIANA served the UK cruise market and the ARCADIA was employed in Australia. In 1981 the ORIANA replaced the ARCADIA in Australia, and the UK was left with just the CANBERRA and the SEA PRINCESS, newly transferred from Australia. CANBERRA was out of P&O service for much of 1982 when she was requisitioned for use in the Falklands War. In 1986 SEA PRINCESS was switched to the Princess Cruises fleet, leaving just the CANBERRA to service the UK.

With the withdrawal of the CANBERRA imminent, P&O Cruises ordered its first new ship for the British market, the ORIANA, which set the standard for all that followed when she was delivered in 1995. CANBERRA was scrapped in 1997 and her replacement was the ARCADIA (formerly STAR PRINCESS and now OCEAN VILLAGE). The P&O cruises fleet is now growing at an impressive rate and the 2005 brochure offered cruises on six ships (including the ADONIA, now transferred back to Princess Cruises as the SEA PRINCESS), a choice not seen since the early 1970's.

P&O Princess Cruises became an independent company on its demerger from the Peninsular & Oriental Steam Navigation Company in 2000. In early 2003 P&O Princess began talks with Royal Caribbean on a possible merger, but shareholders eventually voted for a merger with Carnival Corporation, which occurred in the autumn of that year.

Life President The Lord Sterling of Plaistow **Managing Director** David Dingle

Address Richmond House, Terminus Terrace, Southampton, SO14 3PN, England

Telephone +44 845 355 5333 **Fax** +44 238 052 3720

Website www.pocruises.co.uk

Areas operated Mediterranean, Scandinavia, positioning voyages to the Caribbean and world cruises, all from Southampton. Fly cruises in the Caribbean and South America

ARCADIA	82972t	2005	22.0k	GDEP2	1848p	2388p	866c	289.8m	32.2m	7.8m	BD
ARTEMIS	44588t	1984	21.5k	D2	1200p	1318p	520c	230.6m	29.2m	7.8m	BD
AURORA	76152t	2000	25.0k	DE2	1874p	2290p	850c	270.0m	32.2m	7.9m	UK
OCEANA	77499t	2000	21.0k	DE2	2004p	2272p	875c	261.0m	32.3m	8.0m	UK
ORIANA	69153t	1995	24.0k	D2	1814p	1928p	800c	260.0m	32.2m	7.9m	UK

ARCADIA was laid down for Holland America Line (yard number 6078) by Fincantieri at Monfalcone in Italy. Prior to delivery she was transferred to the Cunard line as the QUEEN VICTORIA. In the spring of 2004, she was again transferred – this time to P&O Cruises as part of a major fleet reorganisation within the British parts of Carnival – to become the ARCADIA when delivered in April 2005. ARCADIA is based in Southampton, and will continue the tradition established by the previous ship of this name as an adults-only vessel. She is the fourth P&O ship to bear the poetic name for an area of what is now the Greek Peloponnese, the peninsula south of the isthmus of Corinth that makes up the southern part of Greece.

ARTEMIS was the first purpose built cruise ship to be ordered by the P&O Group. She was built by Wartsila (yard number 464) at Helsinki, Finland as the ROYAL PRINCESS and delivered in late 1984. Initially used on US based itineraries for Princess Cruises, she has more recently undertaken trips around South America, but spent the summer in European waters. For 2003/2004 she undertook an interesting set of worldwide itineraries, including much of Africa, South America, Antarctica, the Amazon and Europe. In a major redeployment within the British division of Carnival she was transferred to P&O Cruises in spring 2005 as the ARTEMIS, a rather clever, if not entirely appropriate renaming reflecting her connection with Diana, Princess of Wales, who named the ship in 1984. Artemis, daughter of Zeus and Lato, and twin sister of Apollo was a Greek goddess of the chase and protectoress of children and young animals; the Roman equivalent was Diana.

AURORA was built by Jos L Meyer (yard number 640) at Papenburg, Germany as the second purpose built cruise ship for the British market. Ordered in 1998, she was delivered in the spring of 2000 and after an abortive maiden voyage has settled down as a successful member of the P&O Cruises fleet, undertaking an annual world cruise in addition to her European itineraries from Southampton. Engine problems at the start of her World Cruise in 2005 gained much press coverage, but despite the best journalistic efforts it proved extremely difficult to find anyone with a bad word to say about either the company or the ship. Aurora, goddess of the dawn, was the name chosen for the ship as a link to the dawning of a new millennium.

OCEANA was built by Fincantieri (yard number 6044) at Monfalcone, Italy as the OCEAN PRINCESS for Princess Cruises' operations in the Caribbean and to Alaska. In the autumn of 2002 she was renamed OCEANA and transferred to P&O Cruises to serve the British market, operating predominantly from the United Kingdom. Her first season commenced with Caribbean fly-cruises before she took up her Southampton based itinerary. The second ship to bear the name, Oceana is the feminine form of Oceanus, the Roman god of the ocean.

ORIANA was the first purpose built cruise ship for the British market, and when she entered service in 1995 she very quickly became a favourite and set the standard that many others have yet to achieve. This sturdily built, classically elegant ship was ordered from the Jos L Meyer yard (yard number 636) at Papenburg in 1993, becoming, at the time of her delivery, the largest passenger ship to be built in Germany. In addition to cruises from Southampton, the ORIANA has undertaken eight annual world cruises, but for the 2004 UK winter season pioneered a new programme in the Caribbean and around South America. This is the second ORIANA to have served the company, a name given to the poetic huntress and heroine; a character associated with Queen Elizabeth I of England by contemporary writers.

P&O CRUISES (AUSTRALIA)

The Company Although P&O had always had a cruising presence in Australia; until the mid-1970's with regular line voyages and 'between voyage cruising' and in later years with the 1954-built ARCADIA and subsequently the 1960-built ORIANA, the permanent presence ended with the sale of the latter ship to Japan at the end of 1986. That all changed in 1988, however, when P&O acquired Sitmar Line and its Australian based cruise ship, the FAIRSTAR (built in 1957 as the Bibby Line troopship OXFORDSHIRE). A one-ship operation continued with the FAIRSTAR until 1997, then the FAIR PRINCESS until 2000, followed by the PACIFIC SKY until 2003 when the PACIFIC PRINCESS (see Princess Cruises) joined the fleet on a part time basis. Subsequently, the company has benefited from the replacement programmes elsewhere within the group with Carnival's JUBILEE and Costa's COSTA TROPICALE joining the growing fleet. For management purposes the company has recently been re-styled as Carnival (Australia), but it is too soon to know whether the P&O marketing name is likely to disappear in the immediate future.

President of Carnival Australia Gavin Smith

Address Level 10, 160 Sussex Street, Sydney, NSW 2000, Australia

Telephone +61 2 132469 **Fax** +61 2 9364 8862

Website www.pocruises.com.au

Areas operated Australasia, South East Asia and the Pacific Islands

PACIFIC SKY	46087t	1984	21.5k	ST2	1184p	1744p	550c	240.4m	27.8m	8.2m	UK
PACIFIC STAR	33250t	1981	21.0k	D2	1022p	1400p	550c	204.0m	26.3m	7.0m	IT
PACIFIC SUN	47262t	1986	21.5k	D2	1486p	1896p	670c	223.2m	28.0m	7.5m	BA

PACIFIC SKY was ordered by Sitmar Line from Chantiers du Nord et de la Mediterranee (yard number 1436) at La Seyne, France as the FAIRSKY, as an alternative to converting the former Portuguese liner PRINCIPE PERFEITO into a luxury cruise ship. The FAIRSKY was the last major passenger vessel to be built with steam turbine machinery. Delivered in 1984, she was used on west coast USA cruises. Following the takeover by P&O in 1988 she was integrated into the Princess Cruises fleet and renamed SKY PRINCESS, although still under the ownership of P&O Lines. Ownership was transferred to Princess Cruises in 1994, and in 2000 the ship was transferred to P&O Cruises (Australia) and renamed PACIFIC SKY for cruising from Australia.

PACIFIC STAR was the first new cruise ship to be ordered by Carnival Cruise Lines. She was built by Aalborg Vaerft (yard number 234) of Aalborg, Denmark and delivered in December 1980 for service in the Caribbean as the TROPICALE. As the smallest unit in Carnival Cruise Lines' fleet in 2001, she was transferred to Costa Crociere and renamed the COSTA TROPICALE for service in the Mediterranean. In the autumn of 2005 she takes up a new role within the group, being transferred to P&O Cruises (Australia) and renamed PACIFIC STAR.

PACIFIC SUN floated out of her building dock at the Kockums shipyard (yard number 596), Malmo, Sweden in October 1985, and was delivered eight months later to Carnival Cruise Lines as the JUBILEE. In 2004 she was transferred within the group to P&O Cruises (Australia) and renamed PACIFIC SUN.

Princess Cruises PACIFIC PRINCESS has operated cruises marketed by P&O Cruises (Australia) during the southern summer. It has been announced that the DAWN PRINCESS will replace her in 2006.

PRINCESS CRUISES

The Company Princess Cruises began operation in December 1965 when Stanley McDonald, a Seattle industrialist, chartered the 1949-built, Canadian Pacific Railway ship PRINCESS PATRICIA, from where the new company took its name. The first cruises were to the west coast of Mexico, and they were so successful that the ship was chartered again the following year. By the 1967/68 season a larger ship was needed, and the company was fortunate to obtain the charter of the recently completed 12,000-ton ITALIA, marketed as PRINCESS ITALIA but not renamed. During the next season a second ship, Costa Line's CARLA C, marketed as PRINCESS CARLA, joined the ITALIA, allowing that ship to inaugurate cruises to Alaska. In the autumn of 1970 her owners needed the CARLA C, so Princess Cruises was again a one-ship company. The recently built ISLAND VENTURE became unexpectedly available for charter in late 1972, and renamed ISLAND PRINCESS, she quickly established her position in the Princess fleet, where she remained for 27 years. In 1973 the ITALIA was returned to her owners, and in the following year the Peninsular & Oriental Steam Navigation Company, in a move designed to strengthen its American operation, bought out Princess Cruises and transferred the SPIRIT OF LONDON (renamed SUN PRINCESS) to the company, later purchasing the ISLAND PRINCESS and her sister the SEA VENTURE (renamed PACIFIC PRINCESS). The popularity of American cruising undoubtedly received a boost in the mid-1970's when the PACIFIC PRINCESS starred in the television series 'The Love Boat'. The first new ship for the growing Princess company was the 1984-built ROYAL PRINCESS, and two years later the SEA PRINCESS (formerly Swedish America Line's KUNGSHOLM) joined the fleet following a downturn in UK cruising, thus giving Princess five relatively modern ships. By 1988, however, it was apparent that the P&O Group was once again falling behind the market leaders as the US cruise market boomed. P&O had no new ships on order for Princess, and its largest ship, the ROYAL PRINCESS, was only 44,000 tons compared with the 70,000 ton ships that other lines were preparing to take into their fleets. Sitmar Line, facing financial difficulties became available and P&O quickly snapped up this business for $210 million in September 1988, taking into the Princess fleet a mixed bag of older, but popular tonnage, but more importantly contracts for three large ships due for imminent delivery.

Sitmar Line had commenced trading just after the Second World War using two surplus US ships converted to carry around 800 passengers in fairly basic accommodation. Initially the company sailed in the migrant trades between the Mediterranean and Central America and the Caribbean. A little later the company acquired its third ship and entered the emigrant trade from the United Kingdom to Australia. By 1963, the star of the fleet was the former Bibby Line troopship OXFORDSHIRE, now running as the FAIRSTAR. With the acquisition in the late 1960's and the conversion for luxury cruising in 1970/71 of the former Cunard liners CARINTHIA (FAIRSEA) and SYLVANIA (FAIRWIND), the company quickly established itself at the luxury end of the US cruise market. The first new ship for the company was the FAIRSKY (now P&O Australia's PACIFIC SKY), delivered in 1984, and in 1986 the company ordered its largest ship to date, the SITMAR FAIRMAJESTY. However, that ship, along with two slightly larger ships ordered a little later, were to be delivered to the P&O Group, following the takeover.

The Princess story subsequently has been one of rapid expansion, keeping the company at the forefront of the premium US cruise market. The company commissioned two series of new ships in the 1990's. The SUN PRINCESS was the lead ship in a class of four vessels, but the GRAND PRINCESS was the forerunner of a much larger class of similar ships of around 110,000 gross tons. Princess Cruises became part of the new P&O Princess Cruises in 2000, when the cruise operations of the Peninsular & Oriental Steam Navigation Company were de-merged to form a new publicly listed company. Following talks on a possible merger with Royal Caribbean, the shareholders chose instead a merger with Carnival Corporation, which took place in 2003. SEA PRINCESS and OCEAN PRINCESS were sent, with little change to their interiors, to the P&O Cruises fleet in 2003, with the latter company relinquishing its Grand Class ship order to Princess. The transfer back to Princess of the former of this pair may indicate that it's not that easy to quickly adapt large ships from one market to another. With the transfer of ROYAL PRINCESS to P&O Cruises in 2005, and the REGAL PRINCESS to Ocean Village during the following year, the oldest ship in this fleet will be the 1995-built SUN PRINCESS.

Princess Cruises' *Regal Princess* at San Francisco *(Andrew Kilk)*

Princess Cruises' *Sun Princess* at Vancouver *(Andrew Kilk)*

Princess Cruises' **Island Princess** at Skagway *(Andrew Kilk)*

Princess Cruises' **Pacific Princess** on her first call at San Francisco *(Andrew Kilk)*

President and Chief Executive Officer Peter Ratcliffe

Address 24305 Town Centre Drive, Santa Clarita, California 91355, United States of America

Telephone + 1 310 553 1770 **Fax** +1 310 832 0728

Website www.princesscruises.com

Areas operated North and South America, Caribbean, Mediterranean, Scandinavia, Pacific Islands and the Far East

CARIBBEAN PRINCESS	112894t	2004	22.5k	DE2	3114p	3796p	1200c	289.0m	36.0m	8.0m	BD
CORAL PRINCESS	91627t	2002	24.0k	GDE2	1974p	2590p	960c	294.0m	32.2m	8.0m	BD
DAWN PRINCESS	77441t	1997	21.4k	DE2	1950p	2250p	900c	261.3m	32.3m	8.1m	UK
DIAMOND PRINCESS	115875t	2004	22.1k	DE2	2674p	3290p	1100c	290.0m	37.5m	8.0m	BD
GOLDEN PRINCESS	108865t	2001	22.5k	DE2	2600p	3100p	1150c	289.5m	40.2m	8.5m	BD
GRAND PRINCESS	108806t	1998	22.5k	DE2	2592p	3100p	1150c	289.5m	40.2m	8.5m	BD
ISLAND PRINCESS	91627t	2003	24.0k	GDE2	1974p	2481p	960c	294.0m	32.2m	8.0m	BD
PACIFIC PRINCESS	30277t	1999	18.0k	DE2	668p	8002p	373c	181.0m	25.5m	5.8m	GI
REGAL PRINCESS	70285t	1991	19.5k	DE2	1590p	1744p	696c	245.1m	32.3m	8.1m	UK
SAPPHIRE PRINCESS	115875t	2004	22.1k	DE2	2674p	3290p	1100c	290.0m	37.5m	8.0m	BD
SEA PRINCESS	77499t	1998	21.4k	DE2	2004p	2272p	875c	261.3m	32.3m	8.1m	UK
STAR PRINCESS	108977t	2002	22.5k	DE2	2600p	3300p	1150c	289.5m	40.2m	8.5m	BD
SUN PRINCESS	77441t	1995	21.5k	DE2	1950p	2250p	900c	261.3m	32.3m	8.1m	UK
TAHITIAN PRINCESS	30277t	1999	18.0k	DE2	688p	800p	373c	181.0m	25.5m	5.8m	GI

CARIBBEAN PRINCESS, ordered from the Monfalcone, Italy yard of Fincantieri (yard number 6067) was destined for P&O Cruises for service in the growing British cruise market. Following a cascading of ships from Princess to P&O, this vessel was switched to Princess Cruises for service in the Caribbean Sea as the CARIBBEAN PRINCESS. She is currently based at Fort Lauderdale, Florida.

CORAL PRINCESS was built by Chantiers de l'Atlantique (yard number C32) at St Nazaire, France for Princess Cruises as the company's first gas turbine powered ship. She will serve the Panama Canal and Alaska markets.

DAWN PRINCESS is the second ship in the SUN PRINCESS class and was built by Fincantieri (yard number 5955) at Monfalcone, Italy. For 2005 she will cruise in the Mexican Riviera and to Alaska.

DIAMOND PRINCESS was laid down by Mitsubishi Heavy Industries (yard number 2181) in Japan as the SAPPHIRE PRINCESS, but following a major fire on board the DIAMOND PRINCESS while fitting out, the two ships exchanged names. She spends the summer of 2005 in Alaska, before moving to the Far East for a series of cruises based in Bangkok, Thailand and Xingang, China.

GOLDEN PRINCESS was built by Fincantieri (yard number 6050) at Monfalcone, Italy as the second of the GRAND PRINCESS Class. She is the second ship in the Princess fleet to bear this name, the former being a vessel chartered in the 1990's, now the BOUDICCA of Fred. Olsen Cruise Lines. In 2005 she serves the Caribbean and US East Coast markets, but transfers to the Mediterranean Sea in 2006.

GRAND PRINCESS was built as the first 100,000+ ton cruise ship for the P&O Group by Fincantieri (yard number 6956) at Monfalcone, Italy. She is one of a class of three ships. She is scheduled for a 2005 season in the Western Caribbean and the Mediterranean Sea.

ISLAND PRINCESS is the second of a pair of ships built for the company by Chantiers de l'Atlantique (yard number D32) at St Nazaire, France, and a sister to the CORAL PRINCESS. She takes the name of one of the pair of ships upon which the long success of Princess Cruises was founded. Her summer 2005 itineraries centre on the splendours of Alaska, while later in the year she cruises to the Hawaiian Islands from Los Angeles, California.

PACIFIC PRINCESS was built as the R THREE for Renaissance Cruises by Chantiers de l'Atlantique (yard number N31) at St Nazaire, France for year round service in French Polynesia. Renaissance Cruises filed for bankruptcy in the autumn of 2001 and the ship was laid up. P&O Princess Cruises acquired the R THREE in 2002, and renamed her PACIFIC PRINCESS. Her time is to be shared between P&O Cruises Australia (southern summer cruising in the Pacific Islands) and Princess Cruises, based in the Far East. She revives the name of one of the company's early ships.

REGAL PRINCESS was the last ship ordered by Sitmar Line, but was delivered to the P&O Group for service with Princess Cruises by the Monfalcone yard of Fincantieri (yard number 5840). In recent years she has undertaken interesting South East Asian itineraries, and was due to be transferred to fellow group company A'Rosa Cruises in 2004. This transfer did not occur and she remains in the Princess fleet. However, she is now due to transfer to Ocean Village in November 2006. She cruises the Inside Passage from San Francisco, the River Amazon from Fort Lauderdale and has a number of South American cruises based in Buenos Aires, Argentina and Valparaiso, Chile.

SAPPHIRE PRINCESS was laid down as the DIAMOND PRINCESS by Mitsubishi Heavy Industries (yard number 2180) in Japan, but following a major fire and consequent delay in delivery, she exchanged names with her sister under construction at the same yard. She spends summer 2005 in Alaska, and much of the remainder of the year cruising the Mexican Riviera.

SEA PRINCESS was built by Fincantieri (yard number 5998) at Monfalcone, Italy as the SEA PRINCESS for Princess Cruises. As the second ship to bear this name, she subsequently cruised in the Caribbean and to Alaska before being transferred to P&O Cruises as the ADONIA for operation from Southampton in the spring of 2003. With P&O Cruises she operated as an adult-only ship, and in addition to her UK based itineraries undertook a half-world cruise in 2004. The ADONIA transferred back to Princess Cruises in April 2005, reverting to the name SEA PRINCESS, but spent the summer of that year based at Southampton before sailing to New York for a series of cruises to Quebec.

STAR PRINCESS is the third of the GRAND PRINCESS class to be built by Fincantieri (yard number 6051) at Monfalcone, Italy. Her 2003/2004 itineraries included Mexico, Alaska, Australia, Japan, China and the Far East, and a positioning voyage from Bangkok to Venice to commence a summer 2004 season in the Mediterranean. For 2005 she spends the summer season in the Baltic, based in Copenhagen, Denmark before repositioning via the US East Coast to the Caribbean Sea. She is the second ship in the Princess fleet to bear this name.

SUN PRINCESS was built by Fincantieri (yard number 5909) at Monfalcone, Italy, as the lead ship in what was eventually to become series of four. She is expected to cruise in the Caribbean and to Alaska in 2005.

TAHITIAN PRINCESS was built by Chantiers de l'Atlantique (yard number O31) at St Nazaire, France for Renaissance Cruises as the R FOUR. Renaissance Cruises filed for bankruptcy in the autumn of 2001 and the ship was laid up. P&O Princess Cruises acquired the R FOUR in 2002 and renamed her TAHITIAN PRINCESS. She will initially be used for year round cruising based at Tahiti. This appears to be a condition of acquisition of the ship, which received French Government subsidies when built, on the basis that she would be operated for a number of years in French Polynesia.

Cruise ships on order

CROWN PRINCESS	c116000t	2006	22.5k	DE2	2600p	3800p	1100c	289.6m	36.0m	8.5m
EMERALD PRINCESS	c116000t	2007	22.5k	DE2	2600p	3800p	1100c	289.6m	36.0m	8.5m
FINCANTIERI 6132	c116000t	2008	22.5k	DE2	2600p	3800p	1100c	289.6m	36.0m	8.5m

CROWN PRINCESS was ordered from Fincantieri (yard number 6100) in April 2003 in place of the sixth ship in the Holland America Vista class. She will spend the summer of 2006 based in New York.

EMERALD PRINCESS (yard number 6131) and **FINCANTIERI 6132** were ordered from Fincantieri in 2004 and will be built at the Monfalcone yard. The second of these ships may be earmarked for the P&O Cruises fleet and might revive the name CANBERRA.

SEABOURN CRUISE LINE

The Company Seabourn Cruise Line was founded in 1987 with the aim of providing the highest level of personal service to its passengers. In 1991 25% of the company was acquired by Carnival. A further 25% passed to Carnival in 1996, and the remaining stock was acquired in 1998, at which time Seabourn was put under the management of Cunard, Carnival's premium brands division. Cunard's yacht-like SEA GODDESS I and II and the ROYAL VIKING SUN were transferred to the Seabourn operation and appropriately renamed. The Seabourn operation was separated from Cunard in 2005, when the latter company came under the wing of Princess Cruises.

President Deborah L Natansohn **Marketing Director** Linda Schultes

Address Suite 400, 6100 Blue Lagoon Drive, Miami, FL 33126, United States of America

Telephone +1 305 4633000 **Fax** +1 305 4633010

Website www.seabourn.com

Areas operated Worldwide

SEABOURN LEGEND	9961t	1992	19.0k	D2	212p	212p	150c	135.0m	19.0m	5.2m	BA
SEABOURN PRIDE	9975t	1988	19.0k	D2	212p	212p	150c	133.8m	19.0m	5.2m	BA
SEABOURN SPIRIT	9975t	1989	19.0k	D2	212p	212p	150c	133.8m	19.0m	5.2m	BA

SEABOURN LEGEND was to have been the third ship of the series for Seabourn Cruise Line. However, the company did not exercise the option, although Royal Viking Line effectively later took it up. She was delivered to that company by Schichau Seebeckwerft (yard number 1071) as the ROYAL VIKING QUEEN in 1992. By this time the three original Royal Viking ships had left the company, so the fleet consisted of only this ship and the ROYAL VIKING SUN. She was renamed QUEEN ODYSSEY in 1994 and passed to Seabourn in 1996, becoming the SEABOURN LEGEND.

Seabourn Cruise Line's **Seabourn Pride** sailing from Amsterdam *(William Mayes)*

Swan Hellenic's **Minerva II** at Korcula *(Richard Seville)*

Caspi Cruises' **Dream Princess** as Airtour's **Sundream** at Piraeus (*Andrew Kilk*)

Classic International Cruises' **Arion** at Istanbul (*William Mayes*)

SEABOURN PRIDE was ordered from Schichau Seebeckwerft (yard number 1065) at Bremerhaven in Germany as the first of two luxurious mega-yachts by the newly formed Seabourn Cruise Line.

SEABOURN SPIRIT was the second ship to be delivered to Seabourn by Schichau Seebeckwerft (yard number 1070) at Bremerhaven in Germany.

SWAN HELLENIC

The Company The origins of what is now Swan Hellenic go back to the 1930's when the Hellenic Travellers Club ran cruises and tours to Greece and Asia Minor. Following the end of the Second World War, W F & R K Swan, who then owned the club, re-introduced Hellenic Cruises. The first of these cruises was undertaken in 1954 aboard the 1,700 ton 1952-built MIAOULIS. It was in the following year that Sir Mortimer Wheeler, the celebrated archaeologist, began his connection with the firm, of which he was later to become Chairman. In that year the company operated its second cruise aboard the AEGAEON, owned by the Greek Typaldos Lines, and by then more than 40 years old. Swans used another of that company's ships, the MEDITERRANEAN, between 1956 and 1958. Typaldos also provided the ADRIATIKI for ten cruises between 1957 and 1961. By the early 1960's a pattern of three early and three late season cruises aboard the ANKARA, chartered from Turkish Maritime Lines, had emerged. At the start of the next decade the number of cruises undertaken each year had steadily increased and a replacement was sought for the ANKARA, which was by now more than 45 years old, and only partly air-conditioned. The vessel selected was the ORPHEUS of Epirotiki, and she served Swans well for 22 years. In the meantime, P&O had bought Swans Hellenic Cruises in 1983 and continued to develop the business by gradually extending the cruising season. In 1995, the ORPHEUS was replaced by the newly built MINERVA, based on the hull of an unwanted Russian research vessel, but completed and fitted out as a very suitable ship to take the business forward. Initially taken on a four-year charter, this was extended to the spring of 2003, when the laid-up R EIGHT, rather unimaginatively renamed MINERVA II replaced her.

Address Richmond House, Terminus Terrace, Southampton, SO14 3PN England

Telephone +44 238 053 1990 **Fax** +44 238 052 3732

Website www.swanhellenic.com

Areas operated Worldwide, with summers in European waters

MINERVA II	30277t	2001	18.0k	DE2	710p	838p	373c	181.0m	25.5m	5.8m	MI

MINERVA II was built by Chantiers de l'Atlantique (yard number Z31) at St Nazaire, France as the R EIGHT for Renaissance Cruises. Following the failure of that company in the autumn of 2001 she was laid up at Gibraltar. During 2002 it was announced that Swan Hellenic had taken her on a seven-year charter, to commence service in April 2003 following a major re-fit, as a replacement for the smaller MINERVA. Minerva was the goddess of wisdom, whose symbol was an owl.

WINDSTAR CRUISES

The Company Windstar Cruises Inc. has its foundations in the formation in 1984 of Windstar Sail Cruises Limited, a Bahamas registered company set up by Mr Karl Gosta Andren to build and operate the first large commercial sailing vessels since the 1920's. The first two ships were ordered in October 1985 and a third shortly afterwards with an option for a fourth ship, never exercised. The WIND STAR was delivered in October 1986, followed six months later by the WIND SONG. Unfortunately, the company's marketing failed to generate the passenger volume required to fill their ships, so in June 1987 Holland America took on this role, at the same time acquiring a 50% stake in the company. The remaining 50% was purchased in September 1988 and although the company retained an outward appearance of independence, there was a certain amount of integration behind the scenes. In 1994 the head office was moved to Holland America's address in Seattle and the company name was changed to Windstar Cruises Inc. In early 2003 the fourth ship in the fleet was scuttled after an engine room fire, following which the vessel was declared a constructive total loss.

Address 300 Elliott Avenue West, Seattle, WA 98119, United States of America

Telephone +1 206 2863927 **Fax** +1 206 2863229

Website www.windstarcruises.com

Areas operated Mediterranean and Caribbean

WIND SPIRIT	5736t	1988	14.0k	SD1	148p	168p	91c	134.2m	15.8m	4.1m	BA
WIND STAR	5307t	1986	12.0k	SD1	148p	168p	91c	134.2m	15.5m	4.1m	BA
WIND SURF	14745t	1989	12.0k	SDE2	308p	397p	178c	187.2m	20.0m	5.0m	BA

WIND SPIRIT was built, along with her sisters the WIND STAR and the recently lost WIND SONG by Societe Nouvelle de Ateliers et Chantiers du Havre (yard number 272) at Le Havre, France, as a motorised sailing yacht capable of being schooner rigged. She is the fastest of the trio of ships built for the company. Wind assisted she can make 17 knots and has sailed predominantly in the Mediterranean and Caribbean, but did spend part of the 1988 season in Alaska.

WIND STAR was delivered in March 1987 by Ateliers et Chantiers du Havre (yard number 269) and following a positioning cruise spent a season in French Polynesia. She later operated in the Caribbean and Mediterranean.

WIND SURF was built by Societe Nouvelle de Ateliers et Chantiers du Havre (yard number 274) for Club Mediterranee SA (Club Med) of France and on delivery at the beginning of 1990 was registered in Fort de France, Martinique, thus qualifying her for French state subsidies. Wind assisted she is capable of making 14 knots. She operated in the Caribbean and Mediterranean as the CLUB MED 1 until June 1997 when she was bought by Windstar Cruises and renamed WIND SURF. Her operational areas remained unchanged.

CASPI CRUISES

The Company Caspi Cruises is a relatively new entrant to the growing pool of Israeli cruise operators and commenced trading in that sector in the spring of 1999. The DREAM PRINCESS joins the fleet in spring 2005 with a series of short cruises based on Ashdod and Haifa. The arrangement with this ship appears to be an operational franchise rather than a full charter. The company also owns a number of cargo ships.

Chief Executive Officer Yuval Caspi

Address 76 Ha'Atzmaut Street, PO Box 27, Haifa, Israel

Telephone +972 4 867 4444 **Fax** +972 4 867 4456

Website www.caspi-cruise.co.il

Area operated Eastern Mediterranean from Israel

DREAM PRINCESS	22945t	1970	20.5k	D2	1140p	1400p	325c	194.3m	24.0m	6.7m	BA

DREAM PRINCESS was built by Wartsila (yard number 392) at Helsinki, Finland as the SONG OF NORWAY for the new Royal Caribbean Cruise Line, one of an initial series of three revolutionary new ships. Two of the three ships, including the SONG OF NORWAY, were lengthened in 1978-1980. She was sold to Sun Cruises (Airtours) in 1997 and renamed as the SUNDREAM for cruises in the Mediterranean, the Caribbean and around the Atlantic Isles. Sun Cruises withdrew from cruising in 2004 and she was sold to Lance Shipping subsidiary, Tumaco Shipping, taking the new name DREAM PRINCESS. She was franchised to Caspi Cruises in April 2005 to undertake short cruises from Israel to Turkey, Greece and Cyprus.

CLASSIC INTERNATIONAL CRUISES

The Company Classic International Cruises is a trading name of Arcalia Shipping Company Limited, a supplier of cruises to British passengers for more than 20 years. Portuguese officers operate the ships with international crew but employ British cruise staff on cruises marketed in the UK.

Chairman George Potamianos

Address 274 Main Road, Sutton-at-Hone, Dartford, Kent, DA4 9HJ, England

Telephone +44 845 603 1180 **Fax** +44 1322 860751

Website www.classicintcruises.co.uk

Area operated Cruises from the United Kingdom

ARION	5888t	1965	16.0k	D2	328p	350p	150c	118.0m	16.5m	5.3m	PO
ATHENA	16144t	1948	16.5k	D2	550p	638p	185c	160.0m	21.0m	7.6m	PO
FUNCHAL	9563t	1961	16.0k	D2	439p	548p	155c	153.5m	19.5m	6.4m	PO
PRINCESS DANAE	16531t	1955	16.0k	D2	560p	670p	240c	162.4m	21.3m	7.6m	PO

ARION was built by Brodogradiliste Uljanik (yard number 248) at Pula, in what was then Yugoslavia, as the ISTRA for Jadrolinija. She operated initially on a 14-day itinerary from Venice to the far Eastern Mediterranean. She was sold to Caravella Shipping of the Ukraine in 1991 and renamed as the ASTRA. In 1996 she passed to Goring Shipping, another Ukraine owner, who renamed her ASTRA I. Constellation Cruise Holdings, a company within the Arcalia Shipping group, acquired her in 1999 and renamed her ARION for use by Classic International Cruises. Arion was a famous musician who dwelt at the court of Periander, King of Corinth.

ATHENA was built as the transatlantic liner STOCKHOLM for Swedish America Line by the Gotaverken shipyard (yard number 611) in Gothenburg, Sweden. In 1956, while on her regular service between Gothenburg and New York, she famously collided with and sank the Italia Line flagship, the ANDREA DORIA. After repair by the Bethlehem Steel shipyard in Brooklyn the STOCKHOLM re-entered service on her Atlantic route. In 1960 Swedish America Line sold her to VEB Deutsche Seereederie for use by the East German Free Trades Union organisation, which renamed her VOLKERFREUNDSCHAFT. She operated cruises for East German workers until sold on in 1985 to Neptunus Rex Enterprises of Panama. She was renamed VOLKER and laid up at Southampton. She became the FRIDTJOF NANSEN in late 1986 and was moved to Oslo for use as a refugee accommodation ship. Star Lauro acquired the ship in 1989 and intended to have her refurbished and renamed SURRIENTO. In the event, she was laid up in Genoa, renamed ITALIA I and later sold to Nina Compagnia di Navigazione for whom the refit was eventually completed, transforming her appearance. She was then renamed ITALIA PRIMA. She later operated cruises from Havana, Cuba as the VALTUR PRIMA. From 2001 she was laid up at Havana, until chartered by Festival Cruises in late 2003 and renamed CARIBE, but Festival collapsed shortly afterwards and the ship remained unused until taken on a ten-year bareboat charter by Classic International Cruises in 2004 and renamed ATHENA after a refit in Lisbon. She was to have replaced the PRINCESS DANAE, allowing that ship to go for an extended overhaul, but the amount of work required to bring her up to standard was greater than expected. Following her refit she operates two cruises under charter in the German market. Athena, the Greek goddess of wisdom, was the favourite daughter of Zeus.

FUNCHAL was the last of the Portuguese liners, and arguably the most attractive. She was built in Denmark, at the Helsingor Shipyard (yard number 353) for Empressa Insulana de Navegacao of Lisbon, a mini liner, for the almost local service from Lisbon to Madeira, the Azores and the Canary Islands. As built she had two Parsons steam turbines, which gave her a service speed of 20 knots. She was occasionally used as the Portuguese Presidential Yacht, and undertook voyages in that role as far afield as Brazil. She suffered recurring engine problems; however in 1972 her machinery was replaced by diesel engines during a major refit in Amsterdam. Her owner, along with the other Portuguese liner operators, faced severe financial crisis and was merged in 1974 with Companhia Colonial to form Companhia Portuguesa de Transportes Maritimos. By now, the FUNCHAL was used almost exclusively for cruising and undertook a number of charters. Her owner was wound up in 1985 and the FUNCHAL was sold to Great Warwick of Panama, now managed by Arcalia Shipping. She has subsequently been operated by Arcalia Shipping under its own name, but is now marketed by Classic International Cruises. Funchal is the capital of the Portuguese island of Madeira.

PRINCESS DANAE began life as the Port Line cargo ship, PORT MELBOURNE, built by Harland & Wolff (yard number 1483) at Belfast, Northern Ireland, for the company's liner service from London to Australia. By 1971 Port Line was owned by Cunard Line, so when the latter company was acquired by Trafalgar House Investments, the less profitable routes, including that operated by the PORT MELBOURNE, were discontinued. She was sold along with her sister ship the PORT SYDNEY (now the OCEAN MONARCH operated by Hansa Kreuzfahrten (q.v.)), to Greek ship owner J C Karras. The PORT MELBOURNE was renamed THERISOS EXPRESS and was earmarked for conversion into a car ferry. That project never materialised and she was eventually renamed DANAE and converted into a luxury cruise ship. She began her new career in 1977, and two years later was chartered to Costa Line, along with her sister, now named DAPHNE. In 1984 Costa Line purchased the ships. In 1990 the sisters were transferred to a joint venture company Prestige Cruises, in which Costa had a 50% stake. Costa later regained full control, but in 1991, while undergoing a refit the ship caught fire and was subsequently declared a constructive total loss due to the damage caused by smoke, and water from the ship's sprinklers. Renamed ANAR, she was towed to Piraeus, where she was fully refurbished under the name STARLIGHT PRINCESS. She did not operate under that name, but was chartered to the Swedish Baltic Line as the BALTICA. She subsequently undertook further charters to Northern European operators before being sold to Waybell Cruises in 1996 for use by Classic International Cruises as the PRINCESS DANAE. In Greek mythology Danae was the daughter of Acrisius and the mother of Perseus by Zeus.

CLIPPER CRUISE LINE

The Company Barney Ebsworth, a Missouri businessman, established Clipper Cruise Line in 1982. The business was later sold to US luxury tour operator, Intrav. In 1999 Intrav, together with Clipper Cruise Line was acquired by the Swiss tour operator Kuoni Travel Holdings Ltd.

Chief Executive Officer David Drier

Address 11969 Westline Industrial Drive, St Louis, Missouri, 63146-3220, United States of America

Telephone +1 314 655 6700 **Fax** +1 314 655 6670

Website www.clippercruise.com

Area operated Worldwide – Adventurer and Odyssey, North America and the Caribbean Sea – Nantucket and Yorktown

CLIPPER ADVENTURER	4376t	1975	17.0k	D2	122p	122p	79c	100.0m	16.2m	4.7m	BA
CLIPPER ODYSSEY	5218t	1989	18.0k	D2	120p	120p	70c	103.0m	15.4m	4.3m	BA
NANTUCKET CLIPPER	1471t	1984	7.0k	D2	102p	102p	36c	63.1m	11.3m	2.6m	US
YORKTOWN CLIPPER	2354t	1988	10.0k	D2	138p	138p	42c		12.2m		US

CLIPPER ADVENTURER was built by Brodogradiliste Titovo (yard number 408) at Kraljevica in what was then Yugoslavia as the ALLA TARASOVA, one of a series of eight ships for Murmansk Shipping for coastal passenger service. Among her surviving sisters are the LYUBOV ORLOVA and the MARIYA YERMOLOVA. In 1997 she was rebuilt as the cruise ship CLIPPER ADVENTURER for Clipper Cruise Line.

CLIPPER ODYSSEY was built by Nippon Kokan KK (yard number 112) at Tsu, Japan as the OCEANIC GRACE for Oceanic Cruises. In 1997 she was renamed as the OCEANIC ODYSSEY for Spice Island Cruises, but lasted less than a year with that organisation, being sold in 1998, and becoming the CLIPPER ODYSSEY for Clipper Cruise Line.

Classic International Cruises' **Princess Danae** off Calshot *(Alan Ryszka-Onions)*

Clipper Cruise Line's **Clipper Adventurer** at Santander *(William Mayes)*

NANTUCKET CLIPPER was built in 1984 by Jeffboat Inc, at Jeffersonville, Indiana, USA.

YORKTOWN CLIPPER was built in 1988 by First Coast Shipbuilding Inc, at Green Cove Springs, Florida, USA.

CLUB MED CRUISES

The Company Club Med Cruises is a division of the French travel company Club Med.

Address 11 Rue de Cambrai, 75957 Paris Cedex 19, France

Telephone +33 153 353553 **Fax** +33 153 353616

Website www.clubmed.com

Area operated Summer in the Mediterranean Sea and winter in the Caribbean Sea

CLUB MED 2	14893t	1992	15.0k	SD2	392p	419p	181c	187.0m	20.0m	5.0m	WF

CLUB MED 2 was built by Societe Nouvelle des Ateliers et Chantiers du Havre (yard number 282) at Le Havre, France, as one of a pair of sister ships for Club Med. The other of this duo was sold to Windstar Cruises. CLUB MED 2 is managed by V-Ships.

COCO EXPLORER CRUISES

The Company Coco Explorer Cruises is a Filipino company operating weekly adventure cruises around the Philippine Islands.

Address Ground Floor Baywatch Tower, 2057 M.H. Del Pilar St, Malate, Manila, Philippines

Telephone +63 2 523 0319 **Fax** +63 2 526 6903

Website www.cocoexplorer.com

Area operated Philippines

COCO EXPLORER I	1199t	1967	12.0k	D2	120p	120p	53c	60.6m	11.0m	5.3m	PH

COCO EXPLORER I was built by Union Naval de Levante at Valencia, Spain as the SANTA MARIA DE LA CARIDAD for Compania Trasmediterranea for the inter-island service in the Canary Islands. She was sold and became the IRENE in 1984 for Irene Marine. A year later she was the CYPRUS EXPRESS and subsequently the MARIA I. In 1987 she was renamed as the ESTRELLA DO MAR, and spent some time in the waters of East and Southern Africa. She was renamed COCO EXPLORER I in 1999 for Coco Explorer Cruises.

COMPAGNIE DES ILES DU PONANT

The Company Compagnie des Iles du Ponant was established in 1988 and raised the required capital by subscription to purchase and operate the luxury yacht LE PONANT. The company also became a tour agency, but later bought out the other investors to own the ship outright. The purchase of LE LEVANT was financed in the same way and that ship currently has 280 shareholders. In 2003, in conjunction with French tour operator Tapis Rouge Croisieres, the SONG OF FLOWER was acquired from Radisson Seven Seas Cruises and renamed LE DIAMANT. She is operated by Compagnie des Iles du Diamant, a joint venture between 'Ponant' and Tapis Rouge. French container shipping line CMA-CGM is currently the majority shareholder in the company, holding 70% of the stock. The Iles du Ponant are a group of islands off the northern and western coasts of Brittany, France.

Address 60 Boulevard Marechal Alphonse Juin, F44100 Nantes, France

Telephone +33 240 581495 **Fax** +33 240 582702

Website www.ponant.com

Area operated Worldwide

LE DIAMANT	8382t	1974	16.0k	D2	172p	226p	144c	124.2m	16.0m	4.8m	WF
LE LEVANT	3504t	1998	16.0k	D2	90p	90p	49c	100.3m	13.1m	3.0m	WF
LE PONANT	1189t	1991	14.0k	SD1	56p	64p	30c	84.3m	11.9m	4.0m	WF

LE DIAMANT was built by Kristiansands Mekaniske Verksted (yard number 220) at Kristiansand, Norway as one of a pair of ro-ro freighters, the BEGONIA (although she was launched as the FERNHILL) for Oslo ship owners, Fearney & Eger. These ships were immediately transferred to an associated Dutch company. Fearney & Eger reacquired the BEGONIA in 1985 and sent her to the Lloyd Werft yard at Bremerhaven; here she was converted into the exploration cruise ship EXPLORER STARSHIP. On completion she was chartered to Exploration Cruise Line and served initially in the Caribbean and later on the US West Coast and in Alaska. Exploration Cruise Line filed for bankruptcy in 1988 and eventually Fearney & Eger were able to recover their ship. She was soon sold to Seven Seas Cruise Line, a new company set up by the Japanese Kawasaki Kisen Kaisha Line and the

Clipper Cruise Line's **Yorktown Clipper** in the East River, New York *(Theodore W Scull)*

Coco Explorer Cruises' **Coco Explorer 1** *(Jonathan Boonzaier)*

Compagnie des Iles du Ponant's **Le Levant** at Windsor, Ontario *(Andrew Kilk)*

Cruise West's **Spirit of 98** *(Andrew Kilk)*

Norwegian Skaugen concern. Following a refit that converted her to a luxury 214-passenger ship, she entered service from Singapore as the SONG OF FLOWER in February 1990. During the next five years she cruised in most of the then popular cruising areas, but in 1995 the operation was merged with Radisson Diamond Cruises, although her owners retained the ship for a further two years before she was sold to the new Radisson Seven Seas Cruises. No longer in keeping with the remainder of the fleet, she passed to her current operator in 2003 and following a major refit emerged as LE DIAMANT. Diamant translates from French as diamond.

LE LEVANT, the sleek, yacht-like luxury cruise ship was built by Alstom Leroux Naval (yard number 625) at St Malo, France for the company. She has undertaken a number of charters, including one to Classical Cruises International. The ship is named after one of the islands off the coast of Provence, France.

LE PONANT was built by Societe Francaise Construction Navales (yard number 863) at Villeneuv- la-Garenne, France.

CORAL PRINCESS CRUISES

The Company Coral Princess Cruises is an Australian company, founded in 1988.

Address PO Box 2093, Cairns, Queensland, Australia

Telephone +61 7 4040 9999 **Fax** +61 7 4035 5995

Website www.coralprincesscruises.com

Area operated Australia's Great Barrier Reef

CORAL PRINCESS	730t	1988	10.0k	D2	48p	48p	c	35.0m	13.3m	2.4m	AU
CORAL PRINCESS II	729t	1985	10.0k	D2	48p	48p	c	37.3m	12.0m	2.4m	AU
OCEANIC PRINCESS	1838t	2005	16.0k	D2	76p	76p	c	63.1m	13.0m	3.0m	AU

CORAL PRINCESS was built by Carrington Slipways (yard number 204) at Newcastle, New South Wales, Australia.

CORAL PRINCESS II was built by North Queensland Engineers & Agents (yard number 121) at Cairns, Queensland, Australia as the CORAL CAT. In 1990 she was renamed SPICE ISLANDER and took her current name in 1996 when acquired by Coral Princess Cruises.

OCEANIC PRINCESS was built by North Queensland Engineers & Agents (yard number 220) at Cairns, Queensland, Australia for the company.

CROATIAN CRUISE LINE

The Company Croatian Cruise Line is a trading name of Uljanik Shipmanagement Inc, a Croatian shipping company formerly owned by the Uljanik Shipbuilding Group. Uljanik Shipmanagement was established in 1986 in order to acquire and manage three ships that were under construction at the Uljanik Shipyard. Subsequently the company was sold to private investors and currently owns seven ships and offers management services to other owners. The DALMACIJA was purchased from Intercruise in 2001, although Uljanik had managed the ship for the previous four years.

Address Carrarina 6, 52100 Pula, Croatia

Telephone +385 52 212 955 **Fax** +385 52 211 339

Website www.cruiseadriatic.com

Area operated The Dalmatian Coast of Croatia from Venice

DALMACIJA	5619t	1965	16.0k	D2	280p	300p	91c	116.8m	16.5m	5.3m	CR

DALMACIJA was built at the Brodogradiliste Uljanik Shipyard (yard number 243) at Pula, in what was then Yugoslavia for the coastal cruising services of Yugoslavian state operator Jadrolinija. She also made a number of summer cruises in Northern Europe and Scandinavia. She passed to Intercruise in about 1991 and was acquired by her current owner in 2001.

Delta Queen Steamboat Company's **Delta Queen** *(Andrew Kilk)*

Cruise West's **Spirit of Columbia** *(Andrew Kilk)*

CRUCEROS AUSTRALIS

The Company Cruceros Australis is a Chilean company, founded in 1990 to operate short cruises in and around Patagonia.

Address Avenida El Bosque Norte 0440 Piso 11, Las Condes, Santiago 6780235, Chile

Telephone +56 2 442 3110 **Fax** +56 2 203 5173

Website www.australis.com

Area operated Patagonia, Tierra del Fuego and Cape Horn

MARE AUSTRALIS	2664t	2002		D2	126p	126p	c	71.8m	13.4m	3.2m	CL
VIA AUSTRALIS	2750t	2005		D2	128p	128p	c	71.8m	13.4m	3.3m	CL

MARE AUSTRALIS and **VIA AUSTRALIS** were built by Astilleros y Servicios Navales (yard numbers 132 and 145) at Valdivia, Chile for Nisa Navegacion, a Chilean operator of ferries and cargo ships within the same corporate grouping as Cruceros Australis.

CRUISE NORTH EXPEDITIONS

The Company Cruise North Expeditions is part of the Inuit-owned Makivik Corporation, based in Canada.

Address 1111 Dr Frederik-Philips Boulevard, St Laurent, QC, H4M 2X6, Canada

Telephone +1 416 789 3752 **Fax** +1 416 789 1974

Website www.cruisenorthexpeditions.com

Area operated Hudson Strait, Baffin Island and Hudson Bay, Canada

USHUAIA	‡2802t	1968	14.0k	D2	66p	66p	38c	84.8m	15.6m	5.5m	PA

USHUAIA was built as the US Government research vessel RESEARCHER by the American Shipbuilding Co (yard number 198) at Lorain, Ohio, USA. She was renamed as the MALCOLM BALDRIGE in 1988 and was sold to Argentinean company Ushuaia Adventure in 2001, when she took her current name. Cruise North seasonally charter her, commencing in 2005.

CRUISE WEST

The Company The origins of Cruise West go back to 1946, when Chuck West founded Alaska Arctic Travel Service in Fairbanks. The company soon branched out to offer the first small ship tours of Alaska and in 1971 the business, now named Westours, was sold to Holland America Line. Two years later, West founded what is today Cruise West, offering space on the ships of Alaska State Ferries and others. In 1990 the company acquired its first ship, the SPIRIT OF GLACIER BAY, and began to run two-night cruises from Juneau. During the following year, the newly purchased SPIRIT OF ALASKA began cruising from Seattle to Alaska.

Management President Jeff Krida **Chairman and Chief Executive Officer** Richard D West

Address 2301 Fifth Avenue, Suite 401, Seattle, Washington, WA98121-1856

Telephone +1 800 580 0072 **Fax** +1 206 441 4757

Website www.cruisewest.com

Area operated Alaska (all ships except PACIFIC EXPLORER), Costa Rica and Panama (PACIFIC EXPLORER), Mexico and California (SPIRIT OF ENDEAVOUR), Japan and South Pacific (SPIRIT OF OCEANUS), British Columbia (SPIRIT OF COLUMBIA)

PACIFIC EXPLORER	1716t	1970	12.0k	D2	100p	100p	33c	54.9m	11.6m	4.2m	HD
SPIRIT OF 98	1472t	1984	13.0k	D2	96p	99p	26c	58.5m	12.2m	2.9m	US
SPIRIT OF ALASKA	c500t	1980	12.0k	D1	78p	82p	21c	37.6m	8.5m	2.0m	US
SPIRIT OF COLUMBIA	514t	1979	10.0k	D1	78p	80p	21c	37.3m	8.5m	2.0m	US
SPIRIT OF DISCOVERY	910t		13.0k	D2	84p	84p	21c	50.7m	11.2m	2.2m	US
SPIRIT OF ENDEAVOUR	1472t	1983	13.0k	D2	102p	107p	28c	56.2m	11.3m	2.6m	US
SPIRIT OF OCEANUS	4200t	1991	14.5k	D2	114p	129p	64c	90.4m	15.3m	4.0m	BA

PACIFIC EXPLORER was built by American Marine Corporation (yard number 1052) at New Orleans, Louisiana, USA as the FORCE TIDE. She was renamed NORPAC II in 1987, PACIFIC WARRIOR in 1992 and on transfer to Cruceros de Sur in 1995 (Temptress Voyages) TEMPTRESS EXPLORER. In 2001 ownership passed to Transamerica Ship Holding, and in May of the following year she was renamed PACIFIC EXPLORER. Cruise West had previously been marketing voyages on the TEMPTRESS EXPLORER.

Compagnie des Iles du Ponant's **Le Ponant** at Valletta *(Theodore W Scull)*

Croatian Cruise Line's **Dalmacija** at Venice *(William Mayes)*

SPIRIT OF 98 was built by Bender Shipbuilding & Repair Company (yard number 140) at Mobile, Alabama, USA as the PILGRIM BELLE. On sale to Cruise West (West Travel) in 1984 she became the COLONIAL EXPLORER, and in 1988 was renamed again as VICTORIAN EMPRESS. In 1993 she became SPIRIT OF 98.

SPIRIT OF ALASKA was built by Blount Marine Corporation (yard number 234) at Warren, Rhode Island, USA as the PACIFIC NORTHWEST EXPLORER. She became the SPIRIT OF ALASKA in 1988.

SPIRIT OF COLUMBIA was built by Blount Marine Corporation (yard number 225) at Warren, Rhode Island, USA as the NEW SHOREHAM II. She was renamed SPIRIT OF COLUMBIA in 1993.

SPIRIT OF ENDEAVOUR was built by Jeffboat Inc (yard number 82-2542) at Jeffersonville, Indiana, USA as the NEWPORT CLIPPER. She later became SEASPIRIT and took her current name in 1993.

SPIRIT OF OCEANUS was built at the Italian Marina di Carrara yard of Nuovi Cantieri Apuania (yard number 1144) as the RENAISSANCE FIVE for Renaissance Cruises. Sold in 1997 to Sun Viva, she was renamed as the SUN VIVA. When Star Cruises acquired that company in 2000 she became the MEGASTAR SAGITTARIUS, but was quickly sold to Cruise West and renamed SPIRIT OF OCEANUS.

DAMI CRUISES

The Company Dami Cruises is a recent offshoot of the established charter boat company Dami Boats, a Croatian private company. The company also operates the sail-cruiser ROMANSKA, which is too small to include here in detail.

Management Owner Darko Mikulandra

Address Istarska 50a, 51000 Rijeka, Croatia

Telephone +385 51 622 121 **Fax** +385 51 622 121

Website www.damiboats.hr

Area operated The coast of Croatia

DARLI	967t	1959	12.0k	D2	78p	98p	c	56.0m	10.7m	3.1m	CR

DARLI was built by Stord Verft (yard number 50) at Stord, Norway as the HARDANGERFJORD for the Norwegian coastal trade. In 1982 she was briefly renamed HARDANGERFJORD 1 to free up her previous name for a new ship. She was sold later that year becoming the FIRDA. In 1989 she passed to Brand and was renamed BRAND for expedition voyages. She was acquired by her current owner and renamed DARLI in 2004, and following a major refit entered service on the beautiful Croatian coast.

DELPHIN SEEREISEN

The Company Delphin Seereisen is a German company providing cruises for German speaking passengers. The company began operating in 1981 and in the early years chartered such ships as the KAZAKHSTAN and the KAZAKHSTAN II, the latter ship eventually operating as the DELPHIN. The charter of the DELPHIN RENAISSANCE commenced in 2003.

Managing Director Heinz-Herbert Hey

Address Neusalzer Strasse 22e, D 63069 Offenbach, Germany

Telephone +49 69 9840 3811 **Fax** +49 69 9840 3840

Website www.delphin-renaissance.de

Area operated Worldwide

DELPHIN RENAISSANCE	30277t	2000	18.0k	DE2	716p	840p	306c	181.0m	25.5m	6.0m	MI

DELPHIN RENAISSANCE was built as the R SEVEN by Chantiers de l'Atlantique (yard number X31) at St Nazaire, France for Renaissance Cruises. Following the failure of that company she was laid up off Gibraltar before being sold to Cruiseinvest, a company associated with her builders, part of the Alstom Group. She was subsequently chartered by Delphin Seereisen and renamed DELPHIN RENAISSANCE.

DELTA QUEEN STEAMBOAT COMPANY

The Company The origins of the company can be traced back to 1890, when Captain Greene established the Greene Line of Steamers with the purchase at auction of the riverboat H K BEDFORD. Freight services began on the upper Ohio and Kanahwa Rivers, but before long the company started to offer passenger services. In 1948, the DELTA QUEEN entered service for the company, having been bought at auction from the US Navy's reserve fleet. In the early 1950's the company was facing a very uncertain future, but Californian businessman Richard Simonton stepped in and with the help of publicist Betty Blake soon had the company thriving again. Following an emotional campaign, the DELTA QUEEN, with her vast quantities of wood, was granted congressional exception to SOLAS. The company was acquired by Overseas National Airways in 1969, and adopted its current name five years later. In the early 1990's, after another change of ownership, the company acquired the troubled American Hawaii Cruise Line and both companies then became part of the newly formed holding company American Classic Voyages. Following severe financial difficulties after the September 11th attacks on the World Trade Centre the company collapsed, but the steamboat side of the business was rescued by Delaware North Companies Inc.

Address Robin Street Wharf, 1380 Port of New Orleans Place, New Orleans, Louisiana 70130-1890, United States of America

Telephone +1 504 586 0631 **Fax** +1 504 585 0630

Website www.deltaqueen.com

Area operated Mississippi, Arkansas and Ohio Rivers in the Deep South and Heartland of the USA

AMERICAN QUEEN	10159t	1995	10.0k	SR1	444p	481p	180c	127.5m	25.9m	2.6m	US
DELTA QUEEN	‡3360t	1927	10.0k	D1	174p	174p	c	86.9m	17.7m	m	US
MISSISSIPPI QUEEN	‡3364t	1976	12.0k	SR1	414p	414p	c	114.6m	20.4m	m	US

AMERICAN QUEEN was built by the McDermott Shipyard (yard number 296) in Amelia, Louisiana, USA for the Delta Queen Steamboat Company.

DELTA QUEEN was constructed in Scotland and re-assembled in California for the overnight service between San Francisco and Sacramento and entered service in 1927. She served as a troop carrier in San Francisco Bay during the Second World War, but was then mothballed by the US Navy. Greene Line Steamers bought the DELTA QUEEN for $47,000 and boarded her up for her long journey to the Mississippi, via the Panama Canal. Following refurbishment she entered service in 1948 and has been an attraction on the Mississippi River ever since.

MISSISSIPPI QUEEN was built by Jeffboat Inc (yard number 2999) at Jeffersonville, Indiana, USA for the Mississippi Queen Steamboat Company.

DISNEY CRUISE LINE

The Company Disney Cruise Line is part of the Disney Corporation leisure group.

Address PO Box 10238, Lake Buena Vista, Florida 32830-0238 United States of America

Telephone +1 407 566 3500 **Fax** +1 407 566 3541

Website www.disneycruise.com

Area operated Caribbean Sea

| DISNEY MAGIC | 83338t | 1998 | 21.5k | DE2 | 1750p | 2834p | 945c | 294.1m | 32.3m | 8.0m | BA |
| DISNEY WONDER | 83338t | 1999 | 21.5k | DE2 | 1750p | 2834p | 945c | 294.1m | 32.3m | 8.0m | BA |

DISNEY MAGIC and **DISNEY WONDER** were built by Fincantieri (yard numbers 5989 and 5990) at Monfalcone and Breda, Italy (respectively) for the new Disney Cruise Line.

EASYCRUISE

The Company Easycruise is a new and radically different operator, established in 2004, which commenced sailings in May 2005. It remains to be seen whether the 'no frills' concept, so successful in the airline industry, will transform the bottom end of the cruise market in a similar way. The ship offers basic, tiny cabins, which will be serviced at an extra charge. Food is not included, but will be available from a number of outlets. Passengers are able to book for any length of stay on board from two nights upwards and the ship is scheduled to sail overnight between ports allowing much of the day ashore. Easycruise is part of Easygroup.

Chief Executive Officer Stelios Haji-Ioannou

Address The Rotunda, 42/43 Gloucester Crescent, London NW1 7DL England

Telephone +44 207 241 9009

Disney Cruise Line's **Disney Wonder** at Nassau *(Andrew Kilk)*

Elegant Cruises' **Monet** at Dubrovnik *(William Mayes)*

Elysian Cruises' **Grand Victoria** as the **World Renaissance** in Piraeus *(Andrew Kilk)*

Epirotiki Lines' **Iason** at Korcula *(Richard Seville)*

Website www.easycruise.com

Area operated Western Mediterranean in summer, Caribbean in winter

EASYCRUISEONE	4077t	1990	15.5k	D2	170p	170p	54c	88.3m	15.3m	4.0m	CY

EASYCRUISEONE was built by Cantieri Navale Ferrari (yard number 44) at La Spezia, Italy as the RENAISSANCE TWO, the second in a series of eight ships for the new Renaissance Cruises, a company in which the Norwegian ship owner Fearney & Eger were initially involved. She was sold in 1998 as new and larger ships were delivered, and became THE NEPTUNE for Malaysian owners. She was briefly renamed as THE NEPTUNE 2 when sold to Owen Shipping. She was converted from her original luxury to a very basic ship carrying twice the number of passengers in a Singapore shipyard, before entering service in the spring of 2005 for Easycruise as the EASYCRUISEONE in the Western Mediterranean. She is one of an enormous number of ships managed by V-Ships.

EL SALAM MARITIME TRANSPORT

The Company El Salam Maritime Transport Company is an Egyptian company within the El Salam Shipping and Trading Group that might normally be considered to be outside the scope of this book. However, the company's ships are often chartered to Mediterranean operators and the company has, in some recent years, advertised Mediterranean cruises. The fleet is also interesting due to its predominantly European origin. The industrialist Mamdouh Ismail established the El Salam group in 1978. The company operates ferry services in the Red Sea.

Address 30 Yakoub Artten, Heliopolis, Cairo, Egypt

Telephone +202 290 8535 **Fax** +202 291 7032

Website www.elsalammaritime.com

Area operated Mediterranean

AL SALAM PASCOLI 96	11779t	1971	17k	D2	576p	921p	96c	130.9m	20.0m	5.9m	PA

AL SALAM PASCOLI 96 was built by Cantieri Navale del Tirreno e Riuniti (yard number 249) at Palermo, Sicily as the PASCOLI for Tirrenia di Navigazione as a car ferry for domestic Italian services. A major rebuild by INMA occurred in 1991, increasing her passenger accommodation by the addition of two decks of cabins. In 1999 she was sold to El Salam Shipping and Trading and renamed AL SALAM PASCOLI 96. During 2000 she operated as the TERTIUM MILLENIUM on charter for service between Barcelona and Civitavecchia, later taking the name PASCOLI 96, but more recently she has resumed operating as the AL SALAM PASCOLI 96. She sometimes operates cruises in the Mediterranean in the summer.

ELEGANT CRUISE LINE

The Company Elegant Cruise Line is marketed by Elegant Cruises in the USA. A number of other tour companies market space on these ships including Noble Caledonia in the UK. Elegant Cruise Line is a Croatian owned company.

President Mato Stanovik

Address 24 Vanderventer Avenue, Port Washington, New York State, NY 11050, United States of America

Telephone +1 516 767 9302 **Fax** +1 516 767 9302

Website www.elegantcruises.com

Area operated Adriatic and Mediterranean Seas, The Amazon and Antarctica

ANDREA	2549t	1960	16.0k	D1	117p	117p	48p	87.4m	13.3m	4.6m	LB
MONET	1425t	1970	13.3k	D2	60p	61p	30c	68.0m	10.1m	3.3m	SV

ANDREA was built by AS Trondheims Mek. Verksted (yard number 244) at Trondheim, Norway as the HARALD JARL for TFDS for service on the Norwegian Coastal Express (Hurtigruten). She continued to operate in this service until sold in 2002 to Elegant Cruises and refitted for use as a luxury expedition cruise ship. Jadropov International, the manager of the MONET, is also involved in the management of this ship.

MONET was built as the YUSHAR for Northern Shipping. She became the STELLA DALMATIAE in 1997 for Dalmacija Cruise Line and was renamed as the MONET in 1998 for Danaco. She subsequently passed to Ocean Winds in 2001 and Westwind Enterprises in 2003. She is operated by Jadropov International and marketed by Elegant Cruises. The 2005 season is the fifth season that the MONET has operated on the Dalmatian Coast for Elegant Cruises. Frenchman Claude Monet was one of the greatest of the impressionist artists.

ELYSIAN CRUISES

The Company Elysian Cruises appears to be connected with Ravenscroft Shipping of the USA. It is not known if this ship will be operated by Elysian, but her renaming suggests that she might be chartered to Iberojet.

Address 3251 Ponce de Leon Boulevard, Miami, Florida 33134, United States of America

Area operated Unknown at time of publication

GRAND VICTORIA	11429t	1966	18.5k	D2	474p	536p	230c	150.1m	21.0m	6.2m	PA

GRAND VICTORIA was one of the last French built passenger ships destined for a French operator. She was built by Chantiers de l'Atlantique (yard number D23) at St Nazaire as the RENAISSANCE for Paquet's subsidiary Compagnie Francaise de Navigation for service between Marseilles and the ports of the Eastern Mediterranean. Liner services in the Mediterranean were in decline and the ship was gradually transferred to cruising. In 1977 she was sold to Epirotiki Lines of Greece who renamed her as the HOMERIC RENAISSANCE. She was chartered to Costa Cruises fairly quickly and renamed WORLD RENAISSANCE. In the early 1980's she was sub-chartered to Curnow Shipping for service between the UK and St Helena and Cape Town. This was less than successful and the ship reverted to her Costa duties. She later operated for Epirotiki, but in 1995 transferred to Club Awani Travel of Djakarta, Indonesia as the AWANI DREAM. When she returned to Epirotiki in 1998, that company had merged most of its business into Royal Olympic Cruises, so that is where the WORLD RENAISSANCE was employed. When Royal Olympic Cruises finally collapsed in 2004 she was laid up. The ship was acquired at auction in April 2005 and quickly renamed GRAND VICTORIA.

The company also owns the NEW FLAMENCO, on charter to Globalia/Travelplan (q.v.).

EMPRESSA TURISTICA INTERNACIONAL

The Company Empressa Turistica Internacional (ETICA) is an Ecuador owner and operator of expedition cruise ships operating within the Galapagos Islands. Space on most sailings is block-booked by various US and European tour operators.

Management President Eduardo Proano

Address Calle Isla Santa Cruz 103, y Avenida de las Americas, PO Box 09-01-7132, Guayaquil, Ecuador

Telephone +593 4 284666 **Fax** +593 4 280933

Area operated Galapagos Islands

ISABELA II	‡1025t	1979	12.0k	D2	40p	40p	24c	48.8m	11.6m	3.4m	EC
SANTA CRUZ	‡1623t	1995	15.0k	D2	90p	90p	50c	69.6m	11.8m	3.2m	EC

ISABELA II was built by Halter Marine (yard number 848) at Patterson, Louisiana, USA as the CINDY BRILEY. In 1985 she became the CARL B DOWNS and took her present name in 1988 when she passed to ETICA.

SANTA CRUZ was built by Astilleros y Talleres Celaya (yard number 178) at Bilbao, Spain as the SANTA CRUZ for ETICA.

EPIROTIKI CRUISE LINES

The Company The origins of Epirotiki Cruise Lines go back to 1850, when Anastassios Potamianos first began transporting passengers and cargo along the River Danube. When his nephew, George, took over following the death of the founder in 1902, his deep-seated Christianity inspired him to use the Byzantine Cross as the company's emblem, and at the same time the business was renamed Epirotiki. By 1926 the company owned 15 passenger vessels employed in trades in and around Greece. All but one of the company's ships was lost in the Second World War, and in the aftermath the business was slowly reconstructed. The first cruise ship was the SEMIRAMIS of 1954, a 20-year old ship previously named CALABAR. She subsequently became an accommodation ship and was broken up in 1980. In 1965 the 1929-built ARGONAUT joined the cruising fleet, followed over the next few years by, among others, the JASON, ORPHEUS, APOLLON, JUPITER and ATLAS. In the 1970's Epirotiki was the largest cruise ship operator in Greece and the Eastern Mediterranean Sea. Between 1978 and 1984 further acquisitions included OCEANOS, WORLD RENAISSANCE, ODYSSEUS, APOLLO II, PEGASUS and TRITON. By the early 1990's the company had lost its way and needed a partner. In 1993 that partner emerged as Carnival Corporation, and the new arrangement saw the arrival of three large ships, the PALLAS ATHENA and the former Canadian Pacific Empresses, OLYMPIC and APOLLON. The relationship was short-lived and by 1996 the company was again looking for a partner. This time it was the Greek company, Sun Cruises that came to the rescue. Sun brought the STELLA MARIS II, STELLA OCEANIS and STELLA SOLARIS to the now renamed Royal Olympic Cruises. Further financial turmoil led to Louis Cruise Lines of Cyprus taking a 70% stake in Royal Olympic in 1999. However, the final scene had already been set with the ordering of two fast cruise ships from Blohm & Voss in Hamburg the previous year. These ships had been designed to operate a new 'Three Continents in a Week' itinerary, but as the Middle East problems escalated their proposed service was no longer viable and they began to operate itineraries for which slower ships would have been adequate.

By the end of 2004, the company had been declared bankrupt and most of its fleet had been auctioned. The JASON (now slightly renamed as the IASON) had remained within the control of Epirotiki, and it's a sad reflection that she and the day cruise ship HERMES are all that is left of this once impressive company.

President George Potamianos **Vice President** Christos Stoforopoulos

Address 87 Akti Miaouli, Piraeus Greece

Telephone +30 210 459 7211 **Fax** +30 210 429 1641

Website www.epirotiki.gr

Area operated Europe, generally on charters, also day cruises with HERMES (see Passenger Ships in other roles)

| IASON | 4561t | 1965 | 15.0k | D2 | 256p | 325p | 112p | 97.2m | 16.0m | 4.5m | PA |

IASON was built by Cantieri Riunite dell'Adriatico (yard number 1882) at Monfalcone, Italy as the EROS for the Greek Government as part of the Second World War reparations scheme. She was one of three similar ships owned by the Hellenic Tourism Organisation, although each ship was operated by one of the Greek passenger shipping companies. The EROS was allocated to Typaldos Lines, but that company became bankrupt so she went to Epirotiki in 1966 and was renamed JASON. Her name was later restyled as IASON. During 2004 she operated on charter to the French tour operator Rivages. Jason was the son of the King of Iolcus, later famous in Greek mythology for his quest for the Golden Fleece in the ARGO.

FIORDLAND TRAVEL

The Company Fiordland Travel is a New Zealand tour operator.

Address Milford Road PO Box 1, Te Anua, New Zealand

Telephone +64 3 249 7816 **Fax** +64 3 249 7817

Website www.fiordlandtravel.co.nz

Area operated The fjords of New Zealand

FIORDLAND NAVIGATOR	693t	2001		D1	54p	70p	c	38.2m	10.0m	m	NZ
MILFORD MARINER	693t	2000		D2	60p	60p	c	38.2m	10.0m	m	NZ
MILFORD WANDERER	258t	1992		D1	61p	61p	c	28.5m	8.4m	m	NZ

All three ships were built by J K Stevenson Ltd at Invercargill, New Zealand.

FRED. OLSEN CRUISE LINES

The Company The business we know today as Fred. Olsen Cruise Lines has its origins in the ship owning firm founded in 1886 by Frederik Olsen. By the early 1900's the business had expanded to embrace routes between Norway and Europe, Britain and the Mediterranean. The latter was a particularly important development as it introduced the company to the fruit trades from the region. The Canary Islands later became the focus of this trade, and the Olsen family still have significant investments in that area including a ferry operation. In 1906 the company began to carry passengers between Norway and the River Tyne, in northeast England, and Fred. Olsen developed this business, which probably peaked with the introduction of the BRAEMAR on the route from Harwich to Oslo in 1985. Olsen first started to offer what might now be regarded as proper cruises in 1966 with the arrival of the dual purpose BLACK WATCH and BLACK PRINCE. The first of these was jointly ordered by Fred. Olsen and the Bergen Line to serve the latter company's North Sea trades in the summer under the name JUPITER and to begin a new era for the Olsen's by offering cruises to the Canary Islands from London in the winter as the BLACK WATCH. The impressive vehicle deck space was occupied on the northbound leg by Canary Islands fruit, destined for the tables of Northern Europe. The second ship was ordered by Olsen for its own account, but in 1970 the company entered into a similar arrangement with the Bergen Line and she became the VENUS in summer and the BLACK PRINCE in winter. The BLENHEIM, a larger version of the twins was delivered to the company in 1970.

The arrangement between Olsen and the Bergen Line came to an end in 1986 and the BLACK WATCH became the property of the latter. Fred. Olsen retained the BLACK PRINCE and had her converted for full cruise ship operation by Wartsila at Turku in Finland, principally by means of the installation of 125 cabins on her vehicle deck. A second cruise ship, a new BLACK WATCH joined the fleet in 1996. The third ship for this gently expanding company appeared in 2001 in the form of the BRAEMAR and a fourth ship will be in service by the beginning of 2006.

Fred. Olsen Cruise Lines specialises in cruises for British passengers.

Managing Director Mike Rodwell **Marketing Director** Nigel Lingard

Address Fred Olsen House, White House Road, Ipswich, Suffolk, IP1 5LL England

Telephone +44 1473 292200 **Fax** +44 1473 292201

Website www.fredolsencruises.com

Area operated Ex-UK to Scandinavia, the Mediterranean and North Atlantic; Caribbean and Grand Voyages

BLACK PRINCE	11209t	1966	18.5k	D2	412p	451p	200c	141.6m	20.0m	6.4m	BA
BLACK WATCH	28670t	1972	18.5k	D2	761p	902p	330c	205.5m	25.2m	7.5m	BA
BOUDICCA	28388t	1972	20.0k	D2	755p	900p	350c	205.5m	25.2m	7.6m	BA
BRAEMAR	19089t	1993	18.5k	D2	750p	916p	320c	163.8m	22.5m	5.4m	BA

BLACK PRINCE, as noted above, was built for both dual purpose and dual ownership by Lubecker Flender-Werke (yard number 561) at Lubeck, Germany. She initially served Olsen's services between Harwich and Kristiansand and Amsterdam and Kristiansand in summer and joined her sister on the Canary Islands service in winter. She became jointly owned with the Bergen Line in 1970 and continued her dual role until the ending of the agreement in 1986. Following her refit she was equipped with a retractable 'marina' that could be put out from the stern when at anchor for the provision of a number of sporting activities. Her refit had been designed to attract a younger and more active passenger. She was not very successful, and was withdrawn from cruise service. An attempt to employ her on a new ferry service between Copenhagen and Gothenburg, was spectacularly unsuccessful, primarily because her Philippine registry and international crew had caused trouble with local trades unions. She was re-fitted again, but for a British middle-aged market this time and has been an enormous success, with a fiercely loyal following. The days of this 40-year-old ship must now be numbered, but when she goes she will be greatly missed. The BLACK PRINCE also undertakes a number of charters each year, including several with Page & Moy (q.v.). Edward, Prince of Wales (1330-1376), famous for leading the victories at the battles of Crecy and Poitiers, became known as the Black Prince.

BLACK WATCH was built as the first of a trio of ships for the new Royal Viking Line consortium, one of the first purpose-built luxury cruise ships, for worldwide service. When delivered by the Helsinki shipyard of Wartsila (yard number 395) as the ROYAL VIKING STAR she introduced a new and impressive profile. As built she was 21,847 gross tons and carried a mere 539 passengers in luxurious surroundings. She was lengthened in Bremerhaven in 1981, giving her an increased passenger capacity of 829. She was transferred to Kloster Cruise (owners of the Royal Viking Line since 1984) in 1988 and three years later was given the name WESTWARD. She was transferred within the group to Royal Cruise Line in 1994 and renamed as the STAR ODYSSEY. Olsen purchased her in 1996 through an intermediary (Olsen and Kloster were both Oslo shipping families) and following a refit she entered service on ex-UK cruises as the BLACK WATCH. In 2005 she underwent a major refit, including the replacement of her engines. The Scottish army regiment, the Black Watch, was established in 1725 and today only draws its recruits from Perthshire, Angus and Fife.

BOUDICCA was built by Wartsila (yard number 396) at Helsinki, Finland as the ROYAL VIKING SKY for the new Royal Viking Line of Oslo. She was 21,891 gross tons as built. During 1982 Seebeckwerft at Bremerhaven lengthened her by 28m. In 1987 she was transferred to the fleet of Norwegian Caribbean Line (Kloster Cruise), the parent company (Klosters had acquired Royal Viking Line in 1984) and was renamed SUNWARD. In 1992 she passed to Birka Line, an Aland Island based shipping company, and was renamed BIRKA QUEEN for the company's short Baltic cruises. This venture was unsuccessful and the ship was chartered back to Klosters from October 1992 to May 1993. She was then chartered to Princess Cruises as the GOLDEN PRINCESS for Alaska cruising for three years, before passing to Star Cruises in 1996 as the SUPERSTAR CAPRICORN for Asian cruising. Surplus to requirements, in 1998 she was chartered to Hyundai Merchant Marine Co as the HYUNDAI KUMGANG for cruises from Korea. In 2001, at the end of the charter, she reverted to the name SUPERSTAR CAPRICORN and was laid up. In 2004 she operated as the GRAND LATINO for Spanish operator, Iberojet but was sold in early 2005 to Fred. Olsen Cruise Lines, to enter service at the end of 2005 as the BOADICEA. This name was later revised to the less gentle, alternative spelling BOUDICCA. Boadicea, Queen of the Iceni, led her people in battle against the Romans in Britain around 60 A.D., and remains one of Britain's greatest heroines.

BRAEMAR is the third ship in a series ordered by Commodore Cruise Line from the Valencia shipyard of Union Naval de Levante (yard number 198). She was delivered in 1993 as the CROWN DYNASTY. At the end of the following year Commodore Cruise Line entered into an arrangement with Cunard that involved the latter company in the marketing of Commodore's ships. She became the CROWN MAJESTY for a charter to Majesty Cruise Line in 1997, and later that year was renamed as the NORWEGIAN DYNASTY for Norwegian Cruise Line. She reverted to her original name for Commodore again in 1999. Fred. Olsen Cruise Lines acquired the ship as their third vessel in 2001 and following a refit by Blohm & Voss in Hamburg, she entered service in August of that year under the name BRAEMAR. She takes her name from the site on Royal Deeside in Scotland, home to the Highland Games since 1813.

Fred Olsen Cruise Lines' **Black Prince** at Rouen *(William Mayes)*

Fred Olsen Cruise Lines' **Black Watch** off Calshot *(Alan Ryszka-Onions)*

Gap Adventures' **Explorer** at Genoa *(Egidio Ferrighi)*

Glacier Bay Cruises' **Wilderness Discoverer** *(Andrew Kilk)*

GALA TOURS

The Company Gala Tours is a Galapagos Island tour operator.

Address Avenida de los Shyris 1000, y Holanda, Quito, Ecuador

Telephone +593 2 243 0345 **Fax** +593 2 245 0775

Area operated Galapagos Islands

TROPIC SUN	‡790t	1967	12.0k	D2	48p	48p	25c	51.8m	10.1m	3.0m	EC

TROPIC SUN was built by R Dunston (yard number S850) at Hessle in England as the HUMBER GUARDIAN for British Transport Docks Board, which later became Associated British Ports. She passed through a number of owners, only changing name once, in 1993 to TROPIC SUN, before arriving with her current owner in 2002.

GAP ADVENTURES

The Company GAP Adventures was founded at the beginning of the 1990's, pioneering land tours to Ecuador, Belize and Peru. In addition to owning the EXPLORER, the company also markets space on other vessels in the Greek Islands and the Galapagos Islands.

President and Chief Executive Officer Bruce Poon Tip **Vice President Sales & Marketing** Dave Bowen

Address 355 Eglinton Avenue East, Toronto, Canada M4P 1M5

Telephone +1 416 260 0999

Website www.gapadventures.com

Area operated Antarctica, Amazon, North Atlantic and the Arctic

EXPLORER	2398t	1969	14.0k	D1	108p	108p	53c	72.9m	14.0m	4.2m	LB

EXPLORER was built by Uudenkaupungin Telakka Oy at Nystad, Finland as the LINDBLAD EXPLORER as the world's first expedition cruise ship for Lars-Eric Lindblad. In 1985 she became the SOCIETY EXPLORER, under charter to Society Expeditions and in 1992, while under the ownership of Vienna International Shipping, she was renamed EXPLORER for service with Abercrombie & Kent. She passed to Lambeth Navigation in 1996, then Explorer Shipping during the following year. In late 2003 she was sold to Kyris Shipping and her current owner acquired her in September 2004. She has always been employed on expedition type cruises and her managers since 1992 have been V-Ships.

GLACIER BAY TOURS & CRUISES

The Company Glacier Bay Tours and Cruises is a United States of America registered company.

Address 2101 Fourth Avenue, Suite 2200, Seattle, Washington, WA98121, United States of America

Telephone +1 206 623 7110 **Fax** +1 206 623 7809

Website www.glacierbaytours.com

Area operated South East Alaska, Prince William Sound and the Columbia River

WILDERNESS ADVENTURER	c500t	1983	10.0k	D1	68p	76p	20c	47.5m	11.6m	m	US
WILDERNESS DISCOVERER	‡683t	1992	10.0k	D2	84p	98p	22c	53.3m	11.9m	m	US
WILDERNESS EXPLORER	t	1969	9.0k	D1	31p	31p	c	31.6m	6.4m	m	US

WILDERNESS ADVENTURER was built by Blount Marine Corporation (yard number 250) at Warren, Rhode Island, USA as the CARIBBEAN PRINCE for American Canadian Caribbean Line. Glacier Bay Cruiseline purchased her in 1997 and she was renamed WILDERNESS ADVENTURER.

WILDERNESS DISCOVERER was built by Blount Marine Corporation (yard number 280) at Warren, Rhode Island, USA as the MAYAN PRINCE for American Canadian Caribbean Line. She was acquired by Glacier Bay Cruiseline in 1998 and renamed WILDERNESS DISCOVERER.

WILDERNESS EXPLORER was built by Blount Marine Corporation, Warren, Rhode Island, USA as the WILDERNESS EXPLORER. She is recorded as being acquired by her present owner in 2003.

The company also operates the day vessel EXECUTIVE EXPLORER.

Globalia-Travelplan's **New Flamenco** at Valletta *(William Mayes)*

Golden Star Cruises' **Aegean I** at Santorini *(William Mayes)*

GLOBALIA CRUISES / TRAVELPLAN

The Company Travelplan is part of the Spanish Globalia travel and leisure group. The company has the OCEAN COUNTESS of Majestic International on charter for the summer of 2005, after which she becomes the LILI MARLEEN of Holiday Kreuzfahrten.

Director General Marcos Lopez

Address Pl Espana 18, 2 Pl, 28008 Madrid, Spain

Telephone +34 91 540 6006 **Fax** +34 91 548 3637

Website www.globalia-corp.com/travelplan

Area operated Mediterranean Sea and Atlantic Islands

NEW FLAMENCO	17042t	1972	17.0k	D2	792p	983p	350c	163.3m	22.8m	6.5m	BA

NEW FLAMENCO was the first new passenger ship to be bought by the Peninsular & Oriental Steam Navigation Company since the CANBERRA of 1961, and that company's first purpose built cruise ship, although she had not been ordered by P&O, but acquired off the stocks. She was laid down as one of a pair of ships for Kloster's Norwegian Caribbean Cruise Line by Cantieri Navale del Tirreno e Riuniti shipyard (yard number 290) at Riva Trigoso in Italy. Her sister was delivered as the SOUTHWARD (now Louis Cruise Lines PERLA (q.v.)), but due to escalating costs the order for this ship was cancelled. She was to have been named SEAWARD, but was eventually launched for P&O as the SPIRIT OF LONDON. She was initially employed on the US West Coast along with the 1954-built ARCADIA. When P&O acquired Princess Cruises in 1974, the SPIRIT OF LONDON was transferred to that operation and renamed SUN PRINCESS. By 1989 she was the baby of the fleet and no longer fitted in with the larger ships, so was sold to Premier Cruise Line who renamed her STARSHIP MAJESTIC. In 1995 she was chartered to CTC Lines for cruising from the UK and from Australia, and renamed SOUTHERN CROSS. CTC Lines ceased trading in 1997 and the ship was sold to Festival Cruises, becoming the FLAMENCO. After Festival failed in 2004, she was quickly acquired by Elysian Cruises (Ravenscroft Shipping) and renamed NEW FLAMENCO. She commenced a charter with Globalia Cruises/Travelplan in the spring of 2004. Flamenco is a Spanish dance.

GOLDEN STAR CRUISES

The Company Golden Star Cruises is a trading name of Dolphin Hellas Shipping, a privately owned Greek company.

Address 85 Akti Miaouli, Piraeus, 18538, Greece

Telephone +30 210 4290650 **Fax** +30 310 4290660

Website www.goldenstarcruises.com

Area operated The Greek Islands of the Aegean Sea

AEGEAN I	11563t	1974	17.0k	D2	576p	682p	190c	140.5m	20.8m	6.6m	GR

AEGEAN I began life as the ro-ro cargo ship NARCIS of Zim Israel Navigation of Haifa. She was built by Santierul Naval Galatz (yard number 617) at Galatz, Romania. In 1985 she was acquired by Dolphin Hellas Shipping and renamed ALKYON. She was substantially refitted at Perama, Greece and re-delivered in 1988 as the AEGEAN DOLPHIN. During the following year she was renamed as the DOLPHIN, but she reverted to her previous name in 1990. In 1996 she was renamed AEGEAN I and operated at least one cruise for Discovery Cruises. She also undertook a charter to Renaissance Cruises in that year. In 1998 she commenced cruising for Golden Star Cruises.

Gota Canal's *Juno* at Gothenburg *(William Mayes)*

GOTA CANAL CRUISES

The Company Rederi AB Gota Kanal was founded on February 27, 1869. The JUNO was the second of the company's ships, and still remains in service after more than 130 years. The company is now part of the Travel group Stromma.

Address Pusterviksgaten 13, SE41301 Gothenburg, Sweden

Telephone +46 31 806315 **Fax** +46 31 158311

Website www.gotacanal.se

Area operated The Gota Canal between Gothenburg and Stockholm, Sweden

DIANA	269t	1931	10.0k	D1	56p	56p	c	31.6m	6.8m	2.7m	SW
JUNO	254t	1874	10.0k	D2	58p	58p	c	31.5m	6.7m	2.7m	SW
WILHELM THAM	268t	1912	10.0k	D1	50p	50p	c	31.5m	6.7m	2.7m	SW

DIANA was built at the Finnboda Shipyard in Stockholm, Sweden. Built as a steamship, she was the last of that type in regular Swedish canal service. Diana was the Roman goddess of the hunt and of chastity.

JUNO was built by Motala Werkstad, at Motala in Sweden. Her name is that of the Roman goddess of marriage and motherhood. She is the oldest registered ship with overnight cabins.

WILHELM THAM was built by Motala Werkstad, at Motala, Sweden and is named after the Swedish industrialist and director of the Husqvarna Weapons Factory from 1876 to 1911.

HANSA KREUZFAHRTEN

The Company Hansa Kreuzfahrten GmbH is a German company providing cruises for German speaking passengers.

Managing Director Horst Kilian **Marketing Director** Axel Schmidt

Address Contrescarpe 36, D28203 Bremen, Germany

Telephone +49 421 33466 0 **Fax** +49 421 33466 25

Website www.hansakreuzfahrten.de

Areas operated Caribbean (DELPHIN), Atlantic Isles, Mediterranean, Northern Europe, Scandinavia

DELPHIN	16214t	1975	21.0k	D2	466p	520p	235c	156.3m	21.8m	6.2m	MA
OCEAN MONARCH	15833t	1955	17.0k	D2	422p	526p	210c	162.4m	21.3m	7.5m	PO
PALOMA I	12586t	1980	20.0k	D2	342p	528p	170c	133.5m	21.0m	5.3m	SV

DELPHIN was built by the Wartsila Shipyard (yard number 1212) at Turku in Finland as the BYELORUSSIYA for the Black Sea Shipping Company of the Soviet Union. On the break-up of the Eastern Bloc the company became Ukrainian. In 1993 she was renamed KAZAKHSTAN II, but her operators faced severe financial difficulties resulting in the arrest of ships and the eventual collapse of the company. In 1995 she was sold to Lady Lou Shipping, a Cypriot registered but German controlled company. Her ownership was passed to Dolphin Maritime in 1998, another company within the same group and she was renamed DELPHIN. She operates for Hansa Kreuzfahrten on year round charter, in the Caribbean in winter, the Mediterranean and Atlantic Isles in the shoulder seasons and in Northern Europe and Scandinavia in summer.

OCEAN MONARCH was built by Swan Hunter and Wigham Richardson (yard number 1827) at Wallsend on Tyne in England for Port Line as the passenger and cargo ship PORT SYDNEY. In 1972 she was sold to Greek owners for conversion to a passenger and car ferry, but although commenced this conversion was never completed. While undergoing work she was renamed AKROTIRI EXPRESS. She was later rebuilt as a cruise ship, taking the name DAPHNE, and was operated unsuccessfully for a while and eventually chartered to Costa Line, along with her sister (similarly converted and now the PRINCESS DANAE). Costa later purchased the ships and in the late 1980's marketed them under the Prestige Cruises banner. In 1996 she was renamed SWITZERLAND after sale to Leisure Cruises, a Swiss based but Monaco controlled company. In 2000 she passed to Dreamline Cruises, a company under the same control, without a change of name. She was acquired by Majestic International Cruises of Greece in spring 2002 and briefly renamed OCEAN ODYSSEY before adopting her current name. Hansa Kreuzfahrten charters her for most of the summer season.

PALOMA I was built by Stocznia Szczecinska (yard number B492/01) at Szczecin, Poland as the DMITRIY SHOSTAKOVICH for the Black Sea Shipping Company of the Soviet Union. Following the collapse of that company she passed through a number of owners between 1996 and 2000, when she was acquired by Macro Maritime, a Liberian registered company, and renamed PALOMA I. In 2003 D&P Cruises, an Italian company, purchased her. Subsequently she has undertaken a number of charters, including that to Hansa Kreuzfahrten for whom she operates in the Mediterranean and Northern Europe.

Hansa Kreuzfahrten's **Delphin** at Istanbul *(William Mayes)*

Hansa Kreuzfahrten's **Paloma I** at Venice *(William Mayes)*

HEBRIDEAN ISLAND CRUISES

The Company Hebridean Island Cruises was established in 1988 to purchase and convert the car ferry COLUMBA for operation as the small luxury cruise ship HEBRIDEAN PRINCESS in the waters of Western Scotland. The company is now a subsidiary of Hebridean Cruises plc, which purchased HIC from its previous owner in 1998.

Managing Director Mike Deegan

Address Griffin House, Broughton Hall, Skipton, Yorkshire, BD23 3AN, England

Telephone +44 1756 704704 **Fax** +44 1756 704794

Website www.hebridean.co.uk

Area operated Scotland, the Scottish Isles and Norway (Princess), Worldwide (Spirit)

HEBRIDEAN PRINCESS	2112t	1964	14.5k	D2	49p	49p	37c	71.6m	13.3m	2.7m	UK
HEBRIDEAN SPIRIT	4200t	1991	15.5k	D2	80p	80p	65c	90.6m	15.3m	3.6m	UK

HEBRIDEAN PRINCESS, the former MacBrayne car ferry COLUMBA underwent a massive transformation in 1989 to become one of the most exclusive cruise ships in the world. Hall Russell (yard number 912) at Aberdeen, Scotland built her as one of a trio of side-loading car ferries for service to the Western Isles from Oban. In 1973 David MacBrayne and the Caledonian Steam Packet Company (both British Government owned) were merged into Caledonian MacBrayne, and the ship eventually re-registered under that organisation. In 1988 she was sold to Leisure and Marine Holdings (trading as Hebridean Island Cruises) and converted into the luxury country house style cruise ship HEBRIDEAN PRINCESS. In 1998 the company and the ship were sold to Hebridean Cruises plc, but the style of operation remains unchanged.

HEBRIDEAN SPIRIT was built for Renaissance Cruises as the RENAISSANCE SIX by Nuovi Cantieri Apuania (yard number 1145) at Marina di Carrara, Italy as one of a series of eight small luxury cruise ships. She was sold to Sun Cruises of Singapore in 1998 when replaced by impressive new tonnage and renamed as the SUN VIVA 2. Following the loss of the SUN VISTA, that company was taken over by Star Cruises and she was renamed MEGASTAR CAPRICORN in 2000. She was soon sold on, and her purchaser, Hebridean Island Cruises had her refitted, reducing her passenger capacity from 112 to 80, thus producing the exclusive and luxurious HEBRIBEAN SPIRIT in 2001.

HELIOS SHIPPING

The Company Helios Shipping is a Greek company. In addition to the CONSTELLATION, the ORION (see Orion Cruises) is also owned by Helios.

Address 16 Akti Mountsopoulou, 18536 Piraeus, Greece

Telephone +30 210 428 6253 **Fax** +30 210 452 6640

Website www.helios-shipping.gr

Area operated Unknown

CONSTELLATION	2842t	2002	16.0k	D1	92p	96p	56c	88.5m	14.0m	3.6m	SV

CONSTELLATION was built as the SUN BAY II by Schiffswerft u. Maschinenfabrik Cassens (yard number 235) at Emden in Germany for Sun Bay Shipping. She was renamed CORINTHIAN in 2002 and operated for Travel Dynamics International for a while. She was renamed CONSTELLATION in 2003 when sold to Mitridat Shipping, a subsidiary of Helios Shipping.

HOLIDAY KREUZFAHRTEN

The Company Holiday Kreuzfahrten GmbH is a German travel operator providing cruises for German speaking passengers.

Managing Director Herbert Fervers

Address Brusseler Alee 12, 41812 Erkelenz, Germany

Telephone +49 2431 94500 **Fax** +49 2431 9450 450

Website www.ms-monalisa.de

Area operated Northern Europe in summer, Central America, Australia and the Far East

LILI MARLEEN	16795t	1976	18.5k	D2	814p	950p	350c	163.6m	22.8m	5.8m	PO
MONA LISA	28891t	1966	21.5k	D2	728p	782p	336c	201.2m	26.5m	8.6m	BA

LILI MARLEEN started life as one of a pair of second-generation Caribbean cruise ships for Cunard Line. She was built by Burmeister & Wain (yard number 858) at Copenhagen, Denmark as the CUNARD COUNTESS. She served the company for twenty years before being sold for service in the Far East as the AWANI DREAM 2. In 1998 she was acquired by Royal Olympic Cruises and renamed OLYMPIC COUNTESS for service mainly in the Mediterranean. In 2002, under pressure from the International Olympic Committee, the company changed its name to Royal Olympia Cruises and the ship followed suit, becoming the OLYMPIA COUNTESS. Following the collapse of that company she passed to Majestic International Cruises in 2004, and was chartered to Globalia for the summer of 2005. She has now been chartered to Holiday Kreuzfahrten as their second ship and renamed as the LILI MARLEEN. Lili Marleen is a German song, the words of which were written by Hans Leip in 1915, which became popular with German troops during the Second World War, after being set to music by Norbert Schultze in 1938.

MONA LISA was built by John Brown & Co (Clydebank) Ltd (yard number 728) on the River Clyde in Scotland, as the immensely elegant KUNGSHOLM for Swedish America Line's service from Gothenburg to New York. As that trade declined she switched to cruising and was subsequently sold to Flagship Cruises. In 1978 she was acquired by the Peninsular and Oriental Steam Navigation Company and after a drastic conversion, which included the loss of most of the forward funnel, entered service as the SEA PRINCESS. She initially replaced the ARCADIA in February 1979 in the Australian market, where she remained until 1982. She was then transferred to the British market, where she remained until 1986, operating alongside the CANBERRA. She then served Princess Cruises for five years before returning to the United Kingdom in 1991. She was renamed VICTORIA in March 1995, and at the end of 2002 was sold to the Greek controlled Leonardo Shipping and renamed MONA LISA for long-term charter to Holiday Kreuzfahrten to serve the growing German cruise demand. The Mona Lisa, although not the greatest of Leonardo da Vinci's works is certainly his most famous and was painted around 1504.

HURTIGRUTEN (Norwegian Coastal Voyage)

The Company The Hurtigruten, the Norwegian Coastal Express service, covers the 1,300 or so nautical miles from Bergen to Kirkenes, just ten miles from the Russian border in the far north of Norway, in a twelve-day round trip making 34 port calls. Most of the ships carry cars and other vehicles on decks accessed through side doors. All of the vessels perform a year-round lifeline service linking communities who had no other means of transport to the outside world. The Hurtigruten commenced in 1893 at which time the Norwegian Government entered into a four-year agreement with Vesteraalens Dampskibsselskab, providing the subsidy for a weekly service from Trondheim to Hammerfest in summer and to Tromso in winter. However, the story of the coastal service really begins around 1838, when the Norwegian Government paid for the construction and running costs of the steamer PRINDS GUSTAV to trade between Trondheim and Hammerfest in the far north. The service only ran for about seven months each year, and then only sailed during daylight due to the lack of navigation markers north of Trondheim. Initially the service was monthly, but as new ships arrived it was extended south to Kristiansand and increased in frequency. The prime purpose of these early ships was the carriage of passengers and mail; most goods were still travelling in sailing vessels. During the 1860's the route passed in its entirety into the hands of private companies. The failure of the fish harvest in 1875/6 had the eventual result of reducing the lifeline service, as the various operating companies switched their investment to the more lucrative tourist trade. The eventual result was the tendering of the service and the awarding of the agreement referred to above. In 1894 two further companies were licensed to operate the Coastal Express, Bergenske Dampskibsselskab and Nordenfjeldske Dampskibsselskab. Today the route is in the hands of just two companies, and as Government subsidies are again under scrutiny the service is once more turning to tourism as the main source of income on what has often been described as 'The World's Most Beautiful Voyage'.

Website www.hurtigruten.no

Sales Agent UK Norwegian Coastal Voyage Ltd, 3 Shortlands, London W6 8NE

Telephone +44 208 846 2600 **Fax** +44 208 846 2678 **Website** www.norwegiancoastalvoyage.com

Hebridean Island Cruises' **Hebridean Spirit** in London *(William Mayes)*

Holiday Kreuzfahrten's **Mona Lisa** sailing from Venice *(Egidio Ferrighi)*

Hurtigruten – TFDS' **Nordlys** at Trondheim *(William Mayes)*

Hurtigruten – TFDS' **Nordstjernen** *(William Mayes Collection)*

Sales Agent USA Norwegian Coastal Voyage Inc, 405 Park Avenue, New York, NY 10022

Telephone +1 212 319 1300 Fax +1 212 319 1390 Website www.coastalvoyage.com

OVDS

The Company Ofotens og Vesteraalens Dampskibsselskab ASA can trace its origins back to 1881 when Captain Richard With established the Vesteraalens Dampskibsselskab. Ofotens Dampskibsselskab joined the Hurtigruten service in 1936 and in the late 1990's the two companies merged to form OVDS. Today the company employs more than 1,500 people and has recently extended its sphere of operation to include Antarctica and South America.

Director of Hurtigruten Knut Sevaldsen

Address PO Box 43, 8501 Narvik, Norway

Telephone +47 7696 7693

Website www.ovds.no

Area operated Norwegian coast, Spitzbergen, the Lofoten Islands, Chile and Antarctica

FINNMARKEN	15690t	2002	18.0k	D2	638b	372d	85c	135.8m	21.5m	4.9m	NO
LOFOTEN	2621t	1964	16.8k	D1	223b	277d	c	87.4m	13.3m	4.6m	NO
NARVIK	6257t	1982	19.0k	D2	310b	190d	34c	108.6m	16.5m	3.7m	NO
NORDKAPP	11386t	1996	18.0k	D2	481b	210d	59c	123.3m	19.5m	4.7m	NO
NORDNORGE	11384t	1997	18.0k	D2	457b	234d	57c	123.3m	19.5m	4.7m	NI
RICHARD WITH	11205t	1993	18.0k	D2	483b	208d	57c	121.8m	19.2m	4.7m	NO
VESTERALEN	6262t	1983	19.0k	D2	316b	234d	34c	108.6m	16.5m	3.7m	NO

Key: b = berthed passengers d = deck passengers

FINNMARKEN was built by Ulstein Verft (yard number 292) at Ulsteinvik in Norway. Finnmark is Norway's most northerly region, bordering Finland.

LOFOTEN is the last surviving traditional Hurtigruten ship still in regular service. She was built by AS Akers Mekanik Verksted (yard number 547) at Oslo, Norway. She only now operates on the Hurtigruten during the winter, when the NORDNORGE goes south to Antarctica. In the summer she operates cruises to the Lofoten Islands, off the coast of central Norway, from which she takes her name.

NARVIK is the port city that is home to the operating company of this ship. The NARVIK was built by Aker Trondelag AS (yard number 827) at Trondheim, Norway. She is now referred to as a mid-generation ship.

NORDKAPP was built by Kvaerner Kleven Ulsteinvik (yard number 265) at Ulsteinvik in Norway. She is one of two ships that will travel to South America and Antarctica in the winter of 2005/2006. Her name translates as North Cape, the most northerly point of mainland Norway.

NORDNORGE was built by the Kvaerner Kleven Ulsteinvik shipyard (yard number 266) at Ulsteinvik in Norway. She sails south to Antarctica in the winter of 2005/2006.

RICHARD WITH was the name of the founder of the Vesteraalens company, with which Ofotens later merged. This ship was built at Stralsund in Germany by Volkswerft (yard number 103).

VESTERALEN was built by Kaarbos Mek. Verksted (yard number 101) at Harstad, Norway. The very first of the coastal express ships carried the name VESTERALEN, in honour of the Vesteralen Islands, a little to the north of the Lofoten Islands.

TFDS

The Company Troms Fylkes Dampskibsselskab ASA is a major Norwegian ship owner with around 34 vessels. The company was founded in 1867 as Tromso Amts D/S, but assumed its current name in 1925. In 2003 the company became the major shareholder in Fjord Line, the ferry company that links Norway with Denmark and England.

Chairman Steinar Hansen

Address PO Box 6144, 9291 Tromso, Norway

Telephone +47 7764 8100 Fax +47 7764 8180

Website www.tfds.no

Area operated Norwegian coast and Spitzbergen

KONG HARALD	11204t	1993	18.0k	D2	490b	201d	59c	121.8m	19.2m	4.7m	NO

Hurtigruten – TFDS' *Trollfjord* at Bergen *(Andrew Kilk)*

Hurtigruten – OVDS' *Lofoten* *(Clive Harvey)*

MIDNATSOL	16151t	2003	18.0k	D2	648b	174d	74c	135.8m	21.5m	4.9m	NO
MIDNATSOL II	6167t	1982	17.5k	D2	322b	228d	34c	108.6m	16.5m	4.6m	NO
NORDLYS	11204t	1994	18.0k	D2	482b	209d	60c	121.7m	19.2m	4.7m	NO
NORDSTJERNEN	2191t	1956	15.5k	D1	179b	271d	c	80.8m	12.6m	4.5m	NO
POLARLYS	11341t	1996	15.5k	D2	479b	258d	63c	123.0m	19.5m	4.5m	NO
TROLLFJORD	16140t	2002	18.0k	D2	652b	170d	74c	135.8m	21.5m	4.9m	NO

Key: b = berthed passengers d = deck passengers

KONG HARALD is named in honour of the King of Norway, who succeeded to the throne in 1991. She was built in Germany at the Stralsund shipyard of Volksverft (yard number 101).

MIDNATSOL had her hull built at Bruce's Shipyard, Landskrona, Sweden, but was completed by the Fosen Yard (yard number 73) in Norway. Her name means Midnight Sun.

MIDNATSOL II was renamed and laid up in 2003, following the delivery of the new MIDNATSOL. She was built by Ulstein Hatlo (yard number 176) at Ulsteinvik in Norway, as the MIDNATSOL.

NORDLYS takes her name from the Northern Lights, in Latin the Aurora Borealis, or Red Dawn of the North. She was built in Germany at the Stralsund shipyard of Volksverft (yard number 102).

NORDSTJERNEN was built by Blohm & Voss (yard number 787) in Hamburg, Germany as a replacement for a pre-war vessel of the same name for the Bergen Line. From 1994 she has operated the summer run from Tromso to Spitzbergen, acting as a relief Hurtigruten ship as required. Her name translates as North Star.

POLARLYS is a product of the Ulstein Verft yard (yard number 223) at Ulsteinvik, Norway. Her name translates as Polar Lights.

TROLLFJORD's hull was built by Bruce's Shipyard (yard number 246) at Landskrona, Sweden but the ship was completed by the Fosen Yard in Norway, where she acquired the build number 72. Trollfjord is one of the many fjords in the Vesteralen and Lofoten district of Norway.

IBEROJET

The Company Iberojet is a Spanish travel company that has recently entered the growing market for cruising amongst Spaniards. During the early part of 2005 the company was also operating the GRAND LATINO, now Fred. Olsen's BOUDICCA.

Managing Director Alfredo Serrano

Address Valencia 231, 1er Piso, 08007 Barcelona, Spain

Telephone +34 93 488 0220 **Fax** +34 93 487 2762

Website www.cruceros.iberojet.es

Area operated Mediterranean

MISTRAL	47276t	1999	19.0k	DE2	1196p	1667p	516c	216.0m	28.8m	6.9m	MI
VOYAGER	24391t	2000	28.0k	D2	836p	920p	360c	180.4m	25.5m	7.3m	BA

MISTRAL, the first new ship for Festival Cruises was delivered by Chantiers de l'Atlantique (yard number J31), St Nazaire, France. Following the collapse of Festival Cruises she was purchased by her builder, now part of the Alstom Group and eventually chartered to Iberojet. She is marketed as the IBEROSTAR MISTRAL. The Mistral is a strong wind from the northwest affecting the southern coast of France, predominantly from Marseilles to St Tropez.

VOYAGER, another first new ship, was built as one of a pair of high speed cruise ships for Royal Olympic Cruises of Greece by Blohm & Voss (yard number 961) in Hamburg as the OLYMPIC VOYAGER. Political unrest in the Eastern Mediterranean meant that her intended service was curtailed and she was put onto work more mundane than the 'Three Continents in a Week' circuit for which she was built. Difficulties with the International Olympic organisation led to the company restyling itself as Royal Olympia Cruises and the ship was renamed OLYMPIA VOYAGER. The company within ROC that owned the ship filed for bankruptcy, starting the process that led to the complete failure of the group. She ship was auctioned and is now owned within the V-Ships group and chartered to Iberojet. She is marketed as GRAND VOYAGER.

Iberojet's **Grand Voyager** as the **Olympic Voyager** in Istanbul *(William Mayes)*

Iliada Tourism's **Halas** in the Bosphorus *(William Mayes)*

ILIADA TOURISM

The Company Iliada Tourism is a Turkish operator and organiser of exclusive tours in and around Turkey.

Address Haci IzzetPasa Sok, Cam Palas 24/5, 34427 Gumussuyu, Istanbul, Turkey

Telephone +90 212 243 2164 **Fax** +90 212 243 2658

Website www.iliadatourism.com

Area operated Bosphorus and southern coast of Turkey

HALAS	584t	1915	12.0k	D2	30p	30p	c	52.0m	7.9m	2.5m	TU

HALAS is now owned by Il-Tur Isletmeleri of Istanbul and operates on the Turkish coast as a very luxurious cruise vessel. She was built by Fairfield Shipbuilding and Engineering Company (yard number 502) at Govan on the River Clyde in Scotland, as one of the numerous steam ferries for service around Constantinople (now Istanbul) and the Bosphorus. She survived in her original role until the mid 1980's and after a period in lay-up she was rebuilt as the rather splendid ship she is today.

IMPERIAL MAJESTY CRUISE LINE

The Company Imperial Majesty Cruise Line is a relatively new operator, which began sailing with the newly acquired OCEAN BREEZE in 1999.

Address 2950 Gateway Drive, Pompano Beach, Florida, Fl 33069, United States of America

Telephone +1 954 956 9505 **Fax** +1 954 971 6678

Website www.imperialmajesty.com

Area operated Fort Lauderdale to The Bahamas

REGAL EMPRESS	21909t	1953	17.0k	D2	893p	1186p	391c	186.1m	24.1m	8.6m	BA

REGAL EMPRESS was built on a keel originally laid down for an aircraft carrier as the OLYMPIA, the new flagship for the Greek Line, by Alexander Stephen & Sons (yard number 636) in Glasgow, Scotland. She operated sailings for the Greek Line between Piraeus and New York. She was laid up in Piraeus in 1974, not being reactivated until sold to Sally Shipping in 1981. She went to Bremerhaven as the CARIBE for refit where her Parsons steam turbines were replaced by diesels. In 1982 she began operating for Commodore Cruise Line in the Caribbean as the CARIBE I. In 1993 she passed to Regal Cruise Line as the REGAL EMPRESS and was acquired, on the bankruptcy of Regal Cruise Line, by Imperial Majesty Cruise Line in 2003 as a replacement for the OCEAN BREEZE (formerly the SOUTHERN CROSS), without a change of name.

INDIAN OCEAN CRUISES

The Company Indian Ocean Cruises is a new company, part of the South African éLan Group, established as this edition went to press.

Managing Director Trevor Boynton

Address PO Box 35540, Northway, 4065 KwaZulu Natal, Republic of South Africa

Telephone +27 31 576 9600 **Fax** +27 31 576 9601

Website www.elan.co.za/cruise.php

Area operated Indian Ocean based in Durban

MADAGASCAR	3008t	1960	18.5k	D2	180p	180p	c	88.2m	13.4m	4.4m	PA

MADAGASCAR was built by Adler Werft (yard number 19) at Bremen, Germany as the German coastal liner BREMERHAVEN, for service between Bremerhaven and Helgoland. She was purchased by Sun Lines in 1966 and rebuilt as the elegant little STELLA MARIS II. In 1998 she was acquired by Luxembourg-based Viking Cruises and renamed as the VIKING BORDEAUX. Her owners ceased operation in 2003 and the ship was arrested at Eemshaven. In July 2004 it was reported that she had been acquired by Royal African Cruise Line and was to be renamed AFRICAN QUEEN. That never materialised, but later that year she was renamed as the BORDEAUX. It appears that in spring 2005 this ship was acquired by Indian Ocean Cruises and it has been confirmed that she has been renamed MADAGASCAR, although other information indicates that the ship's eventual name might be AFRICAN EXPLORER. Following some charters in the Mediterranean, the ship is scheduled to move to Durban from where she will cruise in the Indian Ocean.

JAPAN CRUISE LINE

The Company Japan Cruise Line is part of SHK Group, a Japanese joint venture between the Shin Nohonkai, Hankyu and Kanpu ferry companies. The ships are marketed as Venus Cruise.

President Yasuo Iritani

Address Herbis Osaka Building 15F, 25-35 Umeda, Kita-ku, JP 530 0001 Osaka, Japan

Telephone +81 6 6347 7521 **Fax** +81 6 6347 0638

Website www.venus-cruise.co.jp

Area operated Asia and worldwide

ORIENT VENUS	‡21884t	1990	18.5k	D2	396p	606p	156c	174.0m	24.0m	6.5m	JP
PACIFIC VENUS	26518t	1998	20.8k	D2	423p	696p	180c	183.4m	25.0m	6.5m	JP

ORIENT VENUS was built by Ishikawajima – Harima Heavy Industries (yard number 2987) at the Tokyo shipyard in Japan. She operated mainly in the charter cruise trades but has been laid up for several years.

PACIFIC VENUS was also built by IHHI (yard number 3095). She operates cruises ranging in length from a few days along the Japanese coast to several months around the world.

KLEINTOURS

The Company Kleintours is a Galapagos Islands based tour and cruise operator, with two smaller yachts that are outside the scope of this book, in addition to the GALAPAGOS LEGEND.

Address Av. Eloy Alfaro N 34-151 & Catalina, Aldaz, Quito, Ecuador

Telephone +593 2 2267 000 **Fax** +593 2 2442 389

Website www.kleintours.com

Area operated Galapagos Islands

GALAPAGOS LEGEND	2890t	1963	15.0k	D2	110p	110p	60c	91.5m	14.3m	4.2m	GE

GALAPAGOS LEGEND was built by Howaldtswerke (yard number 943) at Hamburg, Germany as the HELGOLAND for local services on the North Sea and Baltic coasts of Germany. She had been ordered from the Hanseatische Werft yard in Hamburg, but that yard was declared bankrupt so the order was transferred. She was chartered out from 1964 to 1966 under the name LARVIKSPILEN, but reverted to her original name at the end of that period. From 1966 to 1971 she served as a hospital ship in Vietnamese waters before returning to Europe. In 1972 she was purchased by Stena Reederie of Germany and became the STENA FINLANDICA. Three years later she was renamed BALTIC STAR for Seetouristik (later Forde Reederie) day cruises in the Baltic Sea. She was sold to her current owner in 2001, renamed the GALAPAGOS LEGEND and refitted as an overnight cruise ship.

KRISTINA CRUISES

The Company Kristina Cruises is a Finnish family-owned company, founded in 1985, which acquired its first ship, the KRISTINA BRAHE later that year. In 1987 the former BORE joined the fleet.

Address Kirkkokatu 16, 48100 Kotka, Finland

Telephone +358 5 211 4230 **Fax** +358 5 211 4500

Website www.kristinacruises.com

Area operated Baltic Sea, Finnish lakes, European coast, Canary Islands and Mediterranean Sea

KRISTINA BRAHE	1105t	1943	12.0k	D2	80p	176p	24c	56.5m	10.1m	2.8m	FI
KRISTINA REGINA	4295t	1960	14.5k	D1	238p	381p	55c	99.8m	15.3m	5.5m	FI

KRISTINA BRAHE was built in 1943 by the Pullman Standard Car Manufacturing Company of Chicago, Illinois, USA as the US warship PCE 830, later BEC 4. Subsequently she became the British destroyer HMS KILCHERNAN. She was sold to Norwegian owners and rebuilt as the coastal passenger ferry SUNNHORDLAND. She began cruising as the KRISTINA BRAHE on the coasts and lakes of Finland in 1975, passing to her current owner in 1985. She is named after the wife of the one time Regent of Finland, Peter Brahe.

KRISTINA REGINA was built by AB Oskarshamns Varv (yard number 353) at Oskarshamn in Sweden as the steamship BORE for Bore Line's Baltic Sea services. She was the last steamship to be built for service in Scandinavia. Bore Line was part of the Silja Line consortium. In 1979 she began cruising as the BOREA for Bore Line subsidiary, Jakob Line. Her current owner acquired her in 1987, after a period of lay-up. She was immediately re-engined with diesels and following refurbishment was set to work cruising in the Baltic Sea as

Imperial Majesty's **Regal Empress** at Fort Lauderdale *(Theodore W Scull)*

Japan Cruise Line's **Pacific Venus** at San Francisco *(Andrew Kilk)*

the KRISTINA REGINA. She later had two very substantial interior refits to bring her up to her current high standard. The ship is named after the 17th century Queen Kristina of Sweden and Finland.

LINDBLAD EXPEDITIONS

The Company Lindblad Expeditions was founded in 1979 by Sven-Olof Lindblad, as a development from Lindblad Travel, which had been established some twenty years earlier. From the spring of 2005 Lindblad has teamed up with National Geographic in the marketing and operation of the ENDEAVOUR.

President Sven Lindblad

Address 96 Morton Street, 9th Floor, New York, NY 10014 United States of America

Telephone +1 212 765 7740

Website www.expeditions.com

Area operated Arctic, Northern Europe, the Americas and Antarctica (ENDEAVOUR), Galapagos Islands (POLARIS and ISLANDER), Alaska and Baja California (SEA BIRD and SEA LION)

ENDEAVOUR	3132t	1966	15.0k	D1	124p	138p	63c	89.1m	14.0m	6.6m	BA
ISLANDER	1065t	1995	14.0k	D2	48p	48p	c	49.9m	13.5m	1.9m	EC
POLARIS	2138t	1960	14.0k	D2	82p	82p	32c	64.0m	13.0m	4.3m	EC
SEA BIRD	630t	1992	12.0k	D1	70p	70p	41c	45.7m	9.4m	m	US
SEA LION	630t	1992	12.0k	D1	70p	70p	41c	45.7m	9.4m	m	US

ENDEAVOUR was once a fishing trawler, built by AG Weser (yard number 917) at Bremerhaven, Germany as the MARBURG for German owners. In 1982 she became the LINDMAR and during the following year was converted at Gothenburg into the cruise ship NORTH STAR for Fearney & Eger of Oslo. She entered service for North Star Line in 1983 on Scandinavian cruises, switching to the Mediterranean in the winter. In 1986 she was chartered to Exploration Cruises and Holidays of Seattle, USA for service on the Alaskan coast. Three years later, her charterers were in financial trouble and the NORTH STAR was sold to the Caledonian Steamship Company, renamed CALEDONIAN STAR and chartered to Salen-Lindblad. From 1993 the ship was marketed in the UK by Noble Caledonia and in the USA by Special Expeditions. The latter company acquired the CALEDONIAN STAR in 1997, and in 2000 became Lindblad Expeditions, renaming the ship as ENDEAVOUR during the following year. The most famous ENDEAVOUR was that of Captain James Cook, whose epic voyages of discovery took place between 1768 and 1771.

ISLANDER is operated by Ecoventura and chartered to Lindblad for specific cruises. She was built by Chantiers Navale de Marseille (yard number B210) at Marseilles, France as the RIVAGES GUADELOUPE. Between 2002 and 2004 she was cruising in and around Scotland as the LORD OF THE HIGHLANDS for Highland Lord Steamship Company, but entered service in the Galapagos Islands as the ISLANDER in early 2005.

POLARIS was built by Solvesborgs Varv (yard number 55) at Solvesborg Sweden as the ORESUND, a passenger car ferry for service between Copenhagen, Denmark and Malmo, Sweden. In 1981 she was purchased by Salen Lines and chartered to Lindblad as the expedition ship LINDBLAD POLARIS. She was sold to Lindblad in 1987 and renamed POLARIS.

SEA BIRD is owned by Majestic Alaska Boat Co and operates under charter to Lindblad. She was built by Nichols Bros (yard number S62) at Freeland, Washington State, USA.

SEA LION is registered under the ownership of SPEX Sea Lion and operates under charter to Lindblad. She was built by Nichols Bros (yard number S63) at Freeland, Washington State, USA.

LOUIS CRUISE LINE

The Company Louis began chartering passenger ships soon after the end of the Second World War, but did not actually begin owning its own vessels until the PRINCESSA MARISSA was acquired in 1987. The company also offers management services and is involved in the leisure industry. Louis was a majority shareholder in the recently defunct Royal Olympic Cruises, but has now stepped in to fill the breach with the newly established Louis Hellenic Cruises.

Chairman Costakis Loizou

Address 150A Franklin Roosevelt & Omonias Avenue, PO Box 55612, 3045 Limassol, Cyprus

Telephone +357 2557 0000 **Fax** +357 2557 3320

Website www.louiscruises.com

Area operated Eastern Mediterranean Sea

AQUAMARINE	23149t	1971	21.0k	D2	1056p	1160p	400c	193.3m	24.0m	6.7m	CY
PRINCESA MARISSA	10487t	1966	20.0k	D2	628p	884p	185c	134.4m	19.9m	5.7m	CY

Kristina Cruises' *Kristina Brahe* at Helsinki *(William Mayes)*

Kristina Cruises' *Kristina Regina* at Corfu *(Douglas Cromby)*

| SAPPHIRE | 12263t | 1967 | 19.0k | D2 | 563p | 650p | 240c | 149.0m | 20.7m | 6.4m | MI |
| SERENADE | 14173t | 1957 | 17.0k | D2 | 507p | 698p | 320c | 162.0m | 19.7m | 4.2m | BA |

AQUAMARINE was the second ship in the founding fleet of the new Royal Caribbean Cruise Line when delivered. She was built by Wartsila (yard number 394) in Helsinki, Finland as the NORDIC PRINCE for year-round service in the Caribbean Sea. In 1980 she returned to her builder to have a new 26m mid section inserted, increasing her passenger capacity from 714 to 1194. By 1994 she had served out her useful life with Royal Caribbean and was sold to Airtours, one of the UK's largest package holiday operators. She was placed into service as the CAROUSEL under the Sun Cruises banner. Airtours pulled out of cruising in late 2004 and Louis Cruise Lines acquired the ship and renamed her AQUAMARINE. In keeping with one of Louis' naming schemes, aquamarine is a deep blue coloured gemstone.

PRINCESA MARISSA was built by Wartsila (yard number 377) at Helsinki, Finland as the car ferry FINNHANSA for Finnlines' Baltic Sea services. In 1977 she passed to another Baltic operator, Birka Line, for the 24-hour cruise business between Stockholm and Mariehamn. For this route she was renamed PRINCESSAN. She was laid up in 1986 and during the following year acquired by Louis Cruise Lines for its cruise/ferry service from Piraeus to Rhodes, Limassol and Alexandria. She now carried the name PRINCESA MARISSA. She is currently laid up near Piraeus and her future is uncertain.

SAPPHIRE has had a long and interesting history, as she spends what are likely to be her final years cruising in the Eastern Mediterranean. She was built by Cantieri Navale Felszegi (yard number 76) at Trieste, Italy as the ITALIA for Crociere d'Oltremare of Cagliari, Sicily. She was almost immediately chartered to the newly established Princess Cruises. She was marketed as PRINCESS ITALIA, but not renamed. In 1973 she was chartered to Costa Line for Caribbean cruising, and later that year Costa bought the ship. Seven years later she was sold to Ocean Cruise Lines and renamed OCEAN PRINCESS. In 1990 she was acquired by Croisieres Paquet for whom she operated until sold in 1993 to Ellis Marine of Greece following a partial sinking which rendered her a constructive total loss. She was refurbished in Piraeus and later renamed SEA PRINCE. Later she carried the name SEA PRINCE V, but reverted to SEA PRINCE before being sold to Louis Cruise Lines who renamed her PRINCESA OCEANICA. In 1996 she was chartered to UK tour operator Thomson Holidays for whom she was renamed SAPPHIRE. In 1999 France Croisieres chartered her and she has subsequently operated on other charters and for Louis' own account. Sapphire is a bright blue coloured gemstone.

SERENADE was built by Chantiers de l'Atlantique (yard number 117) at St Nazaire, France as the JEAN MERMOZ for Compagnie de Navigation Fraissinet et Cyprien Fabre of Marseilles, France. She initially operated between her home port and West Africa. In 1965 Nouvelle Compagnie de Paquebots acquired her without a change of name. That company restyled itself, in keeping with changes in sea travel, as Croisieres Paquet in 1970 and the ship was renamed MERMOZ following a conversion to make her more suitable for cruising. In 1998 she was acquired by Prestige Cruises of Nassau, but was sold again at the end of 1999, becoming the SERENADE for Louis Cruise Lines. She currently operates short cruises from Limassol, Cyprus.

Louis Cruise Lines also owns THE EMERALD, mostly chartered to Thomson Cruises (q.v.) but also operated occasionally for its own account, and until recently owned the THOMSON DESTINY. That ship was recently sold to Norwegian investors, but chartered back and is sub-chartered to Thomson. The THOMSON SPIRIT is chartered from Holland America Line and sub-chartered to Thomson.

LOUIS HELLENIC CRUISES

The Company Louis Hellenic Cruises is a new Greek-registered company set up by Louis Cruise Lines principally to operate cruises calling at Turkish ports.

Address 5-7 Kanari Street, 18537 Piraeus, Greece

Telephone +30 210 4528620 **Fax** +30 210 4286140

Website www.louiscruises.com

Area operated Mediterranean Sea

AUSONIA	12609t	1957	20.7k	ST2	505p	750p	210c	159.3m	21.2m	6.9m	CY
CALYPSO	11162t	1967	18.5k	D2	486p	594p	240c	135.4m	19.2m	6.1m	BA
CORAL	13995t	1971	21.0k	D2	676p	912p	285c	148.1m	21.5m	5.9m	GR
PERLA	16710t	1971	21.5k	D2	784p	926p	326c	163.3m	22.8m	6.5m	BA

AUSONIA was the last ship in the post-war rebuilding programme of the major Italian operator, Adriatica of Venice. She was delivered by Cantieri Riuniti dell'Adriatico (yard number 1821) at Monfalcone, Italy and was immediately placed in service between Trieste, Venice, Brindisi, Alexandria and Beirut. She accommodated passengers in three classes and was the first large Italian passenger ship to be fitted with Denny Brown stabilisers. In 1978 she was converted for cruising and placed under the management of Italia Crociere Internazionali. She was later operated by Sicula Oceanica. She was acquired by Louis in 1998 and initially chartered to UK tour operator First Choice. She was subsequently used by Louis for its own account. It was

Lindblad Expeditions' **Polaris** in the Galapagos Islands *(Ben Lyons)*

Lindblad Expeditions' **Sea Lion** on the Columbia River *(Theodore W Scull)*

Louis Cruise Lines' **Sapphire** at Cagliari *(Egidio Ferrighi)*

Louis Cruise Lines' **Serenade** at Limassol *(Bruce Peter)*

suggested that she was to be renamed ITHACA for the 2005 season, but that has not yet happened. The name Ausonia is an ancient name for Italy, taken from Auson, son of Ulysses and father of Ausones.

CALYPSO was built by Navalmeccanica (yard number 645) at Castellammare di Stabia, Italy as the car ferry CANGURO VERDE for Italian operator Traghetti Sardi. She sailed between Genoa and Sardinia in competition with Italian state owned operator, Tirrenia, and along with her sisters was eventually chartered to that company. In 1981 she was sold to a Saudi owner, renamed DURR and set to work as pilgrim carrier. She was sold to Greek ferry operator Strintzis Lines in 1989, along with her sister, the YUM (previously CANGURO BRUNO) and was renamed as the IONIAN HARMONY. She spent two seasons on Adriatic Sea services before being sold again, this time to Danish Cruise Line. She was renamed SUN FIESTA for Caribbean cruising, but it is thought that she never actually entered service. In 1992 she was auctioned by the US Admiralty Marshall and acquired by the owner of Regency Cruise Line and towed to Greece. She was substantially rebuilt and emerged as the cruise ship REGENT JEWEL. She never actually entered service under that name and by the autumn of 1994 she was the CALYPSO, on charter to Germany's Transocean Tours. Her owners eventually collapsed and the National Bank of Greece seized the ship in 1999. Louis Cruise Lines purchased her in 2000, and she continues to operate short cruises in the Eastern Mediterranean. Calypso was the daughter of Atlas, who in Homer's Odyssey entertained Odysseus for seven years.

CORAL was built by the Rotterdam Drydock Company (yard number 329) at Rotterdam in The Netherlands as the CUNARD ADVENTURER for Cunard Line's new venture into Caribbean cruising in purpose built ships. She was replaced by a larger ship and sold to Kloster's Norwegian Caribbean Cruise Line in 1977 when she was renamed SUNWARD II. In 1991 she was acquired by Epirotiki Lines and renamed TRITON for cruising in the Eastern Mediterranean. On the merger with Sun Cruises she became part of the new Royal Olympic fleet, but on the final demise of that business was sold at auction in April 2005 to Louis Cruise Lines. In May 2005 she was renamed CORAL.

PERLA was one of the first generation of purpose-built cruise ships, delivered by Cantieri Naval dell Tirreno e Riuniti (yard number 288) at Riva Trigoso in Italy as the SOUTHWARD for Kloster's Norwegian Caribbean Cruise Line. She served her owner well for almost 25 years before passing to UK tour operator Airtours, whose cruise operation later became Sun Cruises. In her new role she was renamed as the SEAWING. Ownership passed to the Louis group and she continued to operate for Airtours. When Airtours, by now renamed as My Travel, pulled out of cruising in 2004 she was earmarked for further use with Louis Cruise Lines, but has now been switched to Louis Hellenic Cruises, as the PERLA. Perla is pearl in English.

MAGIC 1 CRUISE LINE

The Company Magic 1 Cruise Line is a subsidiary of Israeli run US publicly listed ISRAMCO, a company actively engaged in the oil and energy sectors.

Area Operated Eastern Mediterranean Sea

MIRAGE I		14264t	1973	21.0k	D2	554p	750p	c	141.5m	21.9m	5.7m	BA

MIRAGE I was built by Dubigeon-Normandie (yard number 133) at Nantes, France as the BOLERO for Fred. Olsen Line, initially for service between Travemunde, Germany and Sodertalje, Sweden. In the event she was, instead, chartered to Prinz Linien for North Sea service. She soon travelled west for charters to Commodore Cruise Line in winter for Caribbean cruising, and Prince of Fundy Line in summer for US East Coast cruising. She moved back to Europe in 1976 and sailed between Bergen, Norway and Newcastle, England. From 1978 to 1981 she was on Stena Line's Gothenburg, Sweden to Kiel, Germany service as the SCANDINAVICA while that company was awaiting the very late delivery of some new ships. A planned charter to Brittany Ferries in 1981 didn't materialise, so the ship underwent a major refit to resume Olsen service. Her final days with the Norwegian company were spent on the Newcastle to Bergen service, which was sold along with the BOLERO to Norway's Color Line in 1991. She was renamed as the JUPITER and continued on the same route until 1994. After a short charter to Baltic Sea operator Viking Line, she moved to Central America for a service between Cristobal and Cartagena on charter to Promotora de Navigation as the CRUCERO EXPRESS. In 1997 she began operating from St Petersburg, Florida as the SEMINOLE EXPRESS. The following year she returned to Europe and after another refit became the MAGIC 1 of Magic Cruise Lines. She later served as a Haifa-based cruise ship before returning to the Caribbean to operate for Ocean Club Cruises, a business which failed after only one season. ISRAMCO purchased the ship in March 2004. She has been reported as chartered to a subsidiary of Israeli travel company EGGED for summer 2005, but it is unclear if this means a return to the Mediterranean.

MAGNA CARTA STEAMSHIP COMPANY

The Company Magna Carta Steamship Company is a British registered operator of coastal cruises around Scotland, formed in 1999.

Address 136 Hamilton Terrace, London NW6 9UX

Telephone +44 207 328 1123 **Fax** +44 207 604 3634

Website www.magnacarta.bz

Area operated Scotland

LORD OF THE GLENS	729t	1985	18.0k	D2	54p	54p	c	45.0m	10.5m	3.2m	UK

LORD OF THE GLENS was built in Greece as the VICTORIA. She was renamed VICTORIA II in 1999 and took her current name in 2000.

MAJESTIC CRUISE LINES

The Company Majestic Cruise Lines is an American owned company operating the FREEWINDS on behalf of the International Association of Scientologists.

Address 118 North Fort Harrison Avenue, Clearwater, Florida 33755-4040, United States of America

Telephone +1 727 445 4309 **Fax** +1 727 445 4339

Area operated Caribbean

FREEWINDS	9780t	1968	20.0k	D2	468p	500p	170c	134.3m	19.9m	5.5m	PA

FREEWINDS was built by Wartsila (yard number 1161) at Turku, Finland as the BOHEME for Wallenius Lines for charter to Commodore Cruise Lines for Caribbean cruising. She was sold to Sally Shipping in 1981 and passed to Sally subsidiary Hanseatic Caribbean Shipping later that year. In 1986 she was acquired by the International Association of Scientologists and registered under the ownership of San Donato Properties Corporation and renamed FREEWINDS. She is operated by Majestic Cruises for scientologist members.

MANO CRUISES

The Company Mano Cruises is a division within the Mano Holdings Group, an Israeli private company in the maritime sector. Mordechai Mano founded Mano Maritime in 1945.

President Moshe Mano

Address 2 Pal-Yam St, PO Box 1400, Haifa 33031 Israel

Telephone +972 4 866 7711 **Fax** +972 4 866 1666

Website www.mano.co.il/cruises

Area operated Mediterranean and Black Seas, passenger service between Haifa and Odessa in association with Vival Marine (q.v.)

ROYAL IRIS	14717t	1971	18.0k	D2	720p	850p	330c	142.1m	21.9m	5.5m	PA
THE IRIS	12825t	1982	20.0k	D2	462p	650p	170c	137.1m	21.4m	5.8m	MA
THE JASMINE	12637t	1981	20.0k	D2	460p	650p	150c	134.5m	21.0m	5.6m	SV

ROYAL IRIS began life as the EAGLE for Southern Ferries; a company owned by the Peninsular and Oriental Steam Navigation Company. She was built by Dubigeon-Normandie (yard number 123) at Nantes, France as a car ferry for service between Southampton, Lisbon and Tangiers. In December 1975 she was sold to Nouvelle Compagnie de Paquebots, Marseilles for service in the Mediterranean Sea as the AZUR. In early 1982 she underwent conversion to become a pure cruise ship and she continued to serve her owners until sold to Chandris Lines in 1987, at which time she was renamed as THE AZUR. In 1995 she became the first ship in the new fleet of Festival Cruises, but was not officially renamed, although she carried the name AZUR for some time. When Festival Cruises failed in early 2004, she was laid up at Gibraltar and briefly renamed ELOISE prior to being acquired by Golden Cruises for operation by Mano Cruises. She was renamed ROYAL IRIS in late 2004. At the time of writing the ROYAL IRIS was undergoing refit at the Perama shipyard in Greece.

THE IRIS was built by Stocznia Szczecinska (yard number B492/03) in Szczecin, Poland as the KONSTANTIN SIMONOV, the third of a series of seven ships for the Baltic Shipping Company. She operated as a ferry, serving the ports of Leningrad, Riga and Helsinki. From 1992 she ran for Effjohn Group company, Baltic Line. In 1996 she passed to Pakartin Shipping and was renamed FRANCESCA. Her Australian employment failed and she was eventually laid up in Wilhelmshaven, Germany. In 2000 she was acquired by Silver Cruises and renamed THE IRIS for operation by Mano Cruises.

Louis Hellenic Cruises' **Calypso** in Venice when on charter to Transocean Tours *(Egidio Ferrighi)*

Majestic Cruise Lines' **Freewinds** at Kingstown, St Vincent *(Andrew Kilk)*

Mano Cruises' *The Iris* in Venice *(William Mayes)*

Mediterranean Shipping's *Melody* in Naples *(William Mayes)*

THE JASMINE was built by Stocznia Szczecinska (yard number B492/02) at Szczecin, Poland as the LEV TOLSTOY, the second of a series of seven ships for the Black Sea Shipping Company. In 1986 she underwent a major reconstruction at Lloyd Werft, Bremerhaven, Germany. She first appeared under the Ukrainian flag in 1991 and was chartered to Transocean Tours for four years. She was later laid up in Haifa, Israel before being sold to Columbus Leisure Cruises in 1998, when she was renamed NATASHA. Later that year she was renamed PALMIRA, and chartered to two German operators. In 2001 she was sold to Zenith Cruises for operation by Mano and renamed THE JASMINE.

MEDITERRANEAN SHIPPING CRUISES

The Company Mediterranean Shipping Cruises is part of the Mediterranean Shipping Company of Geneva, Switzerland; the world's largest privately owned shipping business. MSC was established in 1970, with an entry into the cruise market eighteen years later with the acquisition of what was left of Lauro Line. The business was restyled as Star Lauro, but following the loss of the ACHILLE LAURO in 1994, the cruise operation was renamed as Mediterranean Shipping Cruises. MSC operates one of the largest fleets of containerships worldwide, with a total of 134 ships.

Chief Executive Officer Pierfransesco Vago

Address Via A Depretis 31, Naples 80133, Italy

Telephone +39 081 794 2111 **Fax** +39 081 794 2707

Website www.msccruises.com

Area operated Mediterranean and Caribbean Seas

MELODY	35143t	1982	23.5k	D2	1064p	1250p	535c	204.8m	27.4m	7.8m	PA
MONTEREY	20046t	1952	16.0k	ST1	576p	627p	277c	171.8m	23.2m	9.0m	PA
MSC ARMONIA	58714t	2001	21.0k	DE2	1566p	2065p	711c	251.2m	28.8m	6.9m	PA
MSC LIRICA	59058t	2003	20.8k	DE2	1560p	2065p	760c	251.0m	28.8m	6.6m	PA
MSC OPERA	59058t	2004	20.8k	DE2	1756p	2199p	760c	251.2m	28.8m	6.8m	PA
MSC SINFONIA	58714t	2002	21.0k	DE2	1566p	2065p	711c	251.0m	28.8m	6.8m	PA
RHAPSODY	17095t	1977	18.5k	D2	766p	850p	350c	163.6m	22.8m	6.0m	IT

MELODY, formerly Home Lines' second new ship, the ATLANTIC, was built by Construction Navales & Industrielles de la Mediterranee (yard number 1432) at La Seyne, France. She initially operated between New York and Bermuda. Home Lines was sold to Holland America Line in 1988, but the ATLANTIC was not included in the deal. She went instead to Premier Cruise Line, and after a refit in Bremerhaven she emerged as the Caribbean cruise ship STARSHIP ATLANTIC. In 1997 she was sold to Mediterranean Shipping Company and renamed MELODY.

MONTEREY, now more than 50 years old, was built by the Bethlehem Sparrows Point Shipyard (yard number 4507) at Sparrows Point, Maryland, USA as the C4 cargo ship FREE STATE MARINER for the United States Maritime Commission. In 1955 she was sold to Matson Navigation of San Francisco and rebuilt as a passenger ship by Williamette Iron & Steel Corporation, Portland, Oregon. She was redelivered to her new owners in 1956 and given the name MONTEREY. She was operated on liner voyages across the Pacific Ocean until sold to Pacific Far East Line in 1971 for use as a cruise ship. In 1978 she was laid up in San Francisco and sold to World Airways in the following year. In 1980 she passed to American Maritime Holdings, but remained in lay up until 1986, when she was refitted at Portland, Oregon. Over the next 2 years she underwent massive refurbishment and rebuilding in the USA and at Turku in Finland. She finally re-entered service cruising in the Pacific in September 1988, but within six months the company had filed for bankruptcy and the ship was laid up again. In 1990 she was acquired by Star Lauro, the remnants of Lauro Line, which had been absorbed into MSC in 1987.

MSC ARMONIA began as the second new building for Festival Cruises as the EUROPEAN VISION. She was built by Chantiers de l'Atlantique (yard number K31) at St Nazaire, France. Festival Cruises failed in early 2004 and Mediterranean Shipping Cruises quickly snapped up the ship, renaming her MSC ARMONIA.

MSC LIRICA was built by Chantiers de l'Atlantique (yard number K32) at St Nazaire, France for Mediterranean Shipping Cruises. Her current operation includes Europe in summer and the Caribbean Sea in winter.

MSC OPERA, a sister to MSC LIRICA, was delivered by Chantiers de l'Atlantique (yard number L32) in 2004.

MSC SINFONIA was built by Chantiers de l'Atlantique (yard number X31) at St Nazaire, France as the EUROPEAN STARS for Festival Cruises. She was originally advertised to carry the name EUROPEAN DREAM. When Festival Cruises failed, the ship was laid up for some time before being acquired by Mediterranean Shipping Cruises and refitted as the MSC SINFONIA for service beginning in the spring of 2005.

RHAPSODY was built for Cunard as the CUNARD PRINCESS (launched as the CUNARD CONQUEST) by Burmeister & Wain (yard number 859) in Copenhagen, Denmark for service in the Caribbean Sea. She was acquired by Mediterranean Shipping Cruises in 1995 and renamed RHAPSODY.

Cruise Ships on Order

MSC MUSICA	c90000t	2006	k	DE2	2500p		1000c	294.0m	28.8m	PA
MSC ORCHESTRA	c90000t	2007	k	DE2	2500p		1000c	294.0m	28.8m	PA

MSC MUSICA and **MSC ORCHESTRA** are on order from Chantiers de l'Atlantique (yard numbers Q32 and R32) at St Nazaire, France.

METROPOLIS TUR

The Company Metropolis Tur is a Russian tour operator, operating cruises for Russian passengers. The company has operated the DALMACIJA, the ASSEDO and the OLVIA in recent years and is expected to use the ENCHANTED CAPRI in 2006.

Address Moscow, Russia

Telephone +7 095 788 0979 **Fax** +7 095 292 9447

Website www.mkruiz.ru

Area operated Black, Mediterranean and Baltic Seas

ORANGE MELODY	9570t	1980	17.0k	D2	420p	420p	180c	139.3m	17.5m	4.8m	BA

ORANGE MELODY was the ship by which Peter Deilmann entered the ocean cruise market. She was built by Howaldtswerke-Deutsche Werft (yard number 163) at Kiel, Germany as the BERLIN for a consortium of German investors in which Deilmann held a small share. Late in 1982 she was chartered to Blue Funnel Cruises of Singapore, an associated business of the Straits Steamship Company. She was renamed PRINCESS MAHSURI. Her Far East and Australian operation for Blue Funnel was not entirely successful and she was returned to her owners a year early in 1984, when she reverted to her original name. She was lengthened in 1986 at Rendsburg, Germany and continued to operate for Deilmann until that company terminated her charter at the end of 2004, following which she was laid up until purchased by Saga as a replacement for the SAGA PEARL, with delivery at the end of 2005. In the meantime she secured a charter for Metropolitan Tur for the summer of 2005 as the ORANGE MELODY. For her new service with Saga she takes the name SPIRIT OF ADVENTURE.

MITSUI OSK

The Company Mitsui OSK Lines is one of the world's largest shipping companies, with a fleet of 630 ships under the control of its group companies. The cruise business is operated by Mitsui OSK Passenger Lines, or MOPAS for short and also as Nippon Charter Cruise, a joint venture between Mitsui OSK and Japan Cruise Line. Nippon Charter Cruise is recorded as the registered owner of the FUJI MARU. Mitsui OSK was formed in 1964 with the merger of Mitsui Steamship Company (de-merged from its parent in 1942) and the long-established (1884) OSK Line. A further reorganisation took place in 1999 when Navix Line was absorbed into the group.

Chairman Kunio Suzuki **President** Akimitsu Ashida

Address 9-13 Akasaka 1-Chome, Minato-ku, Sankaido Building, 107 8532 Tokyo, Japan

Telephone +81 3 5114 5247 **Fax** +81 3 5114 5270

Website www.mopas.co.jp

Area operated Asia and worldwide for Japanese speaking passengers

FUJI MARU	23235t	1989	20.0k	D2	364p	603p	135c	167.0m	24.0m	6.6m	JP
NIPPON MARU	21903t	1990	18.0k	D2	326p	607p	160c	166.6m	23.6m	6.6m	JP

FUJI MARU was Japan's largest cruise ship when completed in 1989 by Mitsubishi Heavy Industries (yard number 1177) at Kobe, Japan. She has operated mainly on charter cruises within Asia and the Pacific Ocean.

NIPPON MARU is also a product of the Kobe, Japan shipyard of Mitsubishi Heavy Industries (yard number 1188), and carries one of the most prestigious names in Japanese passenger shipping. The ship operates a mixture of cruises ranging from short domestic voyages of a few days to three-month round the world cruises.

Mediterranean Shipping's **Monterey** in Istanbul *(William Mayes)*

Mediterranean Shipping's **MSC Opera** in Genoa *(Egidio Ferrighi)*

Mediterranean Shipping's **Rhapsody** *(William Mayes Collection)*

Metropolis Tur's **Orange Melody**, seen as the **Berlin** in Southampton *(Alan Ryszka-Onions)*

MURMANSK SHIPPING COMPANY

The Company The Murmansk Shipping Company operates a fleet of icebreakers in the Barents Sea and also operates some of them under charter on Arctic and Antarctic expedition cruises. Among the fleet are nine nuclear powered icebreakers, including the YAMAL, operated for Quark Expeditions (q.v.). The company was founded in 1939, but one of the most significant events in the company's history was the expedition by the icebreaker ARKTIKA in 1977 to the North Pole, making that ship the first surface vessel to reach the Pole. In 1993 the company was converted from a state-owned enterprise into a joint-stock company. Murmansk Shipping Company operates a fleet of ice-strengthened cargo ships and tankers and three conventional icebreakers. The only vessels currently carrying passengers are those listed here, and the SOVETSKIY SOYUZ and the YAMAL, both listed elsewhere. It is not known if these two ships are currently chartered out, so they have been listed under their owner.

Director Aleksandr Medvedev

Address Kominterna Street 15, 183636 Murmansk, Russia

Telephone +7 8152 481049 **Fax** +7 8152 481148

Website www.msco.ru

Area operated Polar regions

KAPITAN DRANITSYN	12919t	1980	19.5k	DE3	100p	116p	60c	129.4m	26.5m	8.5m	RU
KLAVDIYA YELANSKAYA	4329t	1977	13.0k	D2	206p	262p	c	100.0m	16.2m	4.6m	RU

KAPITAN DRANITSYN was built by Wartsila (yard number 429) at Helsinki, Finland. In 1997 she rescued 128 passengers from the cruise ship HANSEATIC, which was in danger of sinking.

KLAVDIYA YELANSKAYA would normally be shown in the section headed passenger ships in other roles, as she is a passenger and cargo vessel offering a service from Murmansk. However, she does also offer occasional cruises. She was built by Brodogradiliste (yard number 416) at Kraljevica in what was then Yugoslavia. The ship was used as a vantage point for journalists and relatives during the raising of the sunken Russian submarine KURSK.

NOBLE CALEDONIA

The Company Noble Caledonia is a British operator of exploration, expedition and educational tours and cruises. The company was founded in 1991 and now operates the ISLAND SKY on seasonal charter. The company also sells space on other ships, both ocean and river.

Address 2 Chester Close, Belgravia, London SW1X 7BE

Telephone +44 207 752 0000 **Fax** +44 207 245 0388

Website www.noble-caledonia.co.uk

Area operated Baltic, Black and Mediterranean Seas and the Indian Ocean

ISLAND SKY	4200t	1992	15.5k	D2	114p	114p	72c	90.6m	15.3m	4.1m	BA

ISLAND SKY was built by Nuovi Cantieri Apuania (yard number 1147) at Marina di Carrara in Italy as the RENAISSANCE EIGHT for Renaissance Cruises. She remained with the company until it filed for bankruptcy in the autumn of 2001, following which she was renamed as the RENAI II and laid up. She became the SKY in 2003 and was renamed ISLAND SKY in 2004 when acquired by Mauritius Island Cruises. ISLAND SKY and her sister the ISLAND SUN (now the CORINTHIAN II of Travel Dynamics International (q.v.)) are owned by Danish container operator, Clipper Group and were recently purchased from Mauritius Island Cruises, which has now ceased trading. Noble Caledonia also chartered the ISLAND SKY in 2004.

NORTH STAR CRUISES

The Company North Star Cruises was established in 1987. The new NORTH STAR replaces a 1999-built ship of the same name.

Management Owner Craig Howson

Address PO Box 654, Broome, Western Australia 6725

Telephone +61 8 9192 1829 **Fax** +61 8 9192 1830

Website www.northstarcruises.com.au

Area operated Australia North West coast

TRUE NORTH	630t	2005	13.0k	D2	36p	36p	15c	49.9m	10.0m	1.9m	AU

TRUE NORTH was built by Image Marine Pty Ltd (yard number 287) in Fremantle, Western Australia.

NYK CRUISES

The Company Nippon Yusen Kaisha (NYK) was formed in 1885 with the merger of the Mitsubishi Mail Steamship Company and Kyodo Unyu Kaisha, creating a fleet of 58 ships. Over the ensuing years the company developed an impressive network of liner services that eventually encompassed the whole world. It was not until 1929, however, that the now familiar twin red stripes on a white background was adopted as the company's new funnel marking. NYK emerged from the Second World War with 37 ships and gradually began to re-establish itself, initially in Japanese domestic service, and from 1950 in international trades, although now in freight rather than passengers. The merger in 1964 with Mitsubishi Shipping Company, created a new NYK Group, owning a total of 87 ships. Four years later the company began to containerise its cargo services, and in 1969 NYK disposed of its coastal and domestic operations to concentrate on its liner shipping business. In 1990 Crystal Cruises was established, and in the same year NYK began operating the expedition ship FRONTIER SPIRIT. NYK today operates a fleet of around 800 ships around the world. The company operates a single ship in the Japanese domestic market.

Address 2-3-2 Marunouchi Chiyoda-ku, 100-0005 Tokyo, Japan

Telephone +81 3 3284 5665 **Fax** +81 3 3284 6334

Website www.asukacruise.co.jp

Area operated Japan and worldwide

ASUKA	28856t	1991	21k	D2	584p	604p	243c	192.8m	24.7m	6.6m	JP

ASUKA was built by Mitsubishi Heavy Industries (yard number 2050) at Nagasaki, Japan for operation by NYK in the deluxe sector of the Japanese cruise market. Asuka was the Japanese capital city in 700 AD and home to the ruling dynasty. The ASUKA is heading for German operator Phoenix Reisen (q.v.) as the AMADEA when she is replaced by the CRYSTAL HARMONY (renamed ASUKA II) in December 2005.

CRYSTAL CRUISES

The Company Crystal Cruise was established by NYK in 1990 as a luxury cruise operator geared to the US market. It would appear that the increase in capacity created with the arrival of the CRYSTAL SERENITY in 2003 has not been matched by the increase in passengers, as the company's first ship will transfer to Crystal's parent company at the end of 2005.

Chairman Mitsuhiko Takahashi **President** Gregg Michel

Address 2049 Century Park East, Suite 1400, Los Angeles, California 90067, United States of America

Telephone +1 310 785 9300 **Fax** +1 310 785 0011

Website www.crystalcruises.com

Area operated Worldwide

CRYSTAL HARMONY	48621t	1990	22.0k	DE2	940p	940p	545c	240.9m	29.6m	7.5m	BA
CRYSTAL SERENITY	68870t	2003	22.0k	DEP2	1080p	1140p	635c	250.0m	32.2m	7.6m	BA
CRYSTAL SYMPHONY	51044t	1995	22.0k	DE2	940p	940p	545c	238.0m	30.2m	7.6m	BA

CRYSTAL HARMONY was the first ship for the newly formed Crystal Cruises. She was built by Mitsubishi Heavy Industries (yard number 2100) at Nagasaki, Japan. She will become NYK's ASUKA II in December 2005.

CRYSTAL SERENITY was built by Chantiers de l'Atlantique (yard number H32) at St Nazaire, France.

CRYSTAL SYMPHONY was built by Kvaerner Masa Yards (yard number1323) at Turku, Finland.

OCEAN ADVENTURES

The Company Ocean Adventures SA is an Ecuador registered company, established in 2001.

Address Avenida 12 de Octubre 2449 y Orellana, Edificio Jerico, Planta Baja, Quito, Ecuador

Telephone +593 2 322 8337 **Fax** +593 2 322 7984

Website www.oceanadventures.com.ec

Area operated Galapagos Islands

ECLIPSE	1610t	1998	14.5k	D2	48p	48p	23c	64.0m	12.5m	3.3m	EC

ECLIPSE was built by Astilleros Construcciones at Vigo, Spain as the ECLIPSE.

Mitsui OSK's **Nippon Maru** at San Francisco *(Andrew Kilk)*

Noble Caledonia's **Island Sky** in Istanbul *(William Mayes)*

NYK's **Asuka** at Southampton *(William Mayes)*

Crystal Cruises' **Crystal Harmony** at San Francisco *(Andrew Kilk)*

OCEAN PRINCESS CRUISES

The Company Ocean Princess Group Co Ltd is a Thai registered company within the VAP Group. The company was formed in early 2004 and operates cruises to the islands off the coast of Thailand.

Address 42 Soi Sukhumvit 13 (Saeng-Chan) Klongtoey-Nua, Wattana, Bangkok 10110, Thailand

Telephone +66 2 651 1346 9 **Fax** +66 2 651 1350

Website www.oceanprincess.co.th

Area operated Thailand and the Andaman Islands

OCEAN PRINCESS	6092t	1964	17.0k	D2	300p	377p	c	122.2m	15.9m	5.2m	TH

OCEAN PRINCESS was built by VEB Mathias Thesen Werft (yard number 190) at Wismar, Germany as the BASHKIRIYA for the Black Sea Shipping Company. Following the break-up of the Soviet Bloc, she was owned by Odessa Cruise Song from 1991 and during the following year became the ODESSA SONG. She carried the name ROYAL DREAM in 1997 but was sold the following year to Silver Star Shipping and renamed SILVER STAR. In 2003 she was renamed NANDINI under the ownership of Star Vegas Travel and Resorts. Later that year she became the OLVIAVA. Sold in late 2004 to Ocean Princess Shipping, she was renamed OCEAN PRINCESS.

OCEANIA CRUISES

The Company Oceania Cruises was founded in 2002 by cruise industry veterans Joe Watters and Frank Del Rio.

Address   8120 North West 53rd Street, Miami, Florida 33166 United States of America
UK General Sales Agents The Cruise Line, Softech House, Albourne, West Sussex, BN6 9BN, England

Telephone +1 305 514 2300
UK only 0800 089 0011 **Fax** +44 870 442 6934

Website www.oceaniacruises.com and www.oceanacruise.co.uk

Area operated Europe, South America and the Caribbean Sea, the Far East and China

INSIGNIA	30277t	1998	20.0k	DE2	680p	812p	373p	181.0m	25.5m	5.9m	MI
NAUTICA	30277t	2000	20.0k	DE2	680p	812p	373p	181.0m	25.5m	5.9m	MI
REGATTA	30277t	1998	20.0k	DE2	680p	812p	373p	181.0m	25.5m	5.9m	MI

INSIGNIA was the first of the second generation cruise ships built for Renaissance Cruises by Chantiers de l'Atlantique (yard number H31) at St Nazaire, France as the rather unimaginatively named R ONE. This series of eight ships was decorated in the elegant style of the Edwardian ocean liners. INSIGNIA entered service for Oceania Cruises in 2004.

NAUTICA was built as the R FIVE, the first member of the second quartet of ships for Renaissance Cruises by Chantiers de l'Atlantique (yard number P31) at St Nazaire, France. She operated for Pullmanturs as the BLUE DREAM in 2004, although not officially renamed. NAUTICA began sailing for Oceania Cruises in 2005.

REGATTA was built by Chantiers de l'Atlantique (yard number I31) at St Nazaire, France as the R TWO for Renaissance Cruises. REGATTA entered service for Oceania Cruises in 2003.

Renaissance Cruises collapsed in September 2001 and all of its ships were laid up, many of them at Gibraltar. Subsequently they were all acquired by investment companies connected with the ship builder, as that organisation still had financial commitments. Oceania Cruises subsequently chartered these three ships, introducing them one at a time.

OCEANWIDE EXPEDITIONS

The Company Oceanwide Expeditions is a Netherlands based operator of expedition cruises to the Polar regions. The company also markets space on other ships.

Address Bellamypark 9, 4381 CG Vlissingen, The Netherlands

Telephone +31 118 410 410 **Fax** +31 118 410 417

Website www.ocnwide.com

Area operated Arctic and Antarctic regions

ALEKSEY MARYSHEV	1698t	1990	12.5k	D1	46p	46p	20c	66.0m	12.8m	3.5m	RU
GRIGORIY MIKHEYEV	1729t	1990	12.5k	D1	46p	46p	20c	66.0m	12.8m	3.5m	RU

ALEKSEY MARYSHEV and **GRIGORIY MIKHEYEV** are owned by the Hydrographic Research Institute of St Petersburg, Russia and were built by the Hollming Shipyard (yard numbers 287 and 288) at Rauma in Finland.

Oceania Cruises' **Regatta** *(Clive Harvey)*

Crystal Cruises' **Crystal Symphony** at San Francisco *(William Mayes Collection)*

ORION EXPEDITION CRUISES

The Company Orion Expedition Cruises Pty Ltd is a new Australian entrant to the expanding world of expedition cruise operators.

Managing Director Sarina Bratton

Address 26 Alfred Street, Milsons Point, New South Wales 2061, Australia

Telephone +61 2 9033 8700 **Fax** +61 2 9033 8799

Website www.orioncruises.com.au

Area operated Australia and Antarctica

ORION	3984t	2003	16.0k	D1	106p	140p	70c	102.7m	14.0m	3.8m	BA

ORION was built by Schiffswerft u Maschinenfabrik Cassens (yard number 236) at Emden, Germany as the ORION for Explorer Maritime Ltd of Greece. She began a long-term charter to Orion Expedition Cruises at the beginning of 2005, having previously operated for Travel Dynamics.

PACIFIC CRUISES

The Company China Golden Development Holdings is a Hong Kong-listed cruise company that trades under the marketing name of Pacific Cruises. The company operates cruises between Hainan Island in China, and Halong Bay in Vietnam.

Address 1, Science Museum Road, Tsim Sha Tsui East, Kowloon, Hong Kong

Area operated China and Vietnam

MING FAI PRINCESS	17261t	1972	18.7k	D2	1070p	1800p	c	155.0m	22.8m	6.0m	PA

MING FAI PRINCESS was built in Shimizu, Japan by K K Kanashasi Zosensho (yard number 1008) as the car and freight ferry SHIRETOKO MARU for Nippon Enkai Ferry KK of Tokyo. She was sold to Minoan Lines of Greece in 1988 and completely rebuilt as the passenger and car ferry N KAZANTZAKIS. China Golden Development Holdings purchased her in 2001, renamed her MING FAI PRINCESS and rebuilt her into a cruise ship with numerous gambling facilities.

PAGE & MOY HOLIDAYS

The Company Page & Moy was established more than 40 years ago, although the company began offering its own cruise products somewhat later, and today is one of the United Kingdom's leading travel agents, and is also an important tour operator. In 2004 UK rival, Travelshpere, acquired the business, but both companies have retained their identity for the time being.

Address 136-140 London Road, Leicester LE2 1EB, England

Telephone +44 116 250 7000 **Fax** +44 116 254 9949

Website www.cruisecollection.com and www.1st4cruising.com

Area operated Europe, from UK ports

BLACK PRINCE	11209t	1966	18.5k	D2	412p	451p	200c	141.6m	20.0m	6.4m	BA
OCEAN MAJESTY	10417t	1966	20.0k	D2	544p	613p	235c	130.6m	19.2m	5.4m	PO
OCEAN MONARCH	15833t	1955	17.0k	D2	422p	526p	210c	162.4m	21.3m	7.5m	PO

BLACK PRINCE is owned by Fred. Olsen Cruise Lines (q.v.).

OCEAN MAJESTY was built by Union Naval de Levante (yard number 93) in Valencia, Spain as the car ferry JUAN MARCH for Spain's state carrier, Compania Trasmediterranea. She was one of a series of four ships designed for both the overnight Barcelona to Palma, Majorca run and the longer route from Barcelona to the Canary Islands. She was sold in 1985 to Sol Maritime Services of Limassol, Cyprus. She was renamed SOL CHRISTIANA and placed on a new service linking Piraeus with Crete, Rhodes, Cyprus and Israel. The service was not a success and she was sold to another Cypriot operator, renamed KYPROS STAR and set to work as a ferry serving Rhodes, Cyprus and Egypt from Piraeus. In 1988 she operated for Italy's Adriatica and sailed between Brindisi in Italy and Patras in Greece. Between 1989 and 1994 the ship underwent a total transformation, emerging as the cruise ship OCEAN MAJESTY. She was initially chartered to Epirotiki Line as the OLYMPIC and again for the following year as the HOMERIC. For 1995 the ship was sub-chartered to Page & Moy Holidays for a number of cruises. Subsequently she has made regular appearances in the Page & Moy cruise programme.

OCEAN MONARCH is operated for most of the summer by Hansa Kreuzfahrten (q.v.).

PEREGRINE ADVENTURES

The Company Peregrine Tours is a British and Australian based operator of adventure and exploration tours, including cruises to Antarctica using two chartered ships.

Address First Floor, 8 Clerewater Place, Lower Way, Thatcham, Berkshire, RG19 3RF, England

Telephone +44 1635 872300 **Fax** +44 1635 873758

Website www.peregrineadventures.co.uk

Area operated Antarctica and the Arctic

AKADEMIK IOFFE	6450t	1989	16.0k	D2	110p	118p	53c	117.0m	18.3m	6.1m	RU
AKADEMIK SERGEI VAVILOV	6231t	1988	16.0k	D2	110p	118p	53c	117.0m	18.3m	6.1m	RU

AKADEMIK IOFFE is operated by Peregrine Tours under the marketing name PEREGRINE MARINER. She is owned by the Shirskov Oceanological Institute of Kaliningrad, and was built by the Hollming Shipyard (yard number 266) at Rauma, Finland for the Russian Academy of Sciences. She was transferred to her current owner in 1993. From 1995 she operated under the marketing name MARINE ADVENTURER, but was not officially renamed.

AKADEMIK SERGEI VAVILOV was built by the Hollming Shipyard (yard number 265) at Rauma, Finland for the Russian Academy of Sciences. She is operated by Peregrine Tours under the marketing name PEREGRINE VOYAGER, although not officially renamed. She was transferred to the Shirskov Oceanological Institute of Kaliningrad in 1993. Her owners, under the trading style Poseidon Arctic Expeditions, may also operate the ship.

PETER DEILMANN CRUISES

The Company Peter Deilmann Cruises was founded by Peter Deilmann in 1973 as a company offering cruises in the premium sector. Until 2004 the company also operated the small cruise ship BERLIN, but this has now been returned to her owners. Peter Deilmann died in 2004 and the company is now in the hands of his daughters. The company also operates a fleet of river cruise ships on the waterways of Europe.

Owners Gisa and Hedda Deilmann **Managing Directors** Norbert Becker, Traute Hallmann-Schulze

Address Am Holm 25, 23730 Neustadt, Germany

Telephone +49 4561 3960 **Fax** +49 4561 8207

Website www.deilmann-cruises.com

Area operated Worldwide

DEUTSCHLAND	22496t	1998	20.0k	D2	600p	600p	260c	175.3m	23.0m	5.8m	GY

DEUTSCHLAND was built by Howaldtswerke Deutsche Werft (yard number 328) at Kiel, Germany for grand style cruising for Peter Deilmann Cruises. Initially she was marketed only to German-speaking passengers, but has recently become a bi-lingual German and English ship.

PHOENIX REISEN

The Company Phoenix Reisen is a German tour and travel company.

Address Pfalzer Strasse 14, 53111 Bonn, Germany

Telephone +49 228 726 280 **Fax** +49 228 726 2899

Website www.phoenixreisen.com

Area operated Europe and South America

ALBATROS	28518t	1973	18.5k	D2	884p	1100p	340c	205.5m	25.2m	7.5m	BA
ALEXANDER VON HUMBOLDT	12231t	1996	16.0k	D2	362p	394p	157c	133.0m	20.0m	5.1m	BA
AMADEA	28856t	1991	21.0k	D2	584p	604p	243c	192.8m	24.7m	6.6m	JP
MAXIM GORKIY	24220t	1969	22.0k	ST2	650p	830p	340c	194.7m	26.6m	8.3m	BA

ALBATROS has had a long and varied career. She was built by Wartsila (yard number 397) at Helsinki, Finland as the ROYAL VIKING SEA, the final member of the trio of luxurious first generation vessels for the new Royal Viking Line. She was lengthened in 1983 in Bremerhaven, but just a year later both she and her owners were acquired by Kloster Cruise (Norwegian Cruise Line). Royal Viking Line continued to operate as a separate entity for some time. In 1991 the ship was transferred with the group to Royal Cruise Line and renamed ROYAL ODYSSEY. Later, while NCL was experiencing financial difficulties, the ship was sold to Actinor and chartered back. In 1997 she was renamed NORWEGIAN STAR and chartered to a new company, Norwegian Capricorn Line,

Crystal Cruises' *Crystal Serenity* sailing from Southampton on her maiden voyage *(William Mayes)*

in which Norwegian Cruise Line had an interest. Norwegian Capricorn Line used the ship for cruises from Australia, but was not entirely successful. She passed to Star Holdings in 1999, and in 2001 she was operated by Star Cruises as the NORWEGIAN STAR 1, but did not stay in the Far East for long as, following a charter to Crown Investments for cruising on the Chinese coast, she moved to Mediterranean Sea as the CROWN, serving the Spanish market. By now Club Cruise of the Netherlands owned her. Phoenix Reisen managed to charter the ship at relatively short notice in 2004 to replace the previous ALBATROS, which had suffered mechanical failure and was considered beyond economic repair. From spring 2004 she has sailed as the ALBATROS.

ALEXANDER VON HUMBOLDT was partially constructed by the Sudostroitelnyy Zavod Okean shipyard (yard number 1) at Nikolaev in the Ukraine as the research vessel OKEAN. Her keel was laid in 1987 and she was launched in 1989 but was not completed. She was purchased by V-Ships and towed to the Mariotti shipyard in Genoa for completion as a passenger ship. On completion in 1996 she was chartered to the Peninsular and Oriental Steam Navigation Company for use by Swan Hellenic Cruises as a replacement for the smaller ORPHEUS, and given the name MINERVA. At the end of her charter in 2003, she was returned to V-Ships, who succeeded in setting two new charters for her. For the summer of 2003 she became the SAGA PEARL for the 'over 50' tour operator, Saga Holidays, and in the winter she took the name EXPLORER II for Abercrombie & Kent's expedition cruises. For summer 2004 she was operated by Saga again, reverting to her Saga name. In November 2004 she took up employment with Abercrombie & Kent, but for the summer of 2005 she will operate for Phoenix Reisen as the ALEXANDER VON HUMBOLDT on South American cruises, while continuing to serve Abercrombie & Kent in the winter. Alexander von Humboldt, born in 1769, was described by Charles Darwin as the greatest scientific traveller who ever lived. He was the author of the five-volume Kosmos, the last volume of which was published in 1862, three years after his death.

AMADEA was built by Mitsubishi Heavy Industries (yard number 2050) at Nagasaki, Japan as the ASUKA for operation by NYK in the deluxe sector of the Japanese cruise market. The ASUKA becomes Phoenix Reisen's fourth ship, AMADEA in March 2006 when she is replaced in the NYK fleet by the CRYSTAL HARMONY (renamed ASUKA II) in December 2005.

MAXIM GORKIY was built by Howaldtswerke-Deutsche Werft (yard number 997) in Hamburg, Germany for Deutsche-Atlantik Line of the same city. Completing the pattern, she was named HAMBURG. She was used on the company's service between Cuxhaven and South America. In 1973 she was renamed HANSEATIC, but later that year was laid up after her owners ran into financial difficulties. In 1974 she was acquired by SOVCOMFLOT and renamed MAKSIM GORKIY for service with the Black Sea Shipping Company of Odessa. She was chartered for use as the BRITANNIC in the film Juggernaut. In 1988 she underwent a major modernisation by Lloyd Werft at Bremerhaven, but while on a cruise in June of the following year almost sank after sailing into drifting ice off Spitzbergen. Passengers and crew took to the boats after the pressure of the ice on the hull caused leaks and the ship began to sink. With the assistance of the Norwegian Coastguard the hull was patched and eventually the ship was towed to an inlet to allow more thorough repairs to be carried out. About two weeks later she arrived under her own power at Bremerhaven for permanent repairs. In 1991 she was renamed slightly as the MAXIM GORKIY. She has been a long-term member of Phoenix Reisen's chartered fleet. Maxim Gorkiy was the pseudonym of the writer Aleksei Peshkov (1868-1936).

PLANTOURS & PARTNER

The Company Plantours and Partner GmbH is a German cruise operator, long-term charterer of the VISTAMAR, and operator of European river cruises.

Managing Director A P Traeger

Address Obernstrasse 76, D28195 Bremen, Germany

Telephone +49 421 173690

Website www.plantours-partner.de

Area operated Amazon, Western Europe, Scandinavia, Mediterranean, round Africa

| VISTAMAR | 7478t | 1989 | 16.5k | D2 | 300p | 340p | 110c | 117.4m | 16.8m | 4.5m | SP |

VISTAMAR was built by Union Naval de Levant SA (yard number 175) at Valencia, Spain as the VISTAMAR for Mar Line Universal Shipping, a subsidiary of Hoteles Marinos. In 2000 she was transferred to Vistamar Canarias and two months later to Servicios Maritimos Litoral, based in The Netherlands, both without change of name.

Page & Moy's **Ocean Majesty** at Harwich *(Andrew Kilk)*

Peregrine Adventures' **Akademik Sergei Vavilov** at King George Island, Antarctica *(Andrew Kilk)*

Peter Deilmann's **Deutschland** at Aruba *(Andrew Kilk)*

Phoenix Reisen's **Maxim Gorkiy** at San Francisco *(Andrew Kilk)*

PLEIN CAP CROISIERES

The Company Plein Cap Croisieres is a trading style of French company, Marina Cruises.

Address 251 route de La Colle, 06270 Villeneuve Loubet, France

Telephone +33 4 9320 2120 **Fax** +33 4 9373 7001

Website www.plein-cap.com

Area operated Mediterranean, Red Sea, Indian Ocean, Black Sea and Scandinavia

ADRIANA		4490t	1972	15.0k	D2	250p	298p	100c	103.7m	14.0m	4.5m	SV

ADRIANA was built by the United Shipyard (yard number 54) at Perama, Greece for Hellenic Mediterranean Lines as the AQUARIUS. She was both the first cruise ship for that company and the first such vessel to be built in Greece. With her long raked bow she was a very elegant ship, and made an attractive sight on her Greek Island cruises during the summer. She did spend a few winters in the Caribbean, but served mostly in the Mediterranean. The ACHILLE LAURO hijacking in 1985 had a particularly bad effect on the business of Hellenic Mediterranean Lines, and in 1986 her mortgagees seized the AQUARIUS. She was sold to Adriatic General Shipping, part of the Yugoslav Jadrolinija company and began operating in the Adriatic Sea as the ADRIANA. She often ran cruises on charter to German tour operators. In 1997 she passed to Marina Cruises of Nice and in February of the following year commenced cruising under the Plein Cap banner.

POLAR STAR EXPEDITIONS

The Company Polar Star Expeditions, although Canadian based, is a Norwegian owned company, part of the Karlsen Shipping Company. Polar Star Expeditions was formed in 2000.

Management President Martin Karlsen

Address Karlsen Wharf, 2089 Upper Water Street, PO Box 9510 Station A, Halifax, Nova Scotia, B3K 5S3, Canada

Telephone +1 902 423 7389 **Fax** +1 902 420 9222

Website www.polarstarexpeditions.com

Area operated Antarctic, Arctic and long connecting voyages, UK in 2005, chartered to Spitzbergen Expeditions in summer

POLAR STAR		3963t	1969	11.0k	D3	92p	104p	30c	86.5m	21.2m	6.2m	BB

POLAR STAR was built by Wartsila (yard number 389) at Helsinki, Finland as the icebreaker NJORD for the Swedish Maritime Administration. Karlsen Shipping acquired her in 2000, converted her for use as an expedition ship and renamed her POLAR STAR.

PULLMANTUR CRUISES

The Company Pullmantur is a large Spanish tour company operating its own airline, cruise line and tour bus business. The company was established in 1972, but only entered the cruise business with the establishment of Pullmantur Cruises in 2000. The airline, Pullmantur Air was formed in 2002.

Address C/Orense 16, 1st, 28020, Madrid, Spain

Telephone +34 91556 1114 **Fax** +34 91 418 8790

Website www.pullmanturcruises.com

Area operated Mediterranean and South America

HOLIDAY DREAM	37012t	1981	22.0k	D2	752p	752p	406c	199.6m	28.5m	8.3m	BA
OCEANIC	38772t	1965	27.0k	ST2	1136p	1800p	565c	238.4m	29.4m	8.6m	BA
PACIFIC	20186t	1971	19.0k	D2	648p	723p	300c	168.7m	25.6m	7.7m	BA
R SIX / BLUE STAR	30277t	2000	22.0k	DE2	702p	777p	376c	181.0m	25.5m	6.0m	MI

HOLIDAY DREAM was built by Bremer Vulkan (yard number 1001) at Vegesack, Germany for Hapag-Lloyd of Bremen as the EUROPA. She was widely acclaimed as the most luxurious ship afloat, but after 17 years of worldwide cruising she was sold to Star Cruises, but retained for a further year until the new EUROPA was delivered. She was possibly renamed MEGASTAR ASIA for a very short time, but soon had the name SUPERSTAR EUROPE for cruising the waters of Southeast Asia. In February 2000 she became the SUPERSTAR ARIES and was due to transfer to the Orient Lines fleet in the spring of 2003, but following a general downturn in business, was retained within the Star Cruises fleet. She was sold to Pullmantur in 2003 and renamed HOLIDAY DREAM. Her Caribbean winter cruises are also marketed by Brazilian tour operator CVC.

Plantours & Partner's *Vistamar* at Lisbon *(William Mayes)*

OCEANIC was the first new ship to be built for Home Lines. She was constructed by Cantieri Riunite dell'Adriatico (yard number 1876) at Monfalcone, Italy as the OCEANIC for transatlantic service between New York and Italy. She later sailed between New York and Bermuda and was used extensively for cruising. She was sold to Premier Cruise Lines in 1985, when she became the ROYALE OCEANIC, but was renamed as the STARSHIP OCEANIC later that year. She reverted to her original name in 1998 and two years later was sold to Pullmantur.

PACIFIC was built by Rheinstahl Nordseewerke (yard number 411) at Emden, Germany as the SEA VENTURE for Norwegian Cruiseships of Oslo. She was initially operated by Flagship Cruises between New York and Bermuda, but was soon sold to a joint venture between Oivind Lorentzen and Fearney & Eger. She was sold on to the Peninsular and Oriental Steam Navigation Company in 1975, becoming the PACIFIC PRINCESS for P&O subsidiary Princess Cruises. She was sold to Pullmantur in 2002 and renamed PACIFIC. The ship is operated in conjunction with CVC of Brazil on Brazilian coastal cruises until 2007. Summer cruises include the Fernando de Noronha Islands, while winter itineraries take in the River Amazon.

R SIX is marketed as the BLUE STAR, but not officially renamed. She was built by Ateliers et Chantiers de l'Atlantique (yard number Q31) at St Nazaire, France as one of a series of eight elegantly furnished ships for Renaissance Cruises. Following the collapse of that company in 2001 she, along with many of her sisters, was laid up in Gibraltar. The ships were auctioned and acquired by Cruiseinvest, an offshoot of her builders, who still had a significant financial interest in the ships. Pullmantur eventually chartered her. She is expected to spend the winter operating on the Brazilian coast for tour operator CVC.

QUARK EXPEDITIONS

The Company Quark Expeditions began taking travellers to far flung destinations in 1991 with a voyage aboard the SOVIETSKIY SOYUZ to the North Pole. The KAPITAN KHLEBNIKOV was first used in the following year, and has remained a favourite ever since. Most of the ships are also marketed by other expedition operators, notably the 'Professors' and the LYUBOV ORLOVA.

Address 1019 Post Road, Darien, Connecticut, CT 06820 United States of America

Telephone +1 203 656 0499 **Fax** +1 203 655 6623

Website www.quarkexpeditions.com

Area operated Arctic (July and August), Antarctic (November to March)

KAPITAN KHLEBNIKOV	12288t	1981	18.7k	DE3	108p	112p	c	129.4m	26.5m	8.5m	RU
PROFESSOR MOLCHANOV	1753t	1982	9.0k	D2	49p	49p	23c	71.6m	12.8m	4.5m	RU
PROFESSOR MULTANOVSKIY	1754t	1983	9.0k	D2	49p	49p	23c	71.6m	12.8m	4.5m	RU
LYUBOV ORLOVA	4251t	1976	17.2k	D2	110p	110p	c	100.0m	16.4m	4.7m	MA
YAMAL	20646t	1992	21.0k	D1	100p	100p	c	150.0m	30.0m	11.0m	RU

KAPITAN KHLEBNIKOV was constructed by Wartsila (yard number 430) at Helsinki, Finland as an icebreaker for the Far Eastern Shipping Company of Vladivostok. She was converted for use as an expedition ship by Rickmer Lloyd at Bremerhaven in 1992, and currently operates on charter to Quark Expeditions.

PROFESSOR MOLCHANOV was built for the Government of Russia's Hydrometeorological Institute by Oy Laivateollisuus (yard number 344) at Turku, Finland. The ship passed to the Murmansk Territorial Hydrometeorological Institute in 1994. She operates mainly on charters to Quark Expeditions.

PROFESSOR MULTANOVSKIY was built for the Government of Russia's Hydrometeorological Institute by Oy Laivateollisuus (yard number 346) at Turku, Finland. She is now operated by the Arctic and Antarctic Research Institute to whom she passed in 1994.

LYUBOV ORLOVA was built by Brodogradiliste Titovo (yard number 413) at Kraljevica in what was Yugoslavia for the Far Eastern Shipping Company of Vladivostok as one of a series of eight ships for various Soviet owners. She has been owned by Lyubov Orlova Shipping Company of Novorossiysk since 1996. Lyubov Orlova (1902-1975) was probably the most glamorous and popular actress of the Soviet cinema.

YAMAL was built by the Murmansk Baltic Shipbuilding and Engineering Works (yard number 704) at St Petersburg, Russia as the nuclear powered icebreaker YAMAL for the Murmansk Shipping Company. The Yamal peninsula in Siberia is home to the Nenets, reindeer herders who have occupied the region for more than 1000 years.

Plein Cap Croisieres' **Adriana** (Bruce Peter)

Pullmantur's **Holiday Dream** in Naples (Bruce Peter)

Quark Expeditions' **Kapitan Khlebnikov** *(Doreen Lawes)*

Quark Expeditions' **Professor Molchanov** anchored off St Helena *(Chris Mason)*

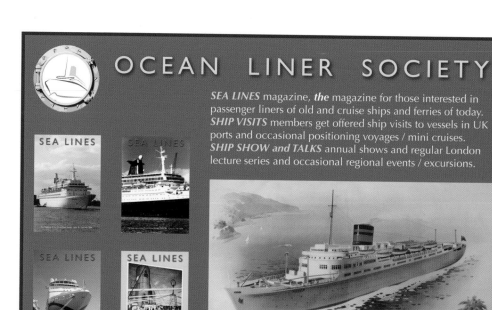

QUASARNAUTICA

The Company Quasarnautica has been operating cruise yachts in the Galapagos Islands since the mid 1980's. The company also operates a number of vessels too small to include here.

President Eduado Diez

Address Brasil 293 y Granda Cento, Edificio IACA, Piso 2, Quito, Ecuador

Telephone +593 2 244 6996

Website www.quasarnauticausa.com

Area operated Galapagos Islands

EVOLUTION		t	12.0k	D2	32p	32p	18c	58.5m	8.9m	3.2m	EC

RADISSON SEVEN SEAS CRUISES

The Company Radisson Seven Seas Cruises is a complicated structure of organisations, partly a joint venture between the US leisure group Carlson (owners of Radisson) and Vlassov (owners of V Ships of Monaco). The company's origins go back to 1992, when Carlson set up a new subsidiary, Diamond Cruise Line, later Radisson Diamond Cruises, to operate the RADISSON DIAMOND. The company later took over Seven Seas Cruises, with its single ship, the SONG OF FLOWER, changing its name at that time to Radisson Seven Seas Cruises, and later took on the lease of the PAUL GAUGUIN. The V Ships joint venture began in 1999 with the delivery of the SEVEN SEAS NAVIGATOR. The company is expected to drop the Radisson prefix from its name in the near future. Cruises on the EXPLORER II (Abercrombie & Kent (q.v.)) are also now marketed by RSSC.

Address 600 Corporate Drive, Suite 410, Fort Lauderdale, FL 33334, United States of America

Telephone +1 800 477 7500 **Fax** +1 954 351 2119

Website www.rssc.com

Areas operated Worldwide

PAUL GAUGUIN	19170t	1997	19.0k	DE2	320p	320p	211c	156.0m	21.6m	5.2m	BA
SEVEN SEAS MARINER	48075t	2001	20.0k	DEP2	712p	780p	445c	216.0m	28.8m	6.8m	WF
SEVEN SEAS NAVIGATOR	28550t	1999	19.5k	D2	504p	542p	324c	170.6m	24.8m	6.8m	BA
SEVEN SEAS VOYAGER	41500t	2003	20.0k	DEP2	706p	769p	447c	177.1m	28.8m	7.1m	BA

PAUL GAUGUIN was built by Chantiers de l'Atlantique (yard number G31) at St Nazaire, France for Services et Transports – Tahiti. She was to have been named TAHITI NUI, but was built with her current name. Initially hotel services were to be provided by Radisson Seven Seas Cruises, but the company then operated the ship under lease. The ship has recently been sold to a consortium incorporating Grand Circle, but for the remainder of 2005 the ship will be operated by RSSC in conjunction with that organization. She continues to operate throughout 2005 in French Polynesia. Paul Gauguin (1848-1903) was one of the leading French painters of the post impressionist period. From 1891 until his death he lived in French Polynesia.

SEVEN SEAS MARINER was built by Chantiers de l'Atlantique (yard number K31) at St Nazaire, France for Radisson Seven Seas Cruises, with a hull based on that of Festival Cruises' MISTRAL. The SEVEN SEAS MARINER is scheduled to operate cruises around South America, US West Coast and Alaska, the Pacific and Far East, moving to the Caribbean Sea in early 2006.

SEVEN SEAS NAVIGATOR's hull was built in St Petersburg, Russia by Admiralteyskiy Sudostroitelnyy Zavod (yard number 02510) as the Ukrainian research vessel AKADEMIK NICOLAY PILYU. Unfinished, the hull was purchased by V-Ships and transferred to the Mariotti shipyard at Genoa for completion as the SEVEN SEAS NAVIGATOR. For 2005 she operates in the Caribbean Sea and East Coast North America, but moves to Europe in spring 2006.

SEVEN SEAS VOYAGER's hull was built by Cantieri Nav. Visentini at Donada, Italy under sub-contract to T. Mariotti of Genoa (yard number MAR001), who completed the construction to the ship. She operates in Europe in the summer of 2005, then undertakes a world voyage from Fort Lauderdale.

Radisson Seven Seas Cruises' *Seven Seas Mariner* at Vancouver *(Andrew Kilk)*

Radisson Seven Seas Cruises' *Seven Seas Voyager* at Nice (*William Mayes*)

RESIDENSEA

The Company Residensea is the company formed to operate THE WORLD. The concept for THE WORLD, the first luxury apartment ship, was that of Knut Kloster Jr, son of the founder of Kloster Cruise (now Norwegian Cruise Line). The original plans were for a ship of twice the size of THE WORLD, but these were scaled back before construction once it became apparent that it would be difficult to sell on the scale originally envisaged. Some apartments are available for rent on a cruise basis.

Address 5200 Blue Lagoon Drive, Suite 790, Miami, Florida 33126, United States of America

Telephone +1 305 264 9090 **Fax** +1 305 264 5090

Website www.residensea.com

Area operated Worldwide

THE WORLD	43188t	2002	19.0k	D2	330p	657p	250c	196.4m	29.2m	6.9m	BA

THE WORLD is one of that select few ships where the hull was built in one yard and the ship completed elsewhere. The hull was constructed at Bruce's Shipyard (yard number 247) in Landskrona, Sweden and towed to the Fosen Yard at Rissa, Norway for completion. The ship was originally to have been about 80,000 tons, but insufficient interest had been generated at a crucial stage in the planning, so the size was scaled back. The ship features 106 two- and three-bedroom apartments, 19 one- and two-bedroom studio apartments and 40 studios. She is currently 90% sold.

RG TOURS

The Company RG Tours is a German tour operator specialising in the Arctic, Antarctica and South America. The company may be the sole charterer of the VIKTOR BUYNITSKIY, but also sells space on the GRIGORIY MIKHEYEV (listed under Oceanwide), the LYUBOV ORLOVA, YAMAL, KAPITAN KLEBNIKOV and the 'Professors' (all listed under Quark Expeditions), and is a non-exclusive marketer of space aboard the SOVETSKIY SOYUZ.

Address Nelkenstrasse 9, D82223 Eichenau, Germany

Telephone +49 81 41 224 888 **Fax** +49 81 41 224 889

Website www.rg-tours.de

Area operated Arctic and Antarctic

SOVETSKIY SOYUZ	20646t	1989	21.0k	ST3	106p	114p	48c	150.0m	30.0m	11.0m	RU
VIKTOR BUYNITSKIY	693t	1986	12.8k	D1	30p	35p	c	49.9m	10.0m	3.6m	RU

SOVETSKIY SOYUZ was built by Baltiyskiy Zavod (yard number 703) at Leningrad, Russia for the Murmansk Shipping Company.

VIKTOR BUYNITSKIY was built by the Valmet Shipyard (yard number 370) at Turku, Finland for the Murmansk Territorial Administration.

ROYAL CARIBBEAN GROUP

CELEBRITY CRUISES

The Company Celebrity Cruises was founded in 1989 as an offshoot of the Chandris Group as an upmarket cruise operation to complement its existing passenger operations, which were generally at the lower end of the market. Chandris gradually disposed of its own fleet and concentrated on a small number of high quality ships within the Celebrity brand. The first ship was the former Italian transatlantic liner GALILEO GALILEI, which entered service after a massive refit in 1990 as the MERIDIAN. The second ship (HORIZON, now ISLAND STAR) was also the first new-build for the company, and began a relationship with the shipbuilder Jos L Meyer which would produce another four ships over the next seven years. Celebrity Cruises became part of the Royal Caribbean Group in 1997. In 2004 the company acquired the small expedition ship XPEDITION to expand its range of cruises to include the Galapagos Islands. For 2005, in a further expansion, Celebrity has teamed up with Quark Expeditions to offer a cruise from Ottawa to the Arctic, and in 2006 the Antarctic from Ushuaia aboard the Russian icebreaker KAPITAN KHLEBNIKOV.

President Dan Hanranhan

Address 1050 Caribbean Way, Miami, Florida 33132, United States of America

Telephone +1 305 262 6677 **Fax** +1 305 406 8630

Website www.celebritycruises.com

Areas operated Caribbean Sea, Alaska, Mexican Riviera, East Coast USA, Europe

Residensea's **The World** *(William Mayes Collection)*

Celebrity Cruises' **Galaxy** at Southampton *(William Mayes)*

CENTURY	70606t	1995	21.5k	D2	1784p	2156p	858c	248.5m	32.2m	7.7m	BA
CONSTELLATION	90280t	2002	24.0k	GEP2	1950p	2449p	999c	294.0m	32.2m	8.2m	BA
GALAXY	76522t	1996	21.5k	D2	1870p	2232p	908c	263.9m	32.2m	7.7m	BA
INFINITY	90228t	2001	24.0k	GEP2	1950p	2449p	999c	294.0m	32.2m	8.2m	BA
MERCURY	76522t	1997	21.5k	D2	1870p	2229p	908c	263.9m	32.2m	7.7m	BA
MILLENNIUM	90228t	2000	24.0k	GEP2	1950p	2449p	999c	294.0m	32.2m	8.2m	BA
SUMMIT	90280t	2001	24.0k	GEP2	1950p	2449p	999c	294.0m	32.2m	8.2m	BA
XPEDITION	2842t	2001	13.5k	D1	92p	96p	56c	88.5m	14.0m	3.6m	EC
ZENITH	47255t	1992	18.0k	D2	1376p	1776p	643c	208.0m	29.0m	7.2m	BA

CENTURY is the lead ship of a trio of ships built by Jos L Meyer (yard number 637) at Papenburg, Germany. Her maiden voyage in 1995 was from Southampton to New York. She is currently employed on Caribbean and European itineraries.

CONSTELLATION was built by Chantiers de l'Atlantique (yard number U31) at St Nazaire, France. She operates in the Caribbean Sea, in Europe and on Canada/New England cruises.

GALAXY is the second member of a trio of ships built by Jos L Meyer (yard number 638) at Papenburg, Germany. She operates Mediterranean Sea and Panama Canal itineraries.

INFINITY is the second of the Millennium class ships built by Chantiers de l'Atlantique (yard number S31) at St Nazaire, France. She operates in Alaska, the Mexican Riviera, South America and the Panama Canal.

MERCURY is third and final member of the trio of ships built by Jos L Meyer (yard number 639) at Papenburg, Germany. Her itineraries include Alaska, the Pacific Northwest and the Mexican Riviera.

MILLENNIUM is the lead ship in a series of four built by Chantiers de l'Atlantique (yard number R31) at St Nazaire, France. She suffered serious problems with her pod propulsion system before delivery and has had to be dry-docked for repairs subsequently. The MILLENNIUM's speciality restaurant has some of the original walnut panels from the White Star Line's Atlantic Liner OLYMPIC, built in 1911. She operates cruises in the Caribbean Sea and in Europe.

SUMMIT was built by Chantiers de l'Atlantique (yard number T31) at St Nazaire, France. Her current programme includes itineraries taking in Alaska, Hawaii, Mexico and the Panama Canal.

XPEDITION was built by Schiffswerft U Maschinenfabrik Cassens (yard number 228) at Emden in Germany as the SUN BAY for Sun Bay Shipping, by whom she is still owned. Celebrity chartered her in 2004 to commence a programme of cruises in the Galapagos Islands. She is marketed as the CELEBRITY XPEDITION.

ZENITH was delivered two years after the HORIZON (now ISLAND STAR) by the Papenburg yard of Jos L Meyer (yard number 620). In 2005 she operates to Bermuda from the new Cape Liberty Cruise Port in New Jersey.

ISLAND CRUISES

The Company Island Cruises is a joint venture between Royal Caribbean International and British tour operator First Choice Holidays that began operating in spring 2002 with a single ship based at Palma de Majorca. For the summer of 2005, Celebrity Cruises' HORIZON joins the fleet.

Managing Director Patrick Ryan

Address Olivier House, 18 Marine Road, Brighton, BN2 1TL, England

Telephone +44 870 850 3927

Website www.islandcruises.com

Areas operated Mediterranean, transatlantic positioning and South America

ISLAND ESCAPE	40171t	1982	18.0k	D2	1542p	1740p	540c	185.0m	27.0m	6.8m	BA
ISLAND STAR	46811t	1990	18.0k	D2	1354p	1752p	642c	207.6m	29.0m	7.2m	BA

ISLAND ESCAPE was built by Dubigeon-Normandie (yard number 164) at Nantes, France for The United Steamship Company (Bahamas) Ltd, a DFDS of Copenhagen subsidiary, as the SCANDINAVIA to operate in the cruise ferry service between New York and the Bahamas for Scandinavia World Voyages. After disappointing results she was transferred to DFDS and put into service on its capital cities car ferry route between Copenhagen and Oslo in 1984. Later that year she was sold to Sundance Cruises of Nassau, Bahamas and after a refit entered service cruising in the Caribbean as the STARDANCER in spring 1985. In 1990 she was sold to Royal Caribbean Cruise Line, renamed VIKING SERENADE and put into service on the West Coast of the USA. During a major refit in 1991 passenger cabins replaced her car decks. She continued to operate for Royal Caribbean until being transferred to a new joint venture with British tour operator First Choice in spring 2002. Renamed as the ISLAND ESCAPE, her itineraries include the Mediterranean in summer and South America in winter.

ISLAND STAR was Celebrity's first new ship and was built by Jos L Meyer (yard number 619) at Papenburg, Germany. When delivered in 1990 as the HORIZON, she was the largest ship to have been completely built in a building hall. She generally operated in the Caribbean and on the East Coast of the USA and Canada in her last years with Celebrity. In autumn 2005 she transfers within the group to Island Cruises with the new name ISLAND STAR. For her first winter with her new owner she operates in Brazil and in summer 2006 moves to the Mediterranean to serve the UK market.

ROYAL CARIBBEAN INTERNATIONAL

The Company Royal Caribbean Cruise Line was founded by Anders Wilhelmsen & Co, I M Skaugen & Co and Gotaas Larsen in 1969 to take a part of the fledgling Caribbean cruise trade. The first ship, the SONG OF NORWAY (now with Caspi Shipping as the DREAM PRINCESS), was delivered during the following year. During the next two years, two further new ships were introduced. By the end of the 1970's the ships were too small for the market they were serving, and two of them were stretched by means of a new mid-section approximately 26 metres in length. By 1988 Anders Wilhelmsen & Co had bought out the other partners, but later entered into a new agreement with other parties in order to raise finance for new-buildings. When delivered in 1988, the 73,000-ton SOVEREIGN OF THE SEAS was the world's largest cruise ship. In 1993 Royal Caribbean became a public company, with a listing on the New York stock exchange, although a major block of stock was retained by Anders Wilhelmsen & Co. The company became Royal Caribbean International in 1997, to better reflect its global operations. By 1998 the three original ships with which the company had laid its foundations had found new homes, and Royal Caribbean was in the middle of a massive building programme. With the entry into service in 1999 of the VOYAGER OF THE SEAS (137,000 tons), the company once again operated the largest cruise ship in the world. In late 2001 a proposed joint venture operation with P&O Princess Cruises was close to becoming a reality before Carnival Corporation stepped in with its own bid for the P&O companies.

President and Chief Executive Officer Richard Fain **Senior Vice-President Marine Operations** William Wright

Address 1050 Caribbean Way, Miami, Florida 33132, United States of America

Telephone +1 305 539 6000 **Fax** +1 305 372 0441

Website www.royalcaribbean.com

Areas operated Caribbean Sea, East Coast North America, Alaska, and Europe

ADVENTURE OF THE SEAS	137276t	2002	23k	DEP3	3114p	3840p	1185c	311.0m	38.6m	8.6m	BA
BRILLIANCE OF THE SEAS	90090t	2002	24k	GEP2	2112p	2501p	859c	293.2m	32.2m	8.1m	BA
EMPRESS OF THE SEAS	48563t	1990	19k	D2	1602p	2020p	671c	210.8m	30.7m	7.1m	BA
ENCHANTMENT OF THE SEAS	74136t	1997	22k	DE2	1954p	2446p	760c	279.1m	32.2m	7.6m	NI
EXPLORER OF THE SEAS	137308t	2000	23k	DEP3	3114p	3840p	1185c	311.0m	38.6m	8.6m	BA
GRANDEUR OF THE SEAS	73817t	1996	22k	DE2	1950p	2440p	760c	279.1m	32.2m	7.6m	BA
JEWEL OF THE SEAS	90090t	2003	24k	GEP2	2126p	2500p	858c	293.2m	32.2m	8.1m	BA
LEGEND OF THE SEAS	69490t	1995	24k	DE2	1804p	2076p	720c	264.3m	32.0m	7.3m	BA
MAJESTY OF THE SEAS	73937t	1992	21k	D2	2356p	2772p	822c	268.3m	32.2m	7.5m	NI
MARINER OF THE SEAS	138279t	2003	23k	DEP3	3114p	3807p	1213c	311.0m	38.6m	8.6m	BA
MONARCH OF THE SEAS	73941t	1991	21k	D2	2354p	2772p	822c	268.3m	32.2m	7.5m	NI
NAVIGATOR OF THE SEAS	138279t	2002	23k	DEP3	3114p	3840p	1185c	311.0m	38.6m	8.6m	BA
RADIANCE OF THE SEAS	90090t	2001	24k	GEP2	2112p	2501p	858c	293.2m	32.2m	8.1m	BA
RHAPSODY OF THE SEAS	78491t	1997	22k	DE2	1998p	2441p	765c	279.0m	32.2m	7.8m	NI
SERENADE OF THE SEAS	90090t	2003	24k	GEP2	2112p	2501p	858c	293.2m	32.2m	8.1m	BA
SOVEREIGN OF THE SEAS	73192t	1987	21k	D2	2276p	2744p	825c	268.3m	32.2m	7.5m	NI
SPLENDOUR OF THE SEAS	69130t	1996	24k	DE2	1804p	2074p	735c	264.3m	32.0m	7.3m	NI
VISION OF THE SEAS	78340t	1998	22k	DE2	1998p	2441p	765c	279.0m	32.2m	7.8m	BA
VOYAGER OF THE SEAS	137276t	1999	22k	DEP3	3114p	3840p	1185c	311.1m	38.6m	8.6m	BA

ADVENTURE OF THE SEAS was built by Kvaerner Masa Yards (yard number 1346) at Turku, Finland as the third and final unit of the original requirement for three Eagle Class ships. Subsequently two further ships were ordered. ADVENTURE OF THE SEAS operates Southern Caribbean cruises.

BRILLIANCE OF THE SEAS is the second ship in a four ship series under construction by Jos L Meyer (yard number 656) at Papenburg, Germany. Her current employment includes Mediterranean Sea, transatlantic and Panama Canal itineraries.

EMPRESS OF THE SEAS was ordered from Chantiers de l'Atlantique (yard number G29) at St Nazaire in France in 1987 by Admiral Cruises as their FUTURE SEAS. Admiral Cruises was merged with Royal Caribbean the following year and the ship was delivered as the NORDIC EMPRESS and employed on shorter Caribbean cruises. In 2004 she was refitted and renamed EMPRESS OF THE SEAS.

Celebrity Cruises' **Millennium** sailing from Venice *(William Mayes)*

Celebrity Cruises' **Summit** drydocked at San Francisco *(Andrew Kilk)*

ENCHANTMENT OF THE SEAS is one of a pair of ships built by Kvaerner Masa Yards (yard number 493) at Helsinki, Finland. She currently operates Caribbean and Canada/New England programmes. During 2005 she is to be lengthened by means of the insertion of a 22-metre mid section, increasing her tonnage to 80,700 and adding a further 151 cabins.

EXPLORER OF THE SEAS is the second of the Eagle Class ships built by Kvaerner Masa Yards (yard number 1345) at Turku, Finland. She operates on the company's Eastern and Western Caribbean cruise programme.

GRANDEUR OF THE SEAS is one of a pair of ships built by Kvaerner Masa Yards (yard number 492) at Helsinki, Finland. She operates in the Caribbean, with a series of cruises to Bermuda and the Caribbean Sea from Baltimore.

JEWEL OF THE SEAS was built by Jos L Meyer (yard number 658) at Papenburg, Germany. Her current areas of operation are Scandinavia and the Caribbean Sea.

LEGEND OF THE SEAS is the lead ship of a pair built by Chantiers de l'Atlantique (yard number A31) at St Nazaire, France. She currently operates for part of the year in Europe, based in Southampton, England. In winter she serves the Caribbean market.

MAJESTY OF THE SEAS is the final member of a trio built by Chantiers de l'Atlantique (yard number B30) at St Nazaire, France. She operates short Caribbean cruises from Miami, Florida.

MARINER OF THE SEAS is the fifth and (for the time being) final unit in the Eagle Class and was built by Kvaerner Masa Yards (yard number 1348) at Turku, Finland. She serves the Eastern and Western Caribbean Sea market from her Port Canaveral base.

MONARCH OF THE SEAS is one of a trio of ships built by Chantiers de l'Atlantique (yard number A30) at St Nazaire, France. She operates cruises to Mexico from Los Angeles.

NAVIGATOR OF THE SEAS was laid down by Kvaerner Masa Yards (yard number 1347) at Turku, Finland as the JOURNEY OF THE SEAS, but renamed during construction. Her programme of Western Caribbean Sea cruises is based on Miami, Florida.

RADIANCE OF THE SEAS is the company's first gas turbine powered ship and was built by Jos L Meyer (yard number 655) at Papenburg, Germany. She is the lead ship in a series of four Panamax vessels. She operates in the Caribbean and Alaska with positioning voyages via Mexico and the Panama Canal.

RHAPSODY OF THE SEAS was built by Chantiers de l'Atlantique (yard number E31) at St Nazaire, France as the first ship of another pair. She is based at Galveston, Texas and operates 7-day Western Caribbean cruises.

SERENADE OF THE SEAS was built by Jos L Meyer (yard number 657) at Papenburg, Germany. Her sphere of operation takes in Alaska, Hawaii and the Caribbean Sea.

SOVEREIGN OF THE SEAS is the lead ship of a trio built by Chantiers de l'Atlantique (yard number A29) at St Nazaire, France. When delivered she was the world's largest cruise ship. She currently operates short Caribbean cruises from Port Canaveral, Florida.

SPLENDOUR OF THE SEAS is the second ship of the first pair built by Chantiers de l'Atlantique (yard number B31) at St Nazaire, France. She operates in the Caribbean and the Mediterranean.

VISION OF THE SEAS was built as the second ship of the second pair by Chantiers de l'Atlantique (yard number F31) at St Nazaire, France. She is one of the company's more widely travelled ships as she operates in Alaska and the Mexican Riviera.

VOYAGER OF THE SEAS was built by Kvaerner Masa Yards (yard number 1344) at Turku, Finland as the lead ship in the Eagle Class of (initially three and later five) massive vessels. The VOYAGER OF THE SEAS became the largest passenger ship ever built when she entered service in the autumn of 1999. She is employed on Caribbean Sea itineraries.

Cruise ships on order

ENDEAVOUR OF THE SEAS	c158000t	2007	22k	DE3	3600p	p	1360c	339.0m	38.6m	8.5m	BA
FREEDOM OF THE SEAS	c158000t	2006	22k	DE3	3600p	p	1360c	339.0m	38.6m	8.5m	BA
UN-NAMED NEWBUILDING	c158000t	2008	22k	DE3	3600p	p	1360c	339.0m	38.6m	8.5m	BA

This series of so called Ultra-Voyager class ships are on order from the Aker Shipyard at Turku, Finland. FREEDOM OF THE SEAS is earmarked for Western Caribbean Sea itineraries.

Island Cruises' *Island Escape* *(William Mayes Collection)*

Royal Caribbean's *Enchantment of the Seas* *(William Mayes Collection)*

Royal Caribbean's **Monarch of the Seas** at San Diego *(Andrew Kilk)*

Royal Caribbean's **Serenade of the Seas** in New York *(Theodore W Scull)*

Royal Caribbean's **Explorer of the Seas** at Calshot (*William Mayes*)

Royal Caribbean's **Jewel of the Seas** off St Peter Port, Guernsey (*William Mayes*)

Royal Caribbean's **Vision of the Seas** (Douglas Cromby)

Saga's **Saga Rose** off Calshot (Alan Ryszka-Onions)

SAGA HOLIDAYS

The Company Saga Shipping Company is a subsidiary of the British financial services and holiday group Saga Group Limited. The company was recently sold by its founding family to its management. Although the company had been selling cruises on other operators' ships for many years, it was not until 1997 that the company acquired its first ship, the SAGA ROSE. Saga cruises are only sold to the over 50's, and are not sold through travel agents.

Address The Saga Building, Embrook Park, High Street, Sandgate, Folkestone, Kent, CT20 3SE, England

Telephone +44 1303 771964 **Fax** +44 1303 771243

Website www.saga.co.uk/travel/cruises

Area operated Europe, North Atlantic, Caribbean and world cruises

SAGA ROSE	24528t	1965	20.0k	D2	587p	650p	350c	188.9m	24.5m	8.3m	BA
SAGA RUBY	24492t	1973	21.0k	D2	677p	732p	400c	191.1m	25.0m	8.2m	BA
SPIRIT OF ADVENTURE	9570t	1980	17.0k	D2	420p	420p	180c	139.3m	17.5m	4.8m	BA

SAGA ROSE was built by Forges et Chantiers de La Mediterranee (yard number 1366) at La Seyne in France as the SAGAFJORD for Den Norske Amerikalinje A/S (Norwegian America Line) for service between Oslo and New York, but with cruising in mind, too. Her liner role had ceased by 1980, and three years later she was sold to Cunard Line Ltd without a change of name. She continued to operate under Norwegian America Cruises for some years, but was later marketed as a Cunard Line ship, although retaining her original name. In 1996 she was chartered to Transocean Tours as the GRIPSHOLM, but suffered damage due to a fire and was withdrawn from service. She was acquired by Saga in 1997 and refitted to become the SAGA ROSE.

SAGA RUBY was delivered in 1973 by Swan Hunter (yard number 39) at Wallsend on Tyne, England as the VISTAFJORD for Den Norske Amerikalinje A/S (Norwegian America Line) and was thus the last passenger liner to be built in the United Kingdom. She was initially employed on line voyages between Oslo and New York, and worldwide cruising. By 1980 she was used exclusively for cruising and was transferred along with her sister the SAGAFJORD to Norwegian American Cruises A/S, but retained her Oslo registry. In 1983 the two ships, together with the Norwegian American Cruises name, were sold to Cunard Line Ltd. and continued to trade under their existing names. Already by then in Cunard colours, the VISTAFJORD was renamed CARONIA following a major refit in 1999. She was the third Cunarder to carry this name, in a short-lived revival of the 'names ending in 'ia' theme'. CARONIA was based in Southampton for cruises from the United Kingdom to Europe and further afield, but in 2004 was sold to Saga Cruises with delivery in November of that year. Following a major refit in Malta, she took up service as the SAGA RUBY with her new owner early in 2005.

SPIRIT OF ADVENTURE was the ship by which Peter Deilmann entered the ocean cruise market. She was built by Howaldtswerke-Deutsche Werft (yard number 163) at Kiel, Germany as the BERLIN for a consortium of German investors in which Deilmann held a small share. Late in 1982 she was chartered to Blue Funnel Cruises of Singapore, an associated business of the Straits Steamship Company. She was renamed PRINCESS MAHSURI. Her Far East and Australian operation for Blue Funnel was not entirely successful and she was returned to her owners a year early in 1984, when she reverted to her original name. She was lengthened in 1986 at Rendsburg, Germany and continued to operate for Deilmann until that company terminated her charter at the end of 2004, following which she was laid up until purchased by Saga as a replacement for the SAGA PEARL, with delivery at the end of 2005. In the meantime she secured a charter for a Russian operator. For her new service with Saga she is expected to take the name SPIRIT OF ADVENTURE, although it was originally thought that she would be renamed SAGA OPAL.

SALAMIS CRUISE LINES

The Company Salamis Cruise Lines is a Cypriot private sector company within the Salamis Tours (Holdings) Group (established in 1959), which is publicly quoted on the Cyprus Stock Exchange. The company previously operated the most regular service on long ferry routes in the Eastern Mediterranean. However the political violence in the state of Israel and the occupied territories of Palestine caused this service to cease in 2002. The company's ro-ro passenger ferry has been variously laid up and chartered to other Mediterranean operators. Salamis Lines has operated short cruises from Cyprus for a number of years, and also owns a small ro-ro freighter that is chartered out.

Managing Director Panagiota Gripeou

Address Salamis House, 125 Franklin Roosevelt Street, 50531 Limassol, Cyprus

Telephone +357 566 1111 **Fax** +357 556 3428

Website www.salamis-tours.com

Area operated Eastern Mediterranean, based in Cyprus

SALAMIS GLORY	10392t	1962	17.5k	D2	444p	480p	190c	150.0m	19.0m	5.6m	CY

Salamis Cruise Lines' **Salamis Glory** arriving at Limassol *(William Mayes)*

Seadream Yacht Club's **Seadream 1** at Livorno *(Egidio Ferrighi)*

SALAMIS GLORY was built by Brodogradiliste Uljanik (yard number 237) at Pula in what was then Yugoslavia as the ANNA NERY for Companhia Nacional de Navegacao Costeira Autarquia of Brazil for the coastal passenger trades. She also operated cruises both in South America and to Europe. She was transferred to Lloyd Brasiliero in 1966, who used her until 1977, when she was laid up. In 1978 she was acquired by the Greek ship owner Kavounides and renamed as the DANAOS. She entered service later that year for Kavounides (Hellenic Cruises) as the CONSTELLATION. Her owners failed in 1987 and the ship was seized by the Greek Development Bank, subsequently being laid up for four years. In 1992 she operated briefly in the Far East as the MORNING STAR, before becoming the REGENT SPIRIT of Regency Cruises. That company, too, was declared bankrupt in 1995 and the ship was arrested in Nice, France. She was sold at auction to a company within the Salamis Shipping Group and has operated since 1996 as the SALAMIS GLORY on short cruises from Limassol, Cyprus.

SEA CLOUD CRUISES

The Company Sea Cloud Cruises is a subsidiary of the German Hansa Truehand Group, a business with interests in ship management, engineering and consultancy. The company also operates two river cruise ships on the waterways of Europe.

Chairman Hermann Ebel

Address Ballindamm 17, D 20095 Hamburg, Germany

Telephone +49 4030 9592 0 **Fax** +49 4030 959 222

Website www.seacloud.com

Area operated Worldwide

| SEA CLOUD | 2532t | 1931 | 12.0k | SD2 | 68p | 74p | 60c | 109.7m | 14.6m | 4.9m | MA |
| SEA CLOUD II | 3849t | 2000 | 14.0k | SD2 | 94p | 94p | 58c | 117.0m | 16.0m | 5.3m | MA |

SEA CLOUD was built by the Krupp Shipyard in Kiel, Germany as the HUSSAR, the largest sailing yacht ever built, for E F Hutton, a wealthy New York businessman. Following divorce in 1935, Hutton handed the ship over to his former wife (who had actually designed the vessel) and she renamed her SEA CLOUD. Following the entry of the United States into the Second World War, the SEA CLOUD was taken up for military service, principally around the Azores and Southern Greenland. She was equipped with weaponry and also served as a weather station under the name IX-99. The ship was returned to her owners at the end of the war, and after a refit lasting four years she re-emerged as good as new. The SEA CLOUD was sold in 1955, becoming the presidential yacht of the Dominican Republic, and renamed ANGELITA. Following the assassination of the president in 1961, she was renamed again, becoming the PATRIA. Five years later, she was back in American hands as the ANTARNA for Operation Sea Cruises. She was subsequently laid up at Colon for eight years before being bought by her German owners and renamed again as the SEA CLOUD. She was refitted in Kiel, and entered service as a sail cruise ship in 1979. Her current owners acquired her in 1994.

SEA CLOUD II was built by Astilleros Gondan (yard number 405) at Castropol, Spain for operation by Sea Cloud Cruises.

SEADREAM YACHT CLUB

The Company Seadream Yacht Club was founded in 2001 by Atle Brynestad (the founder of Seabourn) and Larry Pimentel (former President of Cunard-Seabourn). The company operates two luxury yacht-type vessels.

Chairman Atle Brynestad **President and Chief Executive Officer** Larry Pimentel

Address 2601 South Bayshore Drive, Penthouse 1B, Coconut Grove, Florida 33133, United States of America

Telephone +1 305 631 6101 **Fax** +1 305 856 7599

Website www.seadreamyachtclub.com

Area operated Mediterranean and Black Seas, West Indies, Mexico

| SEADREAM I | 4253t | 1984 | 17.5k | D2 | 110p | 110p | 89c | 104.8m | 14.5m | 4.0m | BA |
| SEADREAM II | 4260t | 1985 | 17.5k | D2 | 110p | 110p | 89c | 104.8m | 14.6m | 4.1m | BA |

SEADREAM I and **SEADREAM II** were built as the SEA GODDESS I and SEA GODDESS II by Wartsila (yard numbers 466 and 467) at Helsinki, Finland for Sea Goddess Cruises of Norway (Norske Cruise) as luxury yacht style vessels. Following a disastrous year for the company in 1986, Cunard Line took the two ships on a twelve-year charter. Cunard continued to market the ships as Sea Goddesses. Following the acquisition of Cunard by Carnival Corporation in 1998, the ships were transferred to Carnival's luxury cruise line, Seabourn, and renamed as SEABOURN GODDESS I and II. In 2001 they were both sold to a new company, Seadream Yacht Club and renamed SEADREAM I and SEADREAM II.

SEVEN OCEAN CRUISES

The Company Seven Ocean Cruises is the manager for Viking Polaris ASA, a Norwegian registered company, previously Brand Polaris. The POLARIS is marketed by a number of tour operators including Norwegian Coastal Voyage.

Address Stoltenberggaten 1, Haugesund, 5527, Norway

Telephone +47 5286 4173 **Fax** +47 5286 4101

Area operated Norway, Iceland and Greenland

POLARIS		2097t	1968	13.0k	D1	92p	96p	36c	70.5m	15.5m	4.4m	BA

POLARIS was built as the DISKO for the local services of Royal Arctic Line within Greenland by Svendborg Skibsvaerft (yard number 122) at Svendborg, Denmark. Her owner was restyled as Arctic Umiaq Line in 1994. She was laid up at Nakskov, Denmark in 1999 and during the following year passed to Scandinavian Cruise Line for whom she was renamed SHEARWATER. Rebuilt at Fredericia in Denmark, she re-entered service later in 2000 cruising around Scotland and the Isles. In 2001 she was renamed as the BRAND POLARIS and two years later took the name VIKING POLARIS. She is now owned by the Murmansk Shipping Company and was renamed POLARIS at the end of 2004.

SHANGHAI WAN BANG CRUISE COMPANY

The Company Shanghai Wan Bang Cruise Company is a subsidiary of the Shenzhen Zhongda Cruise Company of China.

Address Shanghai

Telephone +86 21 5891 6888 **Fax** +86 21 5042 2281

Website www.seatravel.com.cn

Area operated Overnight and weekend domestic cruises in China

JIA RI		10000t	1986	16.0k	D2	400p	400p	200c	120.0m	18.8m	5.2m	CH

JIA RI was built at the Xingang Shipyard in China as the coastal passenger/cargo vessel BAI LING. She was converted into the cruise ship JIA RI by Guangzhou Wenchong Shipyard in 1998, and has since operated short cruises in Chinese waters.

SIAM CRUISE LINE

The Company Siam Cruise line is a Thai registered company established in 1988 and is the longest operating cruise company in the country. It operates cruises to Thailand's tropical islands.

Management Managing Director Prani Yasasindhu

Address 158/1 Aneckvanich Bldg, Sukhumvit Soi 55 Thong Lor, Klongton Nua, Wattanam Bangkok 10110, Thailand

Telephone +66 2 3814 681 **Fax** +66 381 4693

Website www.andamanprincess.com

Area operated Gulf of Thailand (summer), Andaman Sea (winter)

ANDAMAN PRINCESS	5145t	1962	12.0k	D1	276p	335p	200c	101.5m	19.3m	4.8m	TH

ANDAMAN PRINCESS was built by the Finnboda Shipyard (yard number 375) at Stockholm, Sweden as the SVEA JARL for Silja Line's (Rederi AB Svea) Baltic ferry services. In 1976 she was sold to rival consortium Viking Line (Rederi AB Slite) for use as a cruise ship on the lucrative 24-hour cruise service from Stockholm to Mariehamn in the Aland Islands. With the arrival of the new ATHENA in 1989 she was no longer required, and was sold to Thai owners to become the ANDAMAN PRINCESS.

SILJA CRUISE

The Company Silja Cruise AB is part of the Baltic Sea ferry operator, Silja Line, itself now a wholly owned subsidiary of Bermuda-based Sea Containers, the shipping, transport and leisure group.

President Antti Pankakoski

Address Keilaranta 9, PO Box 880, Espoo 02060, Finland

Telephone +358 9 18041 **Fax** +358 9 180 4402

Website www.silja.fi

Shanghai Wan Bang Cruise Company's *Jia Ri* (*Jonathan Boonzaier*)

Silja Cruises' *Silja Opera* at Helsinki (*William Mayes*)

Silversea's **Silver Cloud** in Venice *(Egidio Ferrighi)*

Silversea's **Silver Whisper** at San Diego *(Andrew Kilk)*

Area operated The Baltic Sea

SILJA OPERA	25611t	1980	21.0k	D2	1096p	1452p	180c	158.9m	25.2m	5.6m	SW

SILJA OPERA as we see her now was completed in 1992 by the Rauma Yard at Rauma, Finland as the SALLY ALBATROSS, using the lower hull parts of the previous SALLY ALBATROSS destroyed by fire in 1991 while refitting in Stockholm. That ship had been built in 1980 by Wartsila (yard number 309) at Turku, Finland as the VIKING SAGA for Rederi AB Sally, then part of the Viking Line consortium. She served the Stockholm to Helsinki overnight route until replaced by the OLYMPIA in 1986. She then switched to a new role, cruising mainly from Helsinki. She was later rebuilt with a rather more streamlined forward superstructure. In her current incarnation, she cruised in the Baltic Sea for Sally Line until 1994, when she was chartered to Norwegian Cruise Line and renamed LEEWARD for Caribbean service. At the end of that charter she was taken up by Star Cruises in 2000 and as the SUPERSTAR TAURUS operated for a while in the Far East. She moved to Silja Cruise in 2002 and now offers short cruises in the Baltic as the SILJA OPERA.

SILVERSEA CRUISES

The Company When the Lefebvre family of Rome sold Sitmar Cruises to P&O in 1988, their interest in the cruise industry was undiminished and it was not long before they began to plan for a new top-end cruise line. In 1994 the new Silversea Cruises débuted with its first ship, the SILVER CLOUD. A recent innovation has been to provide personalised voyages allowing embarkation and disembarkation at almost any port, providing a minimum of five nights is spent aboard.

Chief Executive Officer Albert Peter

Address   110 East Broward Boulevard, Fort Lauderdale, Florida 33301, United States of America

European office: 77/79 Great Eastern Street, London, EC2A 3HU, England

Telephone +1 877 760 9052 **Fax** +1 954 522 4499

UK +44 870 333 7030 **Fax** +44 870 333 7040

Website www.silversea.com

Areas operated Worldwide

SILVER CLOUD	16927t	1994	20.0k	D2	296p	296p	185c	155.8m	21.4m	5.3m	BA
SILVER SHADOW	28258t	2000	20.5k	D2	388p	388p	295c	182.0m	24.8m	6.0m	BA
SILVER WIND	16927t	1995	20.0k	D2	296p	296p	185c	155.8m	21.4m	5.3m	BA
SILVER WHISPER	28258t	2001	20.5k	D2	388p	388p	295c	182.0m	24.8m	6.0m	BA

SILVER CLOUD and **SILVER WIND** were built by Cantieri Navali Visentini (yard numbers 775 and 776) at Donada, Italy and completed by Esercizio at Viareggio, Italy.

SILVER SHADOW and **SILVER WHISPER** were built by Cantieri Navali Visentini (yard numbers 981 and 982) at Donada, Italy and completed by T. Mariotti at Genoa, Italy.

SKORPIOS TOURS

The Company Naviera & Turismo Skorpios is a Chilean private sector business.

Address Augusto Leguia Norte 118, Santiago, Chile

Telephone +56 2 231 1031 **Fax** +56 2 232 2269

Website www.skorpios.cl

Area operated Southern Chile

SKORPIOS I		1978	12.0k	D1	74p	74p	24c	50.0m	8.4m	3.0m	CL
SKORPIOS II	‡1263t	1988	12.0k	D1	130p	160p	34c	70.0m	10.0m	2.9m	CL
SKORPIOS III	1597t	1995	14.0k	D1	100p	125p	34c	69.0m	10.0m	3.3m	CL

SKORPIOS II and SKORPIOS III were built by Kochifas Shipyard (yard numbers 1 and 2) at Puerto Montt, Chile.

ST LAWRENCE CRUISE LINES

The Company St Lawrence Cruise Lines, a Canadian business, was founded by Bob Clark in 1981.

Management Chief Executive Officer Bob Clark

Address 253 Ontario Street, Kingston, Ontario, K7L 2Z4 Canada

Telephone +1 613 549 8091 **Fax** +1 613 549 8410

Website www.stlawrencecruiselines.com

Area operated The St Lawrence and Ottawa Rivers in Canada

| CANADIAN EMPRESS | 463t | 1981 | 10.0k | DE2 | 66p | 66p | 14c | 32.9m | 9.2m | 1.5m | CA |

STAD AMSTERDAM

The Company Rederij Clipper Stad Amsterdam is a Dutch company.

Management Executive Director Frank Weermeijer

Address PO Box 12600, 1100AP Amsterdam, The Netherlands

Telephone +31 20 569 5839

Website www.stadamsterdam.nl

Area operated Europe and Caribbean cruises and charters

| STAD AMSTERDAM | 723t | 2000 | | SD1 | 48p | 48p | 25c | 78.0m | 10.5m | 4.2m | NL |

STAD AMSTERDAM is a three-masted square-rigged ship, built by Damen Oranjewerf (yard number 6900) in Amsterdam, The Netherlands.

STAR CLIPPERS

The Company Star Clippers was founded by Swedish entrepreneur Mikeal Krafft in 1991.

Address 7200 NW 19th Street, Suite 206, Miami, Florida 33126, United States of America

Telephone +1 305 442 0550 **Fax** +1 305 442 1611

Website www.starclippers.com

Area operated Caribbean Sea and Far East, all three ships operate in the Mediterranean Sea in summer

ROYAL CLIPPER	4425t	2000	13.5k	SD1	227p	227p	106c	132.7m	16.0m	5.7m	LX
STAR CLIPPER	2298t	1992	12.0k	SD1	170p	170p	70c	111.6m	15.0m	5.5m	LX
STAR FLYER	2298t	1991	12.0k	SD1	170p	170p	70c	111.6m	15.0m	5.5m	LX

ROYAL CLIPPER, inspired by the legendary tall ship, PREUSSEN of 1902, is the only 5-masted sailing ship built since that time. Her 42 sails require a crew of 20 just to handle the canvas. She was built by Stocznia Gdynia (yard number B811/01) at Gdansk, Poland, and was launched as the GWAREK.

STAR CLIPPER and **STAR FLYER** were built by Scheepswerf van Langerbrugge (yard numbers 2184 and 2183) at Ghent, Belgium.

STAR CRUISES GROUP

The Group Star Cruises was established in 1993 by Malaysia's Genting Group. The company revolutionized the Asian cruise industry by operating large, modern cruise ships at internationally accepted levels of service and entertainment. In 2000 Star bought out Norwegian Cruise Lines in a deal that propelled it to the position of the third largest cruise line in the world. The Genting Group has its origins in the Genting Highlands Resort, which was commenced in 1965. The group is now involved in the oil, power generation, property, paper and leisure industries.

CRUISE FERRIES

The Company Cruise Ferries (HK) Ltd is a subsidiary of Star Cruises.

Address Suite 28, 15/F Ocean Centre, 5 Canton Road, Tsimshatsui, Kowloon, Hong Kong

Telephone +852 2957 8188 **Fax** +852 2957 8183

Website www.cruiseferries.com.hk

Area operated Hong Kong

Skorpios II off the San Rafael Glacier, Chile *(John Wiseman)*

Star Clippers' ***Royal Clipper*** in Dominica *(Andrew Kilk)*

Norwegian Cruise Line's *Independence* some years ago in Hawaii *(Theodore W Scull)*

| WASA QUEEN | 16546t | 1975 | 22.0k | D2 | 865p | 1100p | 321c | 155.7m | 22.0m | 6.2m | PA |

WASA QUEEN was built by Dubigeon-Normandie (yard number 143) at Nantes, France as the BORE STAR for Baltic ferry operator Bore Line of Finland, part of the Silja Line consortium, for service between Finland and Sweden. She later passed to consortium member EFFOA of Helsinki and was renamed SILJA STAR. She was refitted in Bremerhaven by Lloyd Werft in 1986 following her sale to Sealink (UK) Ltd, and became the cruise ferry ORIENT EXPRESS for service in the Mediterranean. Later that year she was chartered to Club Sea for Caribbean cruising as the CLUB SEA. She continued to operate as ORIENT EXPRESS on the termination of this charter for a further two years, also undertaking winter charters to Europe Cruise Line as the EUROSUN. In 1990 she reverted to the name ORIENT EXPRESS and cruised in the Mediterranean again. Later in the year she was registered under the ownership of Eurosun Ltd. In 1991 she passed to Sembawang Johnson Shipmanagement of Singapore for cruising from that port as the ORIENT SUN. She moved back to her original area and role in 1992, becoming the WASA QUEEN for Wasa Line's services between Sweden and Finland. She later passed back to Silja Line and continued to operate in the Baltic under the same name. In 2001 she was sold to Star Cruises, who have operated her under the Cruise Ferries brand between Hong Kong and Xiamen in China. Lately she has been operating day and overnight gambling cruises from Hong Kong.

NORWEGIAN CRUISE LINE

The Company The origins of Norwegian Cruise Line date from the mid-1960's when the Norwegian Klosters Rederi ordered a car ferry from a Bergen shipyard to fill what was perceived as a gap in the ferry market, a route from Southern England to Spain. Due to external difficulties the route was quickly abandoned and alternative work was sought for the 11,000 ton SUNWARD. Under the Norwegian Caribbean Line banner she was placed in a new cruise service to the Caribbean, based in Miami, Florida. Such was the success that a second, slightly larger vessel was ordered, the STARWARD, and then another, the SKYWARD. Two further ships were ordered in 1970 from an Italian yard, but after the first (the SOUTHWARD) was delivered the building cost of the second ship escalated dramatically and the company abandoned her. She was subsequently completed as P&O's SPIRIT OF LONDON and is now Globalia Cruises' NEW FLAMENCO. In 1979 the Klosters company acquired the long laid-up transatlantic liner FRANCE and after a major refit she became the world's largest cruise ship – the NORWAY. Further expansion occurred in 1984 with the acquisition by Klosters of another Norwegian owned company, Royal Viking Line, together with its three luxury ships. That company ran for a while as a separate entity, but by 1991 its earlier ships had been absorbed into Norwegian Caribbean Line and Royal Viking Line was left with just two new ships, both of which were eventually sold to units of the now Carnival Group. Royal Cruise Line together with its one remaining ship, the CROWN ODYSSEY, joined the group in 1990. Transfers to that fleet over the next four years included two of the original Royal Viking trio, together with the last ever RV ship, the ROYAL VIKING QUEEN. More new ships came on stream during the 1990's and in a restyling the company adopted the title Norwegian Cruise Line. Following a battle for the company between Carnival Holdings and Star Cruises, the protagonists agreed to take split ownership of Norwegian Cruise Line and its subsidiary, Orient Lines in the ratio of 40 to 60. Subsequently Carnival withdrew and control passed to Star Cruises in 2000. Subsequently several of Star's new-buildings have been allocated to the company.

President and Chief Executive Officer Colin Veitch

Address 7665 Corporate Centre Drive, Miami, Florida 33126, United States of America

Telephone +1 305 436 4000 **Fax** +1 305 436 4120

Website www.ncl.com

Areas Operated North America, Caribbean Sea, South America and Europe

INDEPENDENCE	30293t	1950	22.5k	ST2	802p	1077p	310c	208.0m	27.1m	9.2m	US
NORWAY	76049t	1961	19.0k	ST2	2122p	2548p	900c	315.5m	33.7m	10.0m	BA
NORWEGIAN CROWN	34242t	1988	19.0k	D2	1052p	1225p	470c	187.7m	28.2m	6.8m	BA
NORWEGIAN DAWN	92250t	2002	24.0k	DE2	2224p	2683p	1126c	294.1m	32.2m	8.2m	BA
NORWEGIAN DREAM	50764t	1992	21.0k	D2	1726p	2156p	614c	229.8m	28.5m	6.8m	BA
NORWEGIAN JEWEL	92250t	2005	24.6k	DE2	2376p	2750p	1130c	294.1m	32.2m	8.2m	BA
NORWEGIAN MAJESTY	40876t	1992	21.0k	D2	1460p	1790p	550c	173.1m	27.6m	5.8m	BA
NORWEGIAN SPIRIT	75338t	1998	24.0k	DE2	1960p	2975p	1100c	268.6m	32.2m	7.9m	PA
NORWEGIAN STAR	91740t	2001	24.0k	DE2	2240p	2683p	1126c	294.1m	32.2m	8.0m	BA
NORWEGIAN SUN	78309t	2001	22.6k	DE2	2002p	2400p	968c	258.6m	32.3m	7.6m	BA
NORWEGIAN WIND	50760t	1993	20.3k	D2	1726p	2016p	614c	229.9m	28.5m	7.0m	BA
PRIDE OF ALOHA	77104t	1999	23.0k	DE2	2002p	2450p	800c	258.7m	32.3m	8.0m	US
PRIDE OF AMERICA	c85000t	2005	21.0k	DE2	2110p	2300p	650c	281.3m	32.2m	8.0m	US
UNITED STATES	53329t	1952	35.0k	ST4	1382P	1928P	1093c	301.8m	30.9m	9.8m	US

INDEPENDENCE was built by the Bethlehem Shipbuilding Corporation (yard number 1618) at Quincy, Massachusetts, USA for American Export Lines as the INDEPENDENCE, along with her sister, the CONSTITUTION for the New York to Italy service. The INDEPENDENCE was withdrawn from her Atlantic service in 1967, in the face of air competition. During the following year she ran cruises to the Caribbean and Mediterranean for an American tour operator. This proved unsuccessful and was not repeated in the following year. The ship was laid up until purchased by Hong Kong ship owner C Y Tung in 1974. She was renamed as the OCEANIC INDEPENDENCE and cruised briefly from Hong Kong before suffering a further period of lay-up from 1976 as the SEA LUCK I. C Y Tung formed American Hawaii Cruises in 1980 and began operating the ship under the US flag as the OCEANIC INDEPENDENCE on cruises from Honolulu. In 1983, following a major refurbishment, she reverted to her original name. Four years later the company was sold by Tung and following the terrorist attacks on the USA in 2001, the company filed for bankruptcy. She was laid up in San Francisco, but purchased by Norwegian Cruise Line in 2003, with a possible intention of her being returned to service as a US flag ship. To date nothing has happened and she remains in lay up.

NORWAY was built by Chantiers de l'Atlantique (yard number G19) at St Nazaire, France as the FRANCE for Compagnie Generale Transatlantique's transatlantic service from France to New York. After her maiden voyage in 1962, she spent much of her time on the Atlantic, but also undertook cruises. Following the withdrawal of subsidies by the French Government, the ship was laid up at Le Havre in October 1974, after the resolution of a situation that saw the ship occupied by French trades unionists, necessitating the disembarkation of her final passengers by tender. In 1977, the FRANCE was sold to Saudi Arabian interests, but continued her lay-up at Le Havre. In 1979 she passed to Kloster's of Oslo (Norwegian Caribbean Line) and was renamed NORWAY. Following a major refit she sailed to Miami to begin her second career, as a Caribbean cruise ship. Her forward engine room was closed down and the two outboard shafts and propellers removed. In 1984, all of her steam powered auxiliary equipment was replaced with diesel machinery in a major refit at Bremerhaven, Germany. She then spent much of the next 19 years cruising in the Caribbean, although great marketing opportunities were made of the ship's visits back to Europe for refits and modifications, including the addition of two extra decks in 1990. Following a 'final' transatlantic crossing in September 2001, she reverted to Caribbean cruising. In 2003 she was laid up and later moved to Bremerhaven following a boiler explosion that killed several crewmembers, pending a decision on repairs. By the spring of 2004 it was becoming apparent that the ship was unlikely to return to NCL service and she was subsequently sale-listed. She is now headed for South East Asia and an uncertain future.

NORWEGIAN CROWN was built for the Greek owned Royal Cruise Line by Jos L Meyer (yard number 616) at Papenburg, Germany as the CROWN ODYSSEY. She was to have been one of a pair of ships, but in the event the second vessel was either never ordered or cancelled before work began. Royal Cruise Line became part of the Kloster group around 1990, but the company retained its identity until 1996 when it was absorbed into Norwegian Cruise Line and the ship was renamed NORWEGIAN CROWN. In May 2000 the ship was transferred to Orient Lines and reverted to her original name for 'exploration cruising' worldwide. In early 2003 it was announced that the ship would be returned to Norwegian Cruise Line as the NORWEGIAN CROWN, following a downturn in Orient Lines' business, reverting to her previous NCL name. She currently operates to Bermuda, and handles the longer South American itineraries.

NORWEGIAN DAWN was ordered for Star Cruises from Jos L Meyer (yard number 649) at Papenburg, Germany as the SUPERSTAR SCORPIO but allocated to Norwegian Cruise Line while under construction. Her area of operation is principally the Caribbean.

NORWEGIAN DREAM was built as the DREAMWARD for Kloster Cruise Line of Nassau (Norwegian Caribbean Line) by Chantiers de l'Atlantique (yard number C30) at St Nazaire, France. When built the ship was 39,217 gross tons and had a length of 190 metres. In 1998 she followed her sister, the NORWEGIAN WIND, into the Lloydwerft shipyard in Bremerhaven, Germany to have a new 40 metre mid section fitted, and was renamed NORWEGIAN DREAM for the now re-styled Norwegian Cruise Line. During the following year while on passage to Dover, England at the end of a cruise she was involved in a serious collision with the Evergreen containership EVER DECENT. After disembarking her passengers at Dover she proceeded to Lloydwerft at Bremerhaven for repairs. The NORWEGIAN DREAM spent a number of summer seasons cruising from Dover, England to Baltic and Scandinavian destinations, but now operates in the Caribbean and Alaska.

NORWEGIAN JEWEL commenced her career with three cruises from Dover, England following delivery from Jos L Meyer (yard number 667) at Papenburg, Germany. She then operated a series of cruises on the East Coast of North America before positioning to the Caribbean.

NORWEGIAN MAJESTY was laid down for Birka Line of Mariehamn, Aland Islands by Wartsila (yard number 1312) at Turku, Finland. Following the failure of Wartsila, the ship was completed by Masa Yards for Majesty Cruise Line as the ROYAL MAJESTY and made her maiden voyage from Southampton to New York in July 1992. She was 32,396 tons and 140 metres long as built and subsequently operated for Dolphin Cruise Line. She passed to Norwegian Cruise Line in 1997 and was renamed NORWEGIAN MAJESTY. In 1999 she was lengthened by 33.5 metres by Lloydwerft at Bremerhaven, Germany by means of a new mid-section constructed by Aker MTW at Wismar, Germany. She currently operates Caribbean itineraries.

NORWEGIAN SPIRIT was built by Meyer Werft (yard number 646) at Papenburg, Germany as the SUPERSTAR LEO, the first new ship for Star Cruises. She was transferred to Norwegian Cruise Line in 2004 and renamed NORWEGIAN SPIRIT. She is a sister to the SUPERSTAR VIRGO. Her itineraries include Alaska and the Caribbean.

Norwegian Cruise Line's **Norway** at St Maarten *(Andrew Kilk)*

Norwegian Cruise Line's **Norwegian Dream** at Copenhagen *(Andrew Kilk)*

Norwegian Cruise Line's **Pride of America** in the English Channel (*FotoFlite*)

Norwegian Cruise Line's **Norwegian Star** at Skagway (*Andrew Kilk*)

NORWEGIAN STAR was laid down as the SUPERSTAR LIBRA by Meyer Werft (yard number 648) at Papenburg, Germany for Star Cruises, but switched to subsidiary, Norwegian Cruise Line before completion. She currently cruises in Alaska and the Caribbean.

NORWEGIAN SUN was built by Lloydwerft (yard number 109) at Bremerhaven, Germany for service in the Caribbean and the Alaskan coast.

NORWEGIAN WIND was built as the WINDWARD for Kloster Cruise of Nassau (Norwegian Caribbean Line) by Chantiers de l'Atlantique (yard number D30) at St Nazaire, France. When built the ship was 39,217 gross tons and had a length of 190 metres. In 1998 she went to Lloydwerft at Bremerhaven, Germany to have a new 40 metre mid section inserted and was renamed NORWEGIAN WIND for the now re-styled Norwegian Cruise Line. She currently cruises to Hawaii.

PRIDE OF ALOHA was laid down for Costa Crociere in 1996 as the COSTA OLYMPIA by Bremer Vulkan (yard number 108) at Vegesack, Germany but not completed due to the bankruptcy of the shipyard. The partially built hull was acquired by Norwegian Cruise Line and moved to Lloydwerft at Bremerhaven, Germany to be completed as the NORWEGIAN SKY. She was renamed as the PRIDE OF ALOHA following the partial sinking of the still incomplete PRIDE OF AMERICA in the shipyard at Bremerhaven. She cruises year-round in the Hawaiian Islands.

PRIDE OF AMERICA was ordered by the new United States Lines (part of the American Classic Voyages Grouping) from the Ingalls Shipbuilding yard (yard number 7671) at Pascagoula, Mississippi, USA as one of a pair of what were to be the first ocean passenger ships to be constructed in a US shipyard for more than 40 years. As in other histories in this book, the events of September 11, 2001 had a devastating effect on American Classic Voyages and the company filed for bankruptcy. Norwegian Cruise Line later purchased what there was of these two ships and had the parts towed to Bremerhaven where both ships were to have been completed for the Hawaiian cruise market. While being completed, the PRIDE OF AMERICA as she was now named, was partially sunk during a storm. The shipyard subsequently filed for bankruptcy and it is thought that what little there was of the second ship has now been scrapped or incorporated into another ship. As an 'American built' and US flagged ship she is able to operate in the Hawaii Islands without the need to call at a foreign port.

UNITED STATES, the fastest passenger liner ever built, has been languishing in various ports for more than 35 years, since she was withdrawn from service in 1969. She was built by the Newport News Shipbuilding and Drydock Company (yard number 488) in Newport News, Virginia, USA for the transatlantic service of United States Lines to partner the older and smaller AMERICA. She gained the Blue Riband for the fastest westbound and eastbound crossings of the North Atlantic in 1952 with an eastbound average speed of 35.53 knots, a speed not subsequently beaten by a 'normal' passenger ship. Norwegian Cruise Line acquired the UNITED STATES in 2003, although it is extremely unlikely that she will ever re-enter commercial service, and she remains laid up.

Cruise ships on order

PRIDE OF HAWAII	c92250t	2006	24.0k	DE2	2384p	2750p	1130c	294.1m	32.2m	8.2m	US
MEYER 669	c92250t	2007	24.0k	DE2	2384p	2750p	1130c	294.1m	32.2m	8.2m	BA
MEYER 670	c92250t	2007	24.0k	DE2	2384p	2750p	1130c	294.1m	32.2m	8.2m	BA

PRIDE OF HAWAII (yard number 668), **MEYER 669** and **670** are under construction for the company by Jos L Meyer, at Papenburg, Germany.

The company also operates the NORWEGIAN SEA until September 2005, when she transfers to Star Cruises as the SUPERSTAR LIBRA (q.v.).

ORIENT LINES

The Company Orient Lines was the trading name of a British based company (Shipping and General Services Ltd) formed in 1991 to acquire and operate one of the quintet of Russian liners built in the mid-1960's on exclusive expedition type cruises. The MARCO POLO entered service in 1994 and four years later Orient Lines was sold to Norwegian Cruise Line. Orient Lines has continued to operate with its own identity and the fleet briefly expanded to two ships (with the expectation of a third) before contracting back to a single vessel.

Address 7665 Corporate Centre Drive, Miami, Florida 33126, United States of America

Telephone +1 305 436 4000 **Fax** +1 305 436 4120

Website www.orientlines.com

Areas operated Worldwide

MARCO POLO	22086t	1965	19.5k	D2	848p	922p	450c	176.3m	23.6m	8.2m	BA

MARCO POLO was built in what was then East Germany by Mathias-Thesen-Werft (yard number 125) at Wismar, Germany as one of a series of five liners for the Black Sea Shipping Company and the Baltic Shipping Company. The ALEKSANDR PUSHKIN entered service for the Baltic Shipping Company in the summer of 1965 with a series of cruises before taking up her intended employment on the service from Leningrad to Montreal during the following spring. From 1975 she was mainly used for cruising and from 1979 was on a five-year charter to Transocean. In 1985 she was transferred to the Far Eastern Shipping Company of Vladivostok and over the next few years she undertook charters to CTC Lines for cruising from Sydney, Australia. Following a brief lay-up in Singapore she was sold to Shipping and General and sent to Greece for a major refit that took almost three years to complete. As the MARCO POLO she has subsequently proved to be both popular and successful with her out of the way itineraries. Marco Polo, the great Italian traveller, was born in Venice in 1254. His epic journey along the Silk Road through Asia lasted 24 years and resulted in the production of the greatest travelogue ever written.

STAR CRUISES

The Company From its early foundations in 1993 to the present day, the development of Star Cruises has not been without difficulty, due to a number of regional factors. The company acquired its first ships (the former Viking Line Baltic ferries ATHENA (STAR AQUARIUS) and KALYPSO (STAR PISCES) in the spring of 1994, and these were followed by other good quality second-hand tonnage. It was not until 1998 that the first purpose built ship for the company's South East Asian itineraries entered the fleet, and the story subsequently has been one of alternate expansion and cut back as new markets in the region have been explored and either developed or abandoned. Star Cruises also operates Cruise Ferries.

Chairman, President and Chief Executive Officer Tan Sri Lim Kok Thay

Address Star Cruises Terminal, Pulau Indah, Pelabuhan Barat, 42009 Klang, Selangor, Malaysia

Telephone +60 3 3101 1313 **Fax** +60 3 3101 1406

Website www.starcruises.com

Areas operated South East Asia

MEGASTAR ARIES	3264t	1989	16.0k	D2	72p	72p	80c	82.2m	14.0m	3.4m	PA
MEGASTAR TAURUS	3264t	1989	16.0k	D2	72p	72p	80c	82.2m	14.0m	3.4m	PA
STAR PISCES	40053t	1990	21.3k	D2	1378p	1900p	750c	176.6m	29.0m	6.0m	PA
SUPERSTAR GEMINI	19089t	1992	18.4k	D2	819p	916p	470c	163.8m	22.5m	5.4m	PA
SUPERSTAR LIBRA	42276t	1988	21.5k	D2	1494p	1796p	609c	216.2m	28.4m	7.0m	BA
SUPERSTAR VIRGO	75338t	1999	24.0k	DE2	1964p	2975p	1125c	268.6m	32.2m	7.9m	PA

MEGASTAR ARIES was built by Flender Werft (yard number 648), Lubeck, Germany for the Windsor Cruise Line as the LADY SARAH. She was renamed AURORA II in 1991 when operating for New Frontier Cruises of Hamburg, and passed to Star Cruises in 1995, becoming the MEGASTAR ARIES.

MEGASTAR TAURUS was built by Flender Werft (yard number 647) at Lubeck, Germany for the Windsor Cruise Line as the LADY DIANA, later renamed the LADY DI, before transferring to New Frontier Cruises of Hamburg as the AURORA I. She became the MEGASTAR TAURUS on acquisition by Star Cruises in 1995.

STAR PISCES was built by Masa Yards (yard number 1298) at Turku, Finland as the car ferry KALYPSO for the Swedish partner in the Viking Line consortium, Rederi AB Slite. Following the financial difficulties encountered by that company, receivers were appointed and in 1994 the ship was sold together with her sister, the ATHENA (now DFDS Seaways' PEARL OF SCANDINAVIA) to Star Cruises. She was rebuilt as the cruise ship STAR PISCES and has since been based in Hong Kong. In recent years she has operated overnight cruises out of Hong Kong. While these are geared mainly for gamblers, unlike the rest of the Hong Kong casino cruise fleet, she still offers a full range of cruise-type activities as well.

SUPERSTAR GEMINI was built by Union Naval de Levante (yard number 197) at Valencia, Spain for Effjohn Group's Crown Cruise Line as the CROWN JEWEL. She was marketed by Cunard from 1993 as the CUNARD CROWN JEWEL before passing to Star Cruises in 1995 when she was renamed as the SUPERSTAR GEMINI. She currently operates cruises to Japan from her Taiwan base, but in the autumn of 2005 moves back to Singapore to cruise in the Straits of Malacca and the Andaman Sea.

SUPERSTAR LIBRA was built as the SEAWARD for Kloster's Norwegian Caribbean Cruise Line by Wartsila (yard number 1294) at Turku, Finland and following her naming ceremony in New York she commenced cruising in the Caribbean. In 1997 she was renamed NORWEGIAN SEA. In September 2005 she transfers within the group to Star Cruises and will be renamed SUPERSTAR LIBRA to start a new cruise venture, operating from Mumbai, India.

SUPERSTAR VIRGO was built by Meyer Werft (yard number 647) at Papenburg, Germany for Star Cruises. She is the current flagship of the Star Cruises fleet and is a sister to the NORWEGIAN SPIRIT. She currently operates short cruises from Singapore.

Orient Lines' **Marco Polo** in Copenhagen *(William Mayes)*

Star Cruises' **Superstar Gemini** *(Paul Mason)*

Star Cruises' *Superstar Virgo* (Jonathan Boonzaier)

Transocean Tours' *Astor* at Malaga (William Mayes)

TRANSOCEAN TOURS

The Company Transocean Tours Touristik is a German tour company, operating ocean cruises and river cruises on the waterways of Europe for German-speaking passengers.

Managing Director Peter Waehnert

Address Stavendamm 22, 28195 Bremen, Germany

Telephone +49 421 33360 **Fax** +49 421 3326 100

Website www.transocean.de

Area operated Northern Europe, Mediterranean Sea and South America

ASTOR	20606t	1987	18.0k	D2	590p	590p	300c	176.3m	22.6m	6.1m	BA
ASTORIA	18591t	1981	18.0k	D2	500p	518p	220c	164.3m	22.6m	6.1m	BA

ASTOR was ordered by the South African Marine Corporation as a replacement for the 1981-built ASTOR. She was built by the same yard as the previous ship, Howaldtswerke-Deutsche Werft (yard number 218) at Hamburg, Germany. During construction however, the company decided to abandon its plans to re-start the Cape Town to Southampton liner service and in a complicated series of moves the ship was delivered as the ASTOR to Ireland Blyth and registered in Mauritius. After only eighteen months she was sold to the Black Sea Shipping Company of Odessa as the FYODOR DOSTOEVSKIY. In 1991 she was registered under the ownership of a SOVCOMFLOT group company. She subsequently performed a number of charters and is currently chartered to Transocean Tours as the ASTOR under a ten-year arrangement terminating in 2006.

ASTORIA was built by Howaldtswerke-Deutsche Werft (yard number 165) at Hamburg, Germany as the ASTOR (laid down as the HAMMONIA) for Hadag Cruise Line. In 1984 she was acquired by the South African Marine Corporation of Cape Town for a new liner service between Southampton and Cape Town and for off-season cruising. It became apparent very early that the ship's engines were not powerful enough to maintain the required liner schedule and she was sold to VEB Deutfracht Seereederie of West Germany. She was refitted in Hamburg and as the ARKONA became the replacement for the VOLKERFREUNDSCHAFT (now Classic International Cruises ATHENA (q.v.)). She is currently on a 10-year charter from Astoria Shipping until 2012 as the ASTORIA.

TRAVEL DYNAMICS INTERNATIONAL

The Company Travel Dynamics International, formerly known as Classical Cruises, is an operator of high calibre educational programmes on small ships and was founded in the 1970's.

Address 132 East 70th Street, New York, NY 10021, United States of America

Telephone +1 212 517 7555 **Fax** +1 212 774 1545

Website www.traveldynamicsinternational.com

Area operated Mediterranean Sea

CALLISTO	430t	1963	12.0k	D2	34p	34p	c	46.8m	8.0m	2.3m	GR
CLELIA II	4077t	1991	15.0k	D2	84p	84p	65c	88.3m	15.3m	3.3m	BA
CORINTHIAN II	4200t	2001	15.5k	D2	114p	114p	70c	90.3m	15.3m	4.0m	MA

CALLISTO was the daughter of Lycaon, and associated with Artemis, the goddess of the hunt in Greek Mythology. The ship was built as the MARINA by D W Kremer Sohn at Elmshorn in Germany. She became the ILLYRIA II in 1985 and was renamed CALLISTO in 2000 by Blue Sea Shipping Line. She is operated under charter.

CLELIA II was built by Cantieri Navale Ferrari (yard number 46) at La Spezia, Italy as the RENAISSANCE FOUR for Renaissance Cruises. She became the CLELIA II for Lindos Maritime in 1996. She is currently owned by Goodwin Sands Marine as a private yacht, although she has recently operated for Travel Dynamics from time to time.

CORINTHIAN II was built as the RENAISSANCE SEVEN by Nuovi Cantieri Apuania (yard number 1146) for Renaissance Cruises. She became the REGINA RENAISSANCE in 1992, reverting to her original name in 1998. Sold in 2001 she was renamed as the RENAI I. In 2003 she became the SUN, and in the following year was renamed as the ISLAND SUN. She was then owned by Mauritius Island Cruises, but was sold in 2005 along with her sister the ISLAND SKY (now operated by Noble Caledonia (q.v.)) to the Danish Clipper Group. Mauritius Island Cruises has now ceased to trade. The ship was renamed CORINTHIAN II and following a refit in Piraeus was chartered to Travel Dynamics for service in the Mediterranean Sea.

Travel Dynamics' **Clelia II** at Tunis *(Andrew Kilk)*

Travelscope's **Van Gogh** in Southampton Water *(William Mayes)*

TRAVELSCOPE

The Company Travelscope is a UK based tour operator specialising in Reader Holiday Offers, promoted in national and regional newspapers and in magazines. The company began 2005 by advertising cruises on the REMBRANDT (laid up WALRUS (q.v.)), but the sale to Dutch interests of this vessel and its subsequent charter to Travelscope failed to materialise.

Address Elgin House, High Street, Stonehouse, GL10 2NA, England

Telephone +44 870 380 3333

Website www.travelscope.co.uk

Area operated European cruises from regional UK ports

| VAN GOGH | 15402t | 1975 | 22.0k | D2 | 428p | 640p | 216c | 156.3m | 21.8m | 5.9m | SV |

VAN GOGH is owned by Club Cruise of The Netherlands' subsidiary Maritime & Leasing Ltd and operates on seasonal charter for Travelscope. She was built by Wartsila (yard number 1213) at Turku, Finland as the GRUZIA, one of a series of five ro-ro passenger vessels for the Black Sea Shipping Company of Odessa. She was immediately chartered to the German tour operator, TUI. She subsequently operated for a number of charterers until the early 1990's when, following the break-up of the Soviet Union, the Black Sea Shipping Company was in financial difficulties. In 1994 the ship was chartered to the United States Military Sealift Command. In the following year Blasco, as her owners had become, renamed her as the ODESSA SKY. In 1998 she was converted at Bremerhaven for use as the casino ship CLUB CRUISE 1, and was later renamed simply as CLUB 1. She was acquired by Club Cruise in 1999, converted back to a normal cruise ship and renamed as the VAN GOGH. Her first charter in 2000 was to Nouvelles Frontieres, but she has now become a regular with Travelscope. Vincent Van Gogh (1853-1890) was probably the most famous of the Dutch painters.

Travelscope also charters the FUNCHAL (Classic Cruises q.v.) from time to time.

TUI GROUP

The Group TUI AG, of Germany, is the largest tourism and service group in the world, employing more than 80,000 people in over 500 companies throughout the world.

HAPAG LLOYD CRUISES

The Company Hapag-Lloyd Cruises is part of the giant German shipping group Hapag-Lloyd, itself part of the travel and leisure group TUI. Hapag-Lloyd was formed in 1970 on the amalgamation of Hamburg America Line and Norddeutscher Lloyd. The former had been established in 1847 by a group of Hamburg ship owners and businessmen. The North German Lloyd company was formed ten years later. At the outbreak of the First World War, Hamburg America Line (Hapag) was one of the world's largest shipping companies, with a fleet of 175 ships, including some magnificent transatlantic liners. NGL had 135 ships at this time, and both companies effectively lost all of them. Hapag re-entered the passenger shipping market in 1923 with the liner ALBERT BALLIN, and during the following year NDL introduced the COLUMBUS, the largest and fastest ship in the German fleet. By 1926, Hapag was once again a major ship owner with a fleet of 118 vessels. NDL's BREMEN took the Blue Riband of the North Atlantic in 1929. The Second World War saw the loss of both fleets for the second time, following which NDL concentrated on passenger trades and Hapag on cargo services. The Preussag Group acquired a controlling interest in Hapag-Lloyd in 1997, and five years later acquired the minority interests to become the sole shareholder. In 1998 Hapag-Lloyd acquired a majority shareholding in the major German travel group Touristik Union International. In 2001 Preussag re-branded its tourist businesses as World of TUI. Today, Hapag-Lloyd operates an impressive fleet of large containerships.

Managing Director Gunther Brauer

Address Ballindamm 25, 20095 Hamburg, Germany

Telephone +49 40 3001 4600 **Fax** +49 40 3001 4601

Website www.hlkf.de

Area operated Worldwide

BREMEN	6752t	1990	15.0k	D2	164p	184p	80c	111.5m	17.0m	4.6m	BA
C. COLUMBUS	15067t	1997	18.5k	D2	410p	423p	178c	145.0m	21.5m	5.1m	BA
EUROPA	28437t	1999	21.0k	DE2	408p	408p	270c	198.6m	24.0m	6.1m	BA
HANSEATIC	8378t	1991	14.0k	D2	188p	188p	130c	122.7m	18.0m	4.8m	BA

BREMEN began life as the FRONTIER SPIRIT, an expedition ship for Japan's NYK Line. She was built by Mitsubishi Heavy Industries (yard Number 1182) at Kobe in Japan. She has been used by Hapag-Lloyd as the expedition cruise ship BREMEN since 1993. In 2005 she was to have been chartered to a new business under the name Expedition Leaders in order to promote dual language (German and English) cruises, but that arrangement now appears not to be proceeding. The city of Bremen in Germany, after which this ship is named, has a history going back more than 1,200 years, and played a major role in the Hanseatic League.

C. COLUMBUS was built at the Wismar, Germany yard of MTW Schiffswerft (yard number 451) for operation by Hapag-Lloyd. Her name commemorates one of the greatest of the European discoverers, Genoa-born Christopher Columbus, 1451-1506.

EUROPA was built by Kvaerner Masa Yards (yard number 495) in Helsinki, Finland as a replacement for an earlier, and unusually, larger ship of the same name.

HANSEATIC was built by Rauma Yards (yard number 306) at Rauma in Finland as the SOCIETY ADVENTURER for Society Expeditions. In 1992 she began operating for Hapag-Lloyd as the HANSEATIC under charter, being acquired by the group during the following year. The Hanseatic League was a mercantile league of German and Baltic cities, which began to emerge in the 1240's and which seems to have ceased to have importance in 1669, although never officially dissolved. Hamburg, Lubeck and Bremen are still known as Hanseatic Cities.

THOMSON CRUISES

The Company Thomson Holidays, the long established British package holiday company began offering cruises on other companies ships in the late 1960's, but by 1973 the company was chartering ships on a long-term basis. The first such vessels were the CALYPSO, formerly Shaw Savill & Albion's SOUTHERN CROSS and the rather smaller ITHACA that had been built for Zim Israel as the ZION. Lord Thomson founded the company in 1965, with the purchase of Universal Sky Tours, Britannia Airways and Riviera Holidays. By 1974 Thomson was the largest of the UK package tour operators. Thomson withdrew from the charter market in the early 1980's, but later re-entered the market with the ISLAND BREEZE, THE EMERALD and THE TOPAZ. Thomson Travel Group was floated on the London Stock Exchange by the Thomson Group in 1999, and in the following year was acquired by the German Preussag Group. In 2001 Preussag re-branded its tourist business as World of TUI, encompassing 66 brands within the group.

Managing Director of Tui UK Peter Rothwell **Head of Cruise within Thomson** David Selby

Address Greater London House, Hampstead Road, London NW1 7SD

Telephone +44 207 387 9321 **Fax** +44 207 391 0140

Website www.thomson-cruises.co.uk

Area operated Scandinavia, Mediterranean, Atlantic Islands and the Red Sea

THE EMERALD	26431t	1958	20.0k	D2	960p	1198p	412c	177.9m	25.6m	8.3m	GR
THOMSON CELEBRATION	33933t	1984	21.0k	D2	1210p	1378p	540c	214.7m	27.2m	7.5m	NA
THOMSON DESTINY	37773t	1982	20.5k	D2	1432p	1595p	525c	214.5m	28.4m	7.0m	CY
THOMSON SPIRIT	33930t	1983	21.0k	D2	1210p	1374p	559c	214.7m	27.2m	7.5m	CY

THE EMERALD, built as the SANTA ROSA by Newport News Shipbuilding and Dry Dock Company (yard number 521) at Newport News, USA for Grace Line of New York, served the company's New York to Central America service for only 13 years before being laid up at Hampton Roads. She remained there for 18 years until she was acquired by Coral Cruise Lines in 1989 and towed to Greece for rebuilding. She was renamed PACIFIC SUN, then DIAMOND ISLAND before finally coming back into service as the RAINBOW in 1992 for a Caribbean cruise programme. In 1993 she passed to Regency Cruises as the REGENT RAINBOW, but following the failure of that company she was laid up again. Louis Cruise Lines acquired her in 1996 and she was renamed THE EMERALD, and the following year began a long-term seasonal charter to Thomson Cruises. In the spring of 2005 she operated briefly for Louis Cruise Lines on short itineraries from Piraeus, but for Thomson's season she is based in Corfu for Aegean and Adriatic Sea itineraries.

THOMSON CELEBRATION is one of a pair of cruise ships ordered by Holland America Line from Chantiers de l'Atlantique (yard number X27) at St Nazaire, France in 1980. She was delivered as the NOORDAM in March 1984 and sailed on her maiden voyage from Le Havre, France to Tampa, Florida on 8 April. She subsequently cruised to Alaska in the summer and to Mexico in the winter. In later years she often spent the summer in Europe. In late 2004 she was chartered by Holland America Line to Thomson Cruises and renamed the THOMSON CELEBRATION. Her debut season features ex-UK cruises in the summer, after which she is based in the Canary Islands.

THOMSON DESTINY was the fourth ship to be delivered to the still relatively new Royal Caribbean Cruise Lines, as the SONG OF AMERICA. She was built by Wartsila (yard number 431) at Helsinki, Finland for service in the Caribbean Sea. Replaced by new tonnage she was sold to Airtours of the UK (marketed as Sun Cruises) and renamed as the SUNBIRD in 1999. Airtours later re-styled themselves as My Travel, but that did not stop the losses mounting in other sections of the company from almost pulling the whole business down. The cruise business was sold in 2004, with Louis Cruise Lines taking a number of ships, including the SUNBIRD. For 2005 she has been chartered to Thomson Cruises as the THOMSON DESTINY.

Hapag-Lloyd's *C. Columbus* in Geirangerfjord *(William Mayes)*

Hapag-Lloyd's *Europa* at Copenhagen *(Andrew Kilk)*

Thomson's ***Thomson Celebration*** in refit at Falmouth *(David Trevor-Jones)*

Thomson's ***The Emerald*** at Palma *(Clive Harvey)*

THOMSON SPIRIT was built by Chantiers de l'Atlantique (yard number V27) at St Nazaire, France as the first of a pair of ships of fairly revolutionary appearance for Holland America Line. She was delivered as the NIEUW AMSTERDAM in 1983. In 2000 she was sold to American Hawaii Cruises (part of American Classic Voyages) for use in the Hawaii Islands as the PATRIOT. Following the September 11 terrorist attacks in 2001, the company collapsed and the ship was repossessed by Holland America Line and laid up. She was subsequently chartered to Louis Cruise Lines and then sub-chartered to Thomson Cruises. The THOMSON SPIRIT cruises in the Mediterranean in summer, and for the winter 2005/2006 operates a series of cruises in the Red Sea.

UKRRICHFLOT

The Company UKRRICHFLOT is a major Ukraine operator of river and short sea cargo services. The two ships shown here are principally river vessels, but also cruise from the port of Odessa into the Black Sea. The company was formed in 1992, following the break up of the Soviet Union.

President P I Podlesny

Address 51 Nizhniy Val Str, Kyiv, 04071 Ukraine

Telephone +380 44 4174233

Website www.ukrrichflot.com

Area operated Black Sea and the River Danube

AKADEMIK VIKTOR GLUSHKOV	‡5475t	1983	12.0k	D3	314p	332p	98c	129.1m	16.0m	2.9m	UR
GENERAL LAVRINENKOV	‡5475t	1990	12.0k	D3	314p	332p	98c	129.1m	16.0m	2.9m	UR

AKADEMIK VIKTOR GLUSHKOV and **GENERAL LAVRINENKOV** were built by VEB Elbeverften Boizenburg Rosslau (yard numbers 389 and 397) at Boizenburg, Germany.

VIKING LINE

The Company Today's Viking Line is the sole remaining company from the consortium that formed the original Viking Line in the early 1960's. The company was SF Line AB until it restyled itself in 1995.

Chairman Ben Lundquist **Managing Director** Nils-Erik Eklund

Address Norragatan 4, 22100 Mariehamn, Aland Islands, Finland

Telephone +358 18 26011 **Fax** +358 9 1235292

Website www.vikingline.fi

Area operated 24 hour cruises from Stockholm, Sweden

VIKING CINDERELLA	46398t	1989	21.5k	D2	1828p	2766p	224c	190.9m	29.0m	6.6m	SW

VIKING CINDERELLA was built by the Wartsila shipyard (yard number 1302) in Turku, Finland as the CINDERELLA for the SF Line of Finland, part of the Viking Line consortium. She was initially employed on the overnight intercity route between Stockholm and Helsinki, providing a tandem sailing on alternate nights. She also provided some cruise sailings from Helsinki to Tallinn. From 1993 she became the principal vessel on the Stockholm to Helsinki service, running opposite the MARIELLA.

With the arrival of the GABRIELLA, she switched to full time cruising, initially from Helsinki, but latterly from Stockholm. She was renamed VIKING CINDERELLA in 2003.

VIVAL MARINE

The Company Vival Marine is a Ukraine private sector travel and tour operator, established in 1998. The company also operates the car ferry PALLADA in the Black Sea and offers voyages between Odessa and Haifa in conjunction with Mano Cruises (q.v.).

Address Odessa, Ukraine

Telephone +380 482 375037 **Fax** +380

Website www.vivalmarine.com

Area operated Round trip cruises from Odessa to Istanbul

GLORIYA	5745t	1968	16.0k	D2	p	p	c	124.2m	m	m	UR

GLORIYA was built by VEB Mathias-Thesen-Werft (yard number 186) at Wismar in what was East Germany as the research vessel AKADEMIK VERNADSKIY for the Academy of Science at Sevastopol. She was transferred to the Marine Hydrophysics Institute of the National Academy of Sciences of the Ukraine in 1994 without a change of name. In 2001 she was sold to Hullman International, a business registered in Cambodia and is currently operated under charter by Vival Marine as the GLORIYA.

VOYAGER HOLDINGS

The Company Voyager Holdings is a US registered business.

Address 801 Houser Way North, Renton, Washington State 98055, United States of America

Area operated Unknown

| SEA VOYAGER | 1195t | 1982 | 12.0k | D2 | 63p | 63p | 21c | 51.9m | 11.0m | m | HD |

SEA VOYAGER was built by the Chesapeake Marine Railway Company in Baltimore, USA as the AMERICA. She later became the TEMPTRESS VOYAGER and took her current name in 2002 when acquired by Voyager Holdings.

VOYAGES OF DISCOVERY

The Company Voyages of Discovery is a brand of the United Kingdom registered All Leisure Group. Its origins are in the Schools Abroad business that started offering educational cruises in 1984. The cruises were popular with both adults and children and so the company developed into the mainstream cruise market. Voyages of Discovery has chartered a number of ships over the years including the AEGEAN I and the AEGEAN SPIRIT (formerly Costa's ENRICO C). Until 2004 the company operated the DISCOVERY on a six-month charter from Discovery Cruises, but now also markets itself under that name following its recent acquisition of that business, together with the DISCOVERY.

Managing Director Dudley Smith

Address Lynnem House, 1 Victoria Way, Burgess Hill, West Sussex, RH15 9NF, England

Telephone +44 1444 462150 **Fax** +44 1444 462160

Website www.voyagesofdiscovery.com

Area operated Europe, Red Sea, Scandinavia and South America

| DISCOVERY | 20186t | 1971 | 18.0k | D2 | 698p | 758p | 350c | 168.7m | 24.6m | 7.5m | BD |

DISCOVERY was built by Rheinstahl Nordseewerke (yard number 414) at Emden in Germany as the ISLAND VENTURE for Norwegian Cruiseships (a joint venture between Fearney & Eger and Lorentzen), to be chartered to Flagship Cruises for service between New York and Bermuda, along with her sister, the SEA VENTURE. The service could not support two ships, so the ISLAND VENTURE was put up for charter. Princess Cruises was in search of a replacement for the CARLA C, so chartered her and renamed her as the ISLAND PRINCESS in 1972. She passed to The Peninsular & Oriental Steam Navigation Company, with Princess Cruises in 1974. In 1999 she was sold to Ringcroft Investment and chartered to Hyundai Merchant Marine as the HYUNDAI PUNGAK for cruising from South Korea. Having acquired three ships, the market could not sustain this number of berths and the ship was laid up before being sold to Gerry Herrod, the founder of Orient Lines. She was taken to Tuzla in Turkey and refitted as the PLATINUM in 2001. From 2002 she operated for Herrod's own Discovery Cruises on South American itineraries in winter and on Voyages of Discovery' educational cruises in summer, as the DISCOVERY in both roles. Herrod retired in 2004 and Voyages of Discovery now operate the ship under its own name and as Discovery Cruises. The most famous ship to bear the name DISCOVERY was undoubtedly that of Captain Robert Falcon Scott, used as the ship for the National Antarctic Expedition of 1901-1904. That ship is currently preserved in Dundee, Scotland.

UKRRICHFLOT's **General Lavrinenkov** at Odessa *(William Mayes)*

Vival Maritime's **Gloriya** at Odessa *(William Mayes)*

Voyages of Discovery's **Discovery** at Bermuda *(Theodore W Scull)*

Windjammer's **Amazing Grace** at Nassau *(Andrew Kilk)*

WINDJAMMER BAREFOOT CRUISES

The Company Windjammer Barefoot Cruises was founded in 1947 by former US Navy submariner Mike Burke. The company currently operates an interesting fleet of historic vessels.

President Susan Burke

Address PO Box 190120, Miami Beach, Florida, 33119-0120, United States of America

Telephone +1 305 672 6453 **Fax** +1 305 674 1219

Website www.windjammer.com

Area operated Caribbean Sea and Central America

AMAZING GRACE	1585t	1955	14.0k	D2	92p	92p	44c	78.3m	12.2m	3.8m	TR
LEGACY	1740t	1959	12.0k	SDE2	119p	122p	43c	76.4m	12.6m	6.0m	TR
MANDALAY	420t	1923	9.5k	SD1	72p	72p	30c	61.6m	10.0m	4.9m	GN
POLYNESIA	430t	1939	8.0k	SD1	112p	112p	45c	63.8m	9.9m	5.0m	GN
YANKEE CLIPPER	‡327t	1927	k	SD1	64p	64p	30c	60.0m	8.6m	5.2m	GN

AMAZING GRACE was built as the buoy and lighthouse tender PHAROS by the Caledonian Shipbuilding and Engineering Company (yard number 507) at Dundee in Scotland. She started operating for Windjammer as the AMAZING GRACE in 1988 and now offers cruises on her supply voyages, servicing the company's sailing ships.

LEGACY started out as the meteorological research vessel FRANCE II for the French Government. She was built by Forges et Chantiers de la Mediterranee (yard number 346B) at Le Havre, France. She was acquired by Windjammer in 1989 and refitted as the sailing cruise vessel LEGACY. Her current programme includes the Bahamas, the Virgin Islands, St Lucia and the Windward Islands.

MANDALAY is a barquentine, which was built for E F Hutton by Burmeister & Wain (yard number 323) in Copenhagen, Denmark and named HUSSAR. She was acquired by George Vettlesen in the 1930's and renamed as the VELMA. In later life she operated as a research ship for Columbia University. Windjammer acquired her in 1983, when she was renamed MANDALAY. Her current itineraries include the British Virgin Islands, Antigua and the Eastern Caribbean.

POLYNESIA was built by Scheepswerf de Haan & Oerlemans (yard number 206) at Heusden in The Netherlands as the ARGUS, one of the last of the Portuguese Grand Banks fleet. She moved to Windjammer in 1975 and was renamed POLYNESIA. Later she carried the name OISEAU DE POLYNESIA for the 1984 season, but reverted to her current name in the following year.

YANKEE CLIPPER was built by the Krupp shipyard in Kiel, Germany as the armour plated private yacht CRESSIDA. Later she was renamed CRIMPER. She was later acquired by the Vanderbilts and renamed PIONEER. Windjammer purchased the ship in 1965 and renamed her YANKEE CLIPPER I. She was renamed as the YANKEE CLIPPER in 1996 and currently sails around St Vincent and the Grenadines.

ZEUS CRUISES

The Company The Zeus Group is a Greek registered organisation offering cruises under the brands Harmony Cruises, Galileo Cruises and Casual Cruises. The company was founded in the 1960's as a tour operator and has subsequently developed into yacht cruises.

Management President Lakis Venetopoulos **Vice president** Christina Venetopoulos

Address 2 Papada Street, 11525 Athens, Greece

Telephone +30 210 691 9191 **Fax** +30 210 699 8484

Website www.zeusgroup.gr

Area operated Aegean and Ionian Seas

DIOGENES V	t	1994	10.0k	D2	48p	49p	13c	50.4m	8.2m	3.5m	GR
HARMONY G	498t	2001	11.0k	D2	44p	44p	16c	53.9m	7.1m	3.7m	GR
GALILEO	480t	1995	11.0k	SD2	50p	50p	15c	51.0m	10.0m	2.9m	GR
PANORAMA	674t	1991	12.5k	SD2	46p	50p	18c	52.7m	12.0m	3.0m	GR
VIKING STAR	t	1994	9.0k	SD2	42p	42p	12c	32.2m	8.7m	3.3m	GR
ZEUS II	t	1942	10.0k	D2	34p	34p	9c	32.2m	5.8m	2.9m	GR

HARMONY G was built by N Savvas Shipyard at Eleusis in Greece.

GALILEO was built by Fratsis G Shipyard (yard number 470) at Perama, Greece.

PANORAMA was built by N Kastrinos (yard number 23) at Perama, Greece.

the **leading** *guide to the cruise industry*

section 2

PASSENGER SHIPS IN OTHER ROLES

ANDAMAN CLUB

The Company Andaman Club is a Thai operator of resort hotels and Casinos.

Address 25th A Floor, Lumphini Tower, 1168/71 Pharamthi Road, Yannuawa, Bangkok 10120, Thailand

Telephone +66 2 5154 7558 **Fax** +66 2 5186 1885

Website www.andamanclub.com

Area operated Possibly in use as a hotel ship at Similan, Thailand

KONG OLAV	2637t	1964					87.4m	13.3m	4.6m	TH

KONG OLAV was built by AS Bergens Mek. Verksted (yard number 433) at Bergen, Norway for DSDS, an operator on the Hurtigruten. That company became part of VDS in 1978. She was sold to Thai owners in 1997 and is believed to be in static use as a hotel.

ARTIKMORNEFTEGAZRAVEDKA

The Company Artikmorneftegazravedka is a Russian state-owned oil and gas exploration company, which appears to operate two passenger vessels in conjunction with its exploration activities.

Address Kolskiy Prospekt 1, 183032 Murmansk, Russia

Telephone +7 8152 254647 **Fax** +7 8152 8115

Website www.amngr.ru

Area operated Unknown

ANNA AKHMATOVA	4575t	1988	14.3k	D1	150p	150p	34c	90.0m	17.2m	5.3m	RU
BORIS PASTERNAK	4575t	1989	14.3k	D1	150p	150p	34c	90.0m	17.2m	5.3m	RU

ANNA AKHMATOVA was built by Stocznia im. Komuny Paryskiej (yard number B961/01) at Gdynia, Poland. Anna Akhamatova (1889-1966) was a Ukrainian poet.

BORIS PASTERNAK was built by Stocznia im. Komuny Paryskiej (yard number B961/02) at Gdynia, Poland. Boris Pasternak (1890-1960) was the author of Doctor Zhivago, for which he won the 1958 Nobel Prize for Literature, although he was not allowed to receive it.

ASIA CRUISER CLUB

The Company Asia Cruiser Club is a Hong Kong casino cruise operator.

Address Room 3317, 33rd Floor, China Merchants Tower, Shun Tak Centre, 168-200 Connaught Road Central, Hong Kong, Peoples Republic of China.

Telephone +852 2723 6699 **Fax** +852 2723 0123

Website www.asiacruiser.com

Area operated Hong Kong

OMAR III	18455t	1972	18.0k	D2	600p	600p	380c	168.4m	24.0m	6.3m	PA
OMAR STAR	20295t	1992	12.5k	D2	354p	354p	206c	131.2m	32.0m	8.4m	BA

OMAR III was built as the SUN VIKING for the Wilhelmsen Group for its new joint venture, Royal Caribbean Cruise Lines, by Wartsila (yard number 394) at Helsinki, Finland as one of a trio of revolutionary new Caribbean cruise ships. She was the only one of the three ships not to be lengthened in 1978-80. Her ownership was officially transferred to Royal Caribbean in 1991. In 1994 she was sold to Star Cruises and renamed SUPERSTAR SAGITTARIUS, for a new career cruising in South East Asia. In 1998 she was purchased by Hyundai Merchant Marine of Seoul, South Korea and began offering short cruises as the HYUNDAI PONGNAE. This venture was relatively unsuccessful and after a period of lay-up and brief service in China as the PONGNAE, she was sold to Kong Way of Hong Kong. Renamed OMAR III, she is currently marketed under the Asia Cruiser Club banner.

Epirotiki's *Hermes* at Piraeus *(William Mayes)*

Golden Princess Cruises' *Golden Princess* in Hong Kong *(Andrew Kilk)*

OMAR STAR was built by Finnyards (yard number 310) at Rauma, Finland as the RADISSON DIAMOND for Diamond Cruise Line. Conceived for a conference/seminar/incentive tours market, she has had greater success as a cruise ship. She is still the only SWATH cruise vessel. Her owners merged later with Seven Seas Cruises to become Radisson Seven Seas Cruises. She was sold to Asia Cruiser Club in early 2005 with delivery in June, at the end of her time with Radisson Seven Seas Cruises, for use as the gambling ship OMAR STAR in the Hong Kong casino cruise trade.

CAPTAIN JOHN'S

The Company Captain John's is the local name for the JADRAN, owned and operated by Toronto restaurateur John Letnik.

Area operated Static restaurant ship in Toronto, Canada

JADRAN	2564t	1957	90.1m	13.0m	4.7m

JADRAN was built as the second member of a trio of coastal liners for the services of Jadrolinija along the coast of Yugoslavia. She was built by Brodogradiliste at Split to carry 200 berthed and 1000 deck passengers. She also used to cruise in the off-season. In 1975 she was sold to her current owner and converted for use as a static restaurant ship. Her surviving sister is Epirotiki's HERMES (q.v.).

CHARTER LUXURY YACHTS (various owners)

The Company A broker offering charters on these vessels is Afroudakis in Greece.

Address 14 Sirinon Street, Palaio Faliro, 17561 Greece

Telephone +30 210 9813667 **Fax** +30 210 9883595

Website www.afroudakisyachting.com

Area operated Mediterranean Sea

ALEXANDER	5933t	1966	17.0k	D2	54p	54p	60c	122.0m	16.9m	5.8m	MA
CHRISTINA O	1802t	1943	12.0k	D2	36p	36p	32c	99.1m	11.1m	4.1m	PA
OMEGA	1809t	1985	16.0k	D2	32p	32p	21c	74.0m	11.6m	3.8m	GR
RM ELEGANT	1563t	2005	k	D2	p	p	c	72.4m	12.0m	3.4m	GR
TURAMA	7560t	1990	15.0k	D2	52p	52p	60c	116.4m	17.0m	4.4m	MA

ALEXANDER was built by Lubecker Flender Werke (yard number 558), at Lubeck in Germany as the REGINA MARIS, a small cruise ship for Lubeck Line of Germany. As built she had a small garage for about 40 cars. In 1976 she was sold to Canadian owners, who renamed her MERCATOR ONE. She did one season of Caribbean cruises before being arrested for non-payment of debts. She was laid up until late 1979, when she was sold to Peter Deilmann, and renamed FRANKFURT, although when she entered service as an upmarket ship in 1980 she had reverted to her original name. Sun World Cruises of St Louis chartered her in 1982 and used her for a series of cruises on the St Lawrence in Canada. Deilmann again used the REGINA MARIS for a short series of cruises in 1983, following which she was laid up. In October 1983 she was acquired by John S Latsis and then underwent a two-year refit at Bremerhaven, to emerge as the luxury yacht ALEXANDER (named after Latsis' grandson).

CHRISTINA O, the Onassis yacht for more than twenty years began as the Canadian frigate STORMONT. She was acquired by Onassis in 1948 and converted to a yacht. She has now been restored and is available for charter.

OMEGA was built by Mitsubishi Heavy Industries (yard number 883) at Shimonoseki, Japan as the TOSHIMA. She was renamed KIMA in 2001 and took her current name in 2004 when acquired by Omega Cruises.

RM ELEGANT was built by Kanellos Bros (yard number 586) at Perama, Greece for Marinic Marine Co.

TURAMA was built by Rauma (yard number 305) at Rauma in Finland for Delfin Cruises, an investor group from the Finnish Aland Islands, as the DELFIN CARAVELLE. Delivered in June 1990, the ship operated unsuccessfully until October, when the company ceased operations and the ship was returned to her builder. In 1991 she was chartered to Sally Line as the SALLY CARAVELLE to replace the burnt-out SALLY ALBATROS. At the end of 1991 she was chartered to Odessa Cruise Lines, renamed COLUMBUS CARAVELLE and sub-chartered to the German tour operator, Transocean Tours. In 1994 she moved to Singapore to become a gambling ship, marketed as the LIDO STAR, but her name was never officially changed. Following a lay-up in Singapore, she appears to have been renamed ERNEST HEMINGWAY, but was trading out of Hong Kong as the gambling ship CAPTAIN OMAR by January 2000. In 2004 she was bought by Greek owners, rebuilt as a luxury charter yacht and renamed the TURAMA.

COMPAGNIE POLYNESIENNE DE TRANSPORT MARITIME

The Company Compagnie Polynesienne de Transport Maritime is a French Polynesian registered company providing lifeline services to the Marquesas Islands.

Address PO Box 220, Papeete, Tahiti

Telephone +689 426240 **Fax** +689 434889

Website www.aranui.com

Area operated Passenger cargo service between Tahiti and the Marquesas, French Polynesia

ARANUI 3		2500t	2002	15.0k	D1	200p	200p		c	117.0m	17.6m	5.5m	FP

ARANUI 3 was built by Societatia Comerciala Severnav (yard number 170) at Drobeta, Romania for the company's inter-island service in French Polynesia. Her crew is predominantly Marquesian. In addition to her passengers, she can carry up to 3,800 tons of general cargo. The ship's name means Great Highway in Maori, the name of the first ship purchased for this service from a New Zealand owner in 1959.

DEMAR

The Company Demar is a Mexican company.

Area operated Gambling cruises from Mexico

ENCHANTED CAPRI		15410t	1975	21.2k	D2	460p	650p	250c	156.2m	21.8m	5.9m	BA

ENCHANTED CAPRI was built as one of a series of five passenger/ro-ro vessels for the Black Sea Shipping Company by Wartsila (yard number 1221) at Turku, Finland as the AZERBAYDZHAN. She was chartered to CTC. In 1991 she moved from the Soviet flag to that of Ukraine and five years later was renamed ARKADIYA for a charter to Royal Venture Cruises. During the following year she was chartered to Sea Escape under the name ISLAND HOLIDAY. From 1998 she operated for New Commodore Cruise Line as the ENCHANTED CAPRI. That business collapsed in 2000 and the ship was arrested in New Orleans. She subsequently sailed as a gambling ship from Florida and currently operates for Demar.

DREAM SAILING

The Company Dream Sailing is a Monaco based yacht charter broker.

Telephone +33 6 6403 7020

Website www.dreamsailing.co.uk (charter broker) www.ssdelphine.com (owner)

Area operated Based in Monaco

SS DELPHINE		1961t	1921	9.0k	SE2	26p	28p	24c	78.5m	10.8m	4.5m	PO

SS DELPHINE was built by the Great Lakes Engineering Works at River Rouge, Michigan, USA as the private yacht for Horace Dodge, one of the founders of the Dodge vehicle manufacturing business. The DELPHINE was named after his daughter. In 1926, while in New York, she caught fire and sank. She was raised and restored, and in 1942 was acquired by the US Navy, becoming the USS DAUNTLESS, flagship of Admiral Ernest King. At the end of the Second World War, the Dodge family re-acquired the yacht and restored her again. From 1955 to 1967 she was permanently moored, but in that year she was donated to the People to People Health Foundation. In the following year she became the Lundeberg Maryland Steamship School and was renamed DAUNTLESS. In 1986 she was acquired by New York-based Travel Dynamics, with the idea of a full restoration for luxury cruising. That transformation never materialised, and three years later she was sold to Sun Sea Cruises with a similar plan. She was laid up in the Mediterranean until purchased by an investor who had her towed to Bruges, Belgium. The restoration took five years to complete, and in 2003, following a renaming by Princess Stephanie of Monaco, the elegant SS DELPHINE entered service in the Mediterranean luxury yacht charter market.

EGYPTIAN GOVERNMENT

MAHROUSSA		4560t	1865						128.0m	13.0m	m	EG

MAHROUSSA was built as the paddle steamer EL HORRIA. Her paddle wheel was replaced by screw propulsion in 1905, and she eventually served as the Egyptian Royal Yacht until 1952. She is now a static training ship at Alexandria.

EPIROTIKI CRUISE LINES

The Company Company and contact details can be found under Epirotiki in the Ocean Cruise Ships section.

HERMES		‡2174t	1956	18.0k	D2	130p	700p	c	90.1m	13.0m	4.7m	GR

HERMES is now used as a day cruise ship, operating from Piraeus, Greece. Brodogradiliste (yard number 130) built her at Split, in what was then Yugoslavia, as the JUGOSLAVIA for Jadrolinija for coastal work. She was sold in 1971, becoming the MESSAGER and took her present name in 1976 upon passing to Epirotiki. Her registered owner is currently Short Island Cruises Maritime Company.

GEMI KURTARMA DENIZCILIK

The Company Gemi Kurtarma Denizcilik is a Turkish company, which has taken a 49-year charter on the Turkish Government-owned cruise yacht SAVARONA, expiring in 2038. The company charters the vessel out through charter brokers.

Address Setustu Inebolu Sok., Palanduz Apt, No 9/3, 80040 Kabatas, Istanbul, Turkey

Telephone +90 212 245 4761 **Fax** +90 212 245 4763

Area operated Worldwide

SAVARONA		4701t	1931	18.0k	D2	34p	34p	55c	136.0m	17.5m	6.5m	TU

SAVARONA was built by Blohm & Voss in Hamburg, Germany for Mrs Emily Cadwallader, the grand-daughter of John Roebling, the builder of New York's Brooklyn Bridge, as the world's largest private yacht. The ship was sold to the Government of Turkey in 1938, and was briefly used as a presidential yacht for Kemal Ataturk, the ailing president and founder, in 1923, of the Turkish Nation. The ship was eventually converted for use as a training ship and renamed GUNES DIL. She was almost destroyed by fire in 1979, but following the placing of the charter to her current operator, was rebuilt and currently operates where required.

GOLDEN PRINCE CRUISES

The Company Golden Prince Cruises is a Greek operator.

Address Plateia Peiraios Zotou & Marinelli Streets, 71202 Heraklion, Crete, Greece

Telephone +30 2810 341701 **Fax** + 30 2810 341706

Area operated Day cruises from Heraklion

GOLDEN PRINCE		7735t	1973	19.5k	D1	112b	738d	90c	124.9m	17.2m	5.8m	GR

GOLDEN PRINCE was built by KK Usuki Tekkosho (yard number 1165) at Saiki, Japan as the WAKASHIO MARU for local service in Japan. In 1979 she was renamed as the SUN FLOWER 7. She moved to Greek owners, Epirotiki, in 1991 as the APOLLON and was later converted for use as a day cruise ship. Minoan Lines acquired her in 1995, and renamed her PRINCE, later MINOAN PRINCE. She was sold to Golden Prince Cruises in 2002 and renamed GOLDEN PRINCE.

GOLDEN PRINCESS CRUISES

The Company Golden Princess Cruises is a subsidiary of the Hong Kong-based Emperor Group and operates in the casino trade.

Telephone +852 2893-3918 **Fax** + 852 2292-6388

Website www.goldenprincess.com.hk

Area operated Gambling cruises from Hong Kong

GOLDEN PRINCESS		12704t	1967	20.0k	D2	480p	760p	232c	157.7m	21.0m	6.0m	BA

GOLDEN PRINCESS was built as the ferry FINLANDIA by Wartsila (yard number 383) in Helsinki, Finland. She operated as such for both Finlandia Lines and Finnlines. In 1978 she was converted into the cruise ship FINNSTAR for Mediterranean cruising. This was not a success and she was laid up in 1980. I.M. Skaugen of Norway purchased the ship in 1981, and used her for Far Eastern cruises under the name PEARL OF SCANDINAVIA. The ship, and its operating company Pearl Cruises, were sold to Ocean Cruise Lines in 1987. The ship was again rebuilt, this time becoming OCEAN PEARL, but still operating Far Eastern cruises. Ocean Cruise Lines was sold to Paquet Cruises in 1990, who shortened the name to PEARL in 1994. By this time Paquet was owned by the Costa Line, who took the ship over as COSTA PLAYA in 1995, and used her for cruises from Cuba. The venture was short-lived as Costa was purchased by Carnival Corporation, who shut down the Cuban cruises two years later. In 1995 the ship was sold to Hong Kong casino interests who sailed her in the overnight casino trades as ORIENTAL PEARL and JOY WAVE. The Emperor Group purchased the ship in 2000, and have used her as the GOLDEN PRINCESS in the same trade ever since.

GOVERNMENT OF NEWFOUNDLAND AND LABRADOR

The Company The Government of Newfoundland and Labrador runs a fleet of nine vessels, most of which are cargo carriers. The ship listed here is the sole passenger/cargo ship in the fleet that is not a ro-ro.

Address 6th Floor, Confederation Building Complex, St John's Newfoundland, A1C 5T7, Canada

Telephone +1 709 576 3278

Area operated Newfoundland and Labrador coasts

NORTHERN RANGER	2556t	1986	14.0k	D1	46b	86d	34c	71.9m	15.6m	4.2m	CA

NORTHERN RANGER was built by Port Weller Dry Docks (yard number 75) at St Catherine's, Ontario, Canada.

GOVERNMENT OF THE PEOPLE'S REPUBLIC OF CHINA

The Government of the People's Republic of China controls more than 600 ships of various sizes and types, around 80 of which are said to have cabin accommodation for more than 30 passengers. These two companies have been included because of the size of some of the ships that they operate. Insufficient information is currently available on the other 70 or so vessels to make this topic remotely interesting to the reader, so coverage of those vessels is deferred to a later edition.

CHINA SHIPPING CONTAINER LINES

The company China Shipping Container Lines is a Chinese Government owned company operating a fleet of around 150 ships. The ships listed here have a high passenger capacity, but it is not known if this is utilised.

Address 5th Floor, Shipping Tower, 700 Daming Donglu, Shanghai 200080, Peoples Republic of China

Telephone +86 216 596 6984 **Fax** +86 216 596 6495

Area operated Unknown, but likely to be Chinese coastal

ARAFURA LILY	12307t	1995	20.0k	D2	190p	348p	95c	148.2m	22.7m	6.1m	CH
YU JIN XIANG	12304t	1996	20.0k	D2	190p	348p	93c	148.2m	22.7m	6.1m	CH
ZI YU LAN	16071t	1995	20.0k	D2	244p	392p	95c	150.5m	24.0m	7.2m	CH

ARAFURA LILY was built by the De Merwede Shipyard (yard number 668) in Hardinxveld, The Netherlands as the ZI DING XIANG for the Shanghai Hai Xing Shipping Company. She was renamed ARAFURA LILY for a charter in 1996 and appears not to have reverted to her original name.

YU JIN XIANG was built by De Merwede (yard number 667) at Hardinxveld in the Netherlands.

ZI YU LAN was built by MTW Schiffswerft (yard number 161) at Wismar, Germany.

CHINA SHIPPING PASSENGER LINER

The company China Shipping Passenger Liner was formed in 1997 with the merger of Dalian Marine Transport and Shanghai Shipping Passenger Company. Currently around 28 vessels of varying types are in operation. The ships shown here are all cargo/passenger vessels. Unfortunately information on these vessels is rather sketchy.

Address 1 Minzhu Plaza, Zhongshonqu, 116001 Dalian, People's Republic of China

Telephone +86 411 8263 0160 **Fax** +86 411 8263 0160

Area operated China coastal

CHANG BAI	7670t	1980	18.2k	D1	p	p	c	138.0m	17.6m	6.0m	CH
CHANG SHEN	‡5926t	1976	18.2k	D2	p	850p	c	138.0m	17.6m	6.0m	CH
CHANG XIN	‡3857t	1979	16.0k	D1	p	p	c	106.7m	15.8m	3.8m	CH
HAI HUA	13547t	1972	18.5k	D1	p	72p	62c	161.7m	23.1m	9.9m	CH
RONG XIN	‡3857t	1978	16.0k	D1	p	p	c	106.7m	15.8m	3.8m	CH
TIAN HE	‡5492t	1983	k	D2	p	p	c	120.0m	17.0m	5.8m	CH
TIAN HUAI	‡5002t	1983	k	D2	p	948p	c	120.0m	17.0m	5.8m	CH
WANG XIN	‡3858t	1984	16.0k	D2	p	p	c	106.7m	15.8m	3.8m	CH
XI QUE	7160t	1987	k	D2	p	p	c	120.0m	17.0m	5.8m	CH
XIANG XUE LAN	16071t	1996	20.0k	D1	244p	392p	95c	150.5m	24.0m	7.2m	PA
XIN SHANG HAI YOU LUN	‡3857t	1983	16.0k	D2	p	p	c	106.7m	15.8m	3.8m	CH

CHANG BAI and **CHANG SHEN** were built by the Hudong Shipyard in Shanghai, China.

CHANG XIN was built by the Qiuxin Shipyard in Shanghai, China.

Manila Hotel's **Philippines** at Manila *(Jonathan Boonzaier)*

Mercy Ships' **Anastasis** *(William Mayes Collection)*

HAI HUA was built by Cockerill (yard number 861) at Hoboken, Belgium as the FABIOLAVILLE for CMB. She passed to her current owners in 1989 when she was renamed HAI HUA.

RONG XIN was built by the Qiuxin Shipyard in Shanghai, China.

TIAN HE and **TIAN HUAI** were built by the Xingang Shipyard (yard numbers 239 and 238) at Tianjin, China.

WANG XIN was built by the Qiuxin Shipyard in Shanghai, China.

XI QUE was built by the Xingang Shipyard (yard number 250) at Tianjin, China.

XIANG XUE LAN was built by MTW Schiffswerft (yard number 162) at Wismar, Germany.

XIN SHANG HAI YOU LUN was built by the Qiuxin Shipyard in Shanghai, China as the ZHAN XIN. She was renamed in 1998.

JIMEI GROUP

The Company The Jimei Group is a Hong Kong registered company that operates in the casino cruise trade.

Address 3/F Hyde Center, 221 Gloucester Road, Wan Chai, Hong Kong

Telephone +852 2838 8128 **Fax**: + 852 2838 8567

Website www.jimei.com.hk

Area operated Gambling cruises from Hong Kong

JI MEI	5990t	1966	21.0k	D2	412p	614p	c	140.8m	20.0m	5.8m	PA

JI MEI was built by Kieler Howaldtswerke (yard number 1190) as the Jahre Line ferry PRINSESSE RAGNHILD for the Oslo – Kiel service. After brief stints as JALINA and AMETISTA, she was sold to Fujian Xiamen Shipping of China and renamed JIN JIANG in 1981. Used as a ferry between Hong Kong and Xiamen, her name was later changed to JI MEI. In 1998 she was withdrawn from service and chartered to the newly formed Jimei Group to operate in the casino trades. She was given an extensive internal rebuilding when the company bought her outright in 2000. She operates both day and overnight cruises from Hong Kong, as well as a monthly cruise along the Chinese coast.

KOREA TONGHAE SHIPPING

The Company Korea Tonghae Shipping is a company owned by the government of North Korea. Details about the company and its ships are extremely scarce.

Address Pyongyang, North Korea

Area operated North Korea and Japan

MAN GYONG BONG 92	‡9339t	1992	k	D2	208p	p	c	125.1m	20.4m	5.5m	NK
SAM JI YON	‡8315t	1979	k	D2	400p	p	c	129.3m	m	m	NK

MAN GYONG BONG 92 was built by the Chongjin Shipyard in North Korea as a passenger cargo ship. She operates an irregular service between North Korea and Japan.

SAM JI YON is an attractive looking passenger ship that was built in North Korea. She was employed on an irregular passenger service between North Korea and Japan until replaced by the MAN GYONG BONG 92 in 1992. Since then the ship has not been seen outside of North Korean waters. There have been unconfirmed rumours that she is used as a floating retreat for elite members of North Korea's communist party, although her exact status remains unknown.

KOVALEVSKIY BIOLOGICAL INSTITUTE

The Company Kovalevskiy Biological Institute is a Government of the Republic of Ukraine controlled organisation.

Address Prospekt Nakhimova 2, 99011 Sevastopol, Krym, Ukraine

Telephone +380 692 544110 **Fax** +380 692 557813

Area operated It is not known if this ship is currently carrying passengers

PROFESSOR VODYANITSKIY	1498t	1967	14.0k	D1	32p	p	c	68.9m	11.9m	4.2m	UR

PROFESSOR VODYANITSKIY was built by Oy Lavateollisuus (yard number 312) at Turku, Finland for the Ukraine Academy of Sciences, transferring to her current owner in 1994. It is not known if she currently operates passenger sailings.

LOGINN HOTEL

The Company Loginn Hotel is a waterfront hotel in Stockholm, Sweden.

Address Krukmakargatan 20, 11851 Stockholm, Sweden

Telephone +46 8 442 4420 **Fax** +46 8 442 4421

Website www.loginn.se

Area operated Static hotel in Stockholm, Sweden

KRONPRINSESSE MARTHA	906t	1929						58.6m	9.5m	4.2m	SW

KRONPRINSESSE MARTHA was built for Stavanger Steamships for a Norwegian domestic service between Oslo and Bergen by Danziger Werft in Poland as the KRONPRINSESSE MARTHA. In 1934 she saved 553 people from the sinking German luxury liner DRESDEN, off the Norwegian coast. Following the German occupation of Norway she was renamed RYFYLKE, reverting to her original name in 1945. Four years later her steam engine was replaced by a second-hand diesel engine. Following a sinking in 1956, she was completely rebuilt with a rather more modern appearance. She ceased operating along the Norwegian coast in 1974 and for a short time became a static hotel ship at Stavanger, Norway. At the end of that year she was sold for use as a hotel ship in Sweden and renamed KOSTER. Following a major refurbishment in 1979 she became the SPORT VENTURE for West Indies activity cruises. Her owners were declared bankrupt in the following year and she eventually returned to Europe and served for some years as a static casino ship in The Netherlands. In 1987 she was purchased by Magellan Cruises and went to Falmouth, England to be refitted for service in the Caribbean. That venture never materialised and in 1990 she reverted to her original name. In 1998 she became the EMERALD SEA but reverted to KRONPRINSESSE MARTHA in 2001 when she moved back to Sweden to become a hotel ship again.

LYDIA

Address Avenue de la Grande Plage, Le Barcares, Languedoc-Roussillon 66420 France

Area operated Static hotel ship at Le Barcares on the French Mediterranean coast

LYDIA	2696t	1931						91.1m	13.5m	4.8m	FR

LYDIA was built by Burmeister & Wain in Copenhagen, Denmark for the Adelaide Steamship Company as the MOONTA for Australian coastal work from Adelaide. In 1955 she was acquired by Hellenic Mediterranean Lines for service between Marseilles, Greece and the Eastern Mediterranean. For her new role she took the name LYDIA. She was sold to French owners in 1967 and following her engine removal she was permanently moored in a basin at Le Barcares for use as a hotel, nightclub and casino, as part of a larger leisure complex.

MACAU SUCCESS

The Company Macau Success Ltd is a publicly listed Hong Kong company in the travel, finance, entertainment and property sectors. The company operates in the Hong Kong casino ship trade.

Chairman Sonny Yeung Hoi Sing **Executive Directors** William Chan, Cheung Lee Siu

Address Unit 411-413, 4th Floor Tower A, New Mandarin Plaza, 14 Science Museum Road, Tsim Sha Tsui East, Kowloon, Hong Kong, Peoples Republic of China

Telephone +852 3107 1111 **Fax** +852 2303 4489

Website www.macausuccess.com

Area operated Hong Kong

MACAU SUCCESS	9848t	1974	21.0k	D2	474p	509p	200c	130.2m	19.5m	5.3m	BA

MACAU SUCCESS was built by Helsingor Vaerft (yard number 404) at Helsingor, Denmark as the GOLDEN ODYSSEY for the new Royal Cruise Line of Greece. She initially operated cruises in the Mediterranean and later spent winter seasons in South America and the Caribbean Sea. From 1985 she began to spend her winters in South East Asia, and from the following year cruised in Alaskan waters in the summer. In 1989 Royal Cruise Line was sold to Norwegian Cruise Line and although there was little change to the operation, the GOLDEN ODYSSEY was re-flagged to the Bahamas. By 1994 she no longer fitted in with the rest of the fleet and was chartered to Mitsui-OSK Line. Later that year she was sold to Deutsche Seereederie, renamed ASTRA II and chartered to German tour operator Neckermann. She passed to Kong Wing (Asia Cruisers Club) in 2000 and was renamed as the OMAR II for gambling cruises from Hong Kong. She moved to her current operator in 2004 and was renamed MACAU SUCCESS.

MANILA FLOATING HOTEL & RESTAURANT

Address 1000 Corner of San Marcelino Street & United Nations Avenue, Manila, Philippines

Area operated The PHILIPPINES is berthed by the Manila Hotel, Manila, Philippines

PHILIPPINES	27090t	1952	21.0k	D2	1000p	1186p	440c	207.4m	26.6m	8.5m	PH

PHILIPPINES was built by Cantieri Riunite dell'Adriatico (yard number 1757) at Trieste in Italy as the AUGUSTUS for the Italian Line. She was the second major passenger ship to be delivered to the company as part of its post-war rebuilding programme and was immediately placed on the service to South America. Following the loss of the ANDREA DORIA, the AUGUSTUS was transferred to Italia's North Atlantic service in 1957. She returned to the South Atlantic in 1961 following the delivery of the new LEONARDO DA VINCI. She had a long career as a transatlantic liner until she was sold to Emilio Yap, owner of Philippine President Lines, in 1976. The ship then went into a semi-retirement at anchor in various Far Eastern ports. During this time she has had frequent name changes including GREAT SEA, OCEAN KING, PRESIDENT, ASIAN PRINCESS and more recently, PHILIPPINES. Despite almost three decades of lay-up, the ship has always been well maintained and fully crewed. Her only voyages have been occasional private cruises for the Yap family and their friends. In recent years the ship has been tied up at a pier next door to the Manila Hotel, where her public rooms are available for private parties.

MAURITIUS SHIPPING

The Company Mauritius Shipping Corporation is a Government of Mauritius owned operator of two cargo/passenger ships serving Mauritius, Rodriques, Reunion and Madagascar.

Address Suite 417/418 St James Court, St Dennis Street, Port Louis, Mauritius

Telephone +230 210 5944 **Fax** +230 210 5176

Website www.mauritiusshipping.intnet.mu

Area operated Local services in the Indian Ocean from Mauritius

MAURITIUS PRIDE	5234t	1980	14.5k	D2	12b	248d	52c	99.5m	17.0m	6.5m	MU
MAURITIUS TROCHETIA	5492t	2001	14.5k	D2	112p	112p	37c	107.9m	17.5m	6.2m	MU

MAURITIUS PRIDE was built by the Husumer Shipyard (yard number 1505) at Husum, Germany for the company.

MAURITIUS TROCHETIA was built by the Hudong Shipyard (yard number H1260A) at Shanghai, China for the company.

MERCY SHIPS

The Company Mercy Ships, a global charity, has operated a growing fleet of hospital ships in developing nations since 1978. In the organisation's own words 'Following the example of Jesus, Mercy Ships brings hope and healing to the poor, mobilising people and resources worldwide'. The organisation was founded in 1978, with the purchase of the VICTORIA (at a cost of $1m) being completed in October of that year. The ANASTASIS, as the VICTORIA was renamed, is currently the world's largest non-government hospital ship. She was joined in 1994 by the CARIBBEAN MERCY and five years later by the AFRICA MERCY, which is still being refitted as a hospital ship with six operating theatres and an 80-bed ward.

Chief Executive Officer Don Stephens

Address PO Box 2020, Garden Valley, Texas 75771-2020, United States of America

Telephone +1 903 939 7000 **Fax** +1 903 882 0336

Website www.mercyships.org

Area operated Worldwide

AFRICA MERCY	16071t	1980	19.0k	D2	152.0m	22.8m	6.0m	MA
ANASTASIS	11701t	1953	19.5k	D2	159.1m	20.7m	7.2m	MA
CARIBBEAN MERCY	2125t	1952	13.0k	D1	80.0m	12.2m	4.5m	PA

AFRICA MERCY was built by Helsingor Vaerft (yard number 418) at Helsingor, Denmark as one of a trio of Inter-City train ferries for Danske Statsbanner (DSB – Danish State Railways) for service between Korsor and Nyborg on the Great Belt. As the DRONNING INGRID she served until the opening of the Great Belt Bridge in 1997 and was then laid up at Nakskov, Denmark. She was purchased for Mercy Ships, renamed AFRICA MERCY, and has been undergoing conversion on the River Tyne in North East England for some years.

ANASTASIS was built as the VICTORIA for Lloyd Triestino by Cantieri Riunite dell'Adriatico (yard number 1765) at the San Marco shipyard in Trieste, Italy. She was built for the service from Italy to the Far East, which she

MS Georg Buchner at Rostock *(William Mayes)*

The museum ship **Hikawa Maru** at Yokohama *(Andrew Kilk)*

served for fourteen years, before switching to the Karachi service via Cape Town following the closure of the Suez Canal in 1967. Line voyages were on the decline so in 1974, in a reorganisation among the fleets controlled by the mighty Finmare Group, she was transferred to Adriatica for local Mediterranean services and cruising. She only lasted another three years before being laid up. In 1978 she was acquired by the American organisation Youth with a Mission for use as floating church. She was renamed as the ANASTASIS. She was refurbished in Piraeus from 1979 to 1982, when she passed to Mercy Ministries of Malta. In 1990 she was registered under the ownership of Mercy Ships.

CARIBBEAN MERCY was built as the POLARLYS by Aalborg Vaerft (yard number 98) in Aalborg, Denmark for TFDS, one of the Norwegian Coastal Express operators. She passed to Mercy Ships in 1994 and was renamed CARIBBEAN MERCY.

MORSKAYA KOMPANIYA SAKHALIN-KURILY

The Company Morskaya Kompaniya Sakhalin-Kurily is a Government of the Russian Federation controlled company.

Address ul Sovetskaya 111 A, Kholmsk, Sakhalinskaya Oblast, 694620 Russia

Area operated In the Sakhalin region of Eastern Russia, possibly carrying oil workers

IGOR FARKHUTDINOV	4575t	1991	14.3k	D1	150p		p	c	90.0m	17.2m	5.3m	RU
MARINA TSVETAYEVA	4575t	1989	14.3k	D1	150p		p	c	90.0m	17.2m	5.3m	RU

IGOR FARKHUTDINOV was built for Yuzhmorgeologiya as the research vessel NEVA by Stocznia im Komuny Paryskiey (yard number B961/06) at Gdynia, Poland as one of a series of similar research vessels. She was renamed as the ADMIRAL LAZAREV in 1996 and passed to her current owner in 2003 when she took the name IGOR FARKHUTDINOV, honouring the former Governor of the Region of Sakhalin.

MARINA TSVETAYEVA was built by Stocznia im Komuny Paryskiey (yard number B961/03) at Gdynia Poland for Glavmorneft. Marina Tsvetayeva (1892-1941) was a Russian poet, born in Moscow.

MS GEORG BUCHNER

The Company The GEORG BUCHNER is a floating youth hostel, moored in Rostock.

Address Am Stadhafen 72, 18057 Rostock, Germany

Telephone +49 381 6700 320 **Fax** +49 381 6700 321

Area operated Rostock, Germany

GEORG BUCHNER	11060t	1951	153.7m	19.6m	8.4m	GY

GEORG BUCHNER was built by Cockerill (yard number 743) at Hoboken, Belgium as the CHARLESVILLE for Cie Maritime Belge for service from Antwerp to the Belgian Congo and Angola. She was the last ship in a series of five passenger/cargo liners, each with accommodation for around 200 first class passengers. In 1967 she was sold to the East German Merchant Marine for use as a cadet training ship and renamed GEORG BUCHNER, but by 1991 she had become a hotel ship in Rostock. She is named after Georg Buchner (1813-1837), the German author, playwright and academic.

MUSEUM SHIPS

FINNMARKEN	2188t	1956	Hurtigruten ship now at Stokmarknes, Norway
GREAT BRITAIN	3270t	1843	Brunel's famous ship now at Bristol, England
HIKAWA MARU	11622t	1930	Former NYK liner now at Yokohama, Japan
KEEWATIN	3856t	1907	Museum ship at Douglas, MI, USA
MILWAUKEE CLIPPER	4272t	1905	Museum ship at Muskegon, MI, USA

NEW CENTURY CRUISE LINES

The Company New Century Cruise Lines is a Singapore-based casino cruise operator.

Address 51 Ubi Avenue 1, #05-30, Singapore, 408399

Telephone +65 6846 3225 **Fax** +65 6846 6930

Website www.nctoursonline.com

Area operated Singapore and Malaysia

AMUSEMENT WORLD	12764t	1967	18.0k	D2	635p	635p		c	141.2m	22.5m	5.5m	BA
LEISURE WORLD	15653t	1969	16.0k	D2	580p	850p		c	160.3m	22.8m	6.3m	BA

LEISURE WORLD I	4077t	1989	16.0k	D2	100p	111p	c	88.3m	15.3m	4.0m	MY

NOTE: New Century ships carry a significant number of day cruise passengers who do not occupy cabins. Their numbers are not factored into above statistics. Furthermore, the ships have very large casino staffs. Some of these occupy passenger cabins, while others commute to the ships by ferry on a daily basis.

AMUSEMENT WORLD was built as Swedish Lloyd's ferry PATRICIA for service between the UK and Spain, by AB Lindholmens Varv (yard number 1095) in Gothenburg, Sweden. She was sold to Stena Line and became STENA OCEANIC in 1978. Since then she has sailed for numerous operators in a variety of roles under the names STENA SAGA, LION QUEEN, CROWN PRINCESS VICTORIA, PACIFIC STAR and SUN FIESTA. She was sold to New Century in 1997, and operated briefly as PUTRI BINTANG before becoming the casino ship AMUSEMENT WORLD. She operates mainly out of Penang in Malaysia. The ship made headlines in December 2000, when police in Singapore discovered the karaoke lounge was also being operated as a brothel.

LEISURE WORLD was built by AG Weser Werk Seebeck (yard number 942) at Bremerhaven, Germany as the SKYWARD for Klosters Rederi, Oslo (Norwegian Caribbean Cruise Line) for cruising in the Caribbean Sea. She was sold for Asian cruising in 1991 as the SHANGRI-LA WORLD and during the following year became the ASEAN WORLD. Later in 1992 she was renamed as the FANTASY WORLD, then in 1993 as the CONTINENTAL WORLD. Later in 1993 she became the LEISURE WORLD for gambling cruises. She continues to operate in this trade and is usually anchored in international waters off Singapore, with gamblers shuttled to and fro by high speed ferry.

LEISURE WORLD I was built as the RENAISSANCE for Renaissance Cruises by Cantieri Navale Ferrari (yard number 43) at La Spezia, Italy. Her career with the line was short-lived as she was placed on long term charter to casino cruise operator Universal Cruise Lines of Singapore two years later. Universal later bought the ship outright and renamed her THE MERCURY. She was laid up when Universal went bankrupt in 2002. Ownership then passed to a Malaysian company called Viking Lines, who continued to keep the ship in lay-up until she was sold to New Century at the beginning of 2004. She operates overnight casino cruises from Singapore and ports in Malaysia as the LEISURE WORLD I.

NOVOSHIP

The Company Novoship is a major Russian ship owner, operating a fleet of about 70 ships, mainly tankers and bulk carriers. The company also operates a single passenger vessel linking the Russian port of Novorossiysk with Istanbul in Turkey.

President Tagir Izmaylov

Address ul Svobody 1, 353900 Novorossiysk, Krasnodarskiy Kray, Russia

Telephone +7 8617 601684 **Fax** +7 8617 601060

Website www.novoship.ru

Area operated The Black Sea

MARIYA YERMOLOVA	4364t	1974	17.0k	D2	206p	262p	c	100.0m	16.2m	4.7m	RU

MARIYA YERMOLOVA was one of a series of eight ships built by Brodogradiliste Titovo (yard number 406) at Kraljevica, in what was then Yugoslavia, for the Murmansk Shipping Company. Other vessels were delivered to other Russian operating companies.

OCEAN FIVE

The Company Ocean Five is a trading name of King Crown International, a newly formed Taiwanese cruise line that is scheduled to begin service in 2005.

Website http://www.gogojp.com.tw/royalpacific/ship-index.htm#

Area operated Cruises from Keelung in Taiwan to ports in Japan

ROYAL PACIFIC	9805t	1967	20.0k	D2	486p	p	c	130.6m	19.2m	5.4m	PA

ROYAL PACIFIC was built by Union Naval de Levante (yard number 94) at Valencia, Spain as the Spanish ferry LAS PALMAS DE GRAN CANARIA and was operated by Trasmediterranea until laid up in 1984. She then underwent a long conversion into the cruise ship CROWN DEL MAR and was operated by Crown Cruise Lines between 1988 and 1990. After a further extended lay up, she was re-acquired by Trasmediterranea in 1994 and used by their subsidiary Royal Hispana Cruises for Mediterranean cruises under the name DON JUAN. Success was again elusive and she was laid up until being sold to Naviera Tapias in 2000, who renamed her RIVIERA I. The only employment the ship managed to obtain was a short-lived charter to Toronto-based World Cruise Co. The ship was scheduled to do several world cruises, but only made it as far as Tahiti before World Cruise Co collapsed. The ship returned to Spain where she was laid up. In late 2004 she was sold to King Crown, who plan to use her for short cruises out of Taiwan as the ROYAL PACIFIC, aimed primarily at the gambling market.

New Century Cruise Lines' *Leisure World I* (Jonathan Boonzaier)

New Century Cruise Lines' *Leisure World* (Jonathan Boonzaier)

OGASAWARA KAIUN

The Company Ogasawara Kaiun Co Ltd is a Japanese company.

Address Asahi Building, 29-19 Shiba 5-chome, Minato-ku, Tokyo 108, Japan

Telephone +81 3 3451 5171 **Fax** +81 3 3541 4522

Website www.ogasawarakaiun.co.jp

Area operated Long distance Japanese domestic service from Tokyo

OGASAWARA MARU	‡6679t	1997	22.5k	D2	198b	833d	49c	131.0m	17.2m	5.7m	JP

OGASAWARA MARU was built by Mitsubishi Heavy Industries (yard number 1030) in Japan. She is a passenger and cargo vessel, serving the long route south from Tokyo to Bonin Island. She is likely to be replaced by a large ro-ro catamaran in 2005.

OPERATION MOBILIZATION

The Company Operation Mobilisation is a missionary organisation taking its floating bookshops to the ports of the world. The first ship, the UMANAC was purchased from the Danish Government in 1970 and became the LOGOS. The DOULOS joined the fleet in 1977 and the LOGOS II was purchased as a replacement for the LOGOS, which was lost after running onto rocks in South America in 1988.

International Director and Founder George Verwer

Address Postfach 1561, D74819 Mosbach, Germany

Telephone +49 6261 9470

Website www.omships.org

Area operated Worldwide

DOULOS	6804t	1914	13.0k	D1				130.4m	16.5m	5.6m	MA
LOGOS II	4804t	1968	10.0k	D2				105.9m	16.1m	5.1m	MA
LOGOS HOPE	12252t	1973	22.0k	D2				129.0m	20.8m	4.9m	FA

DOULOS was built by the Newport News Shipbuilding and Dry Dock Company (yard number 176) as the cargo ship MEDINA for the US East Coast to Gulf of Mexico service of the Mallory Steamship Company. This unremarkable little ship survived both world wars and was sold in 1948 for conversion as an emigrant ship for the trade from Europe to Australia. Renamed as the ROMA she carried 287 first class passengers and almost 700 in tourist class. Costa Line purchased the ship in 1952 and she was rebuilt as that company's FRANCA C. Modern Fiat diesels replaced her coal-fired boilers and triple expansion steam engine. She ran between Italy and South America until 1959, following which she was used for cruising. Re-engined again in 1970, she cruised for a further seven years before, at the age of 63, she passed to Operation Mobilisation and was renamed DOULOS for use as a Christian missionary ship and floating bookshop. Doulos is Greek for servant.

LOGOS II was built as the Spanish ferry ANTONIO LAZARO by Union Naval de Levante (yard number 100) at Valencia, Spain for Cia. Trasmediterranea's Mediterranean Sea car ferry services. She was acquired by Operation Mobilisation in 1988 and renamed ARGO. Later that year she was renamed again as the LOGOS II.

LOGOS HOPE was built by Werft Nobiskrug (yard number 678) at Rendsburg, Germany as the GUSTAV VASA for Saga Line's Baltic Sea car ferry services. In 1983 Smyril Line of the Faeroes bought her and she was renamed NORRONA for her long journeys between Denmark and Torshavn and Iceland. On the delivery of a new NORRONA she was renamed NORRONA 1 and laid up in Esbjerg, Denmark. OM acquired her in 2004 and she is currently in Malta awaiting a decision on where she will go to be refitted. She is now named LOGOS HOPE.

ORIANA

The Company Oriana is operated by the Hangzhou Songchen Group as a tourist and leisure attraction.

Area operated Dalian China

ORIANA	‡41915t	1960	27.0k	D2				245.1m	30.5m	9.6m	CH

ORIANA was the last in a long line of Orient Liners, laid down in September 1957 by Vickers Armstrong (Shipbuilders) Ltd (yard number 1061) at Barrow-in-Furness, England. Her Royal Highness Princess Alexandra launched the ORIANA on November 3, 1959. During trials she achieved a speed of 30.64 knots, but once in service the company was happy with a speed of 27.5 knots, shaving a week off the voyage to Australia. The Orient Steam Navigation Company was fully merged with the Peninsular & Oriental Steam Navigation Company to become P&O – Orient Lines in 1960. The ORIANA enjoyed a period of 14 years sailing between the UK and Australia on regular line voyages, but as the years progressed she was employed more and more on cruising. From 1973 she was used almost exclusively for cruising, initially still as a two class ship, but from 1974 as a

Novoship's **Mariya Yermolova** at Istanbul *(William Mayes)*

Ocean Five's **Royal Pacific** *(Arturo Mazorra)*

Operation Mobilisation's **Doulos** at Southampton *(William Mayes)*

Oriana at Southampton during her days with P&O *(William Mayes Collection)*

one-class vessel. In 1981, the ORIANA sailed from Southampton for the last time to begin a new career based in Australia. She operated until 1986, when she was withdrawn from service in the face of competition from Sitmar, CTC and others. She was sold to Japanese interests to become a hotel and museum ship at Beppu Bay, Japan. The venture was not particularly successful and she was sold to Chinese interests in 1995 and used for three years as a Chinese Government accommodation ship. In 1998 she was sold to become a tourist attraction in Shanghai. She was opened to the public in February 1999, but closed within 18 months as she was not meeting her costs. She was acquired by Hangzhou Songchen Group at auction and towed to Dalian where she became a tourist attraction again. During a storm in June 2004 she partially capsized, having taken on a great deal of water. Current reports suggest that she is now almost upright again but will need a great deal of money spent on her to bring her back into service.

PACIFIC SEAWAYS

The Company Pacific Seaways is a subsidiary of Care Offshore.

Address L'Oujonnet, PO Box 5, 1195 Bursinel, Switzerland

Area operated Unknown

KAY		4575t	1990		D1	150p	150p		c	122.0m	17.6m	5.3m	SV

KAY was built by Stocznia im. Komuny Paryskiej (yard number B961/05) at Gdynia, Poland as the VLADIMIR CHIVILIKHIN for Dalryba. She later passed to Vladivostok Trawling and in 1998 was registered as the KAY for Falkland Investments. Her current owner acquired her in 1999. Her current use is unknown, but she may be in use as transport for oil workers.

PALM BEACH CASINO LINE

The Company Palm Beach Casino line

Address One East 11th Street, Riviera Beach, Florida 33404, United States of America

Telephone +1 561 845 SHIP

Website www.pbcasino.com

Area operated Gambling cruises from Palm Beach, Florida

PALM BEACH PRINCESS	6659t	1964	17.0k	D2	850p			128.3m	16.4m	4.4m	PA

PALM BEACH PRINCESS was built by Wartsila (yard number 375) at Helsinki, Finland as the ILMATAR for Finska Angfartygs of Helsinki for its passenger and car ferry service from that city to Stockholm. From her earliest days, in addition to her ferry duties, she operated short cruises in the Baltic. In 1970, she appeared in Silja Line livery for the first time, although her owner had been trading as part of the Silja consortium for some years. For a change of route, and a greater emphasis on cruising she was sent to Germany in 1973 for lengthening by about 20 metres, and for the installation of additional engines. She re-entered service, now trading between Helsinki and Travemunde as a three-screw vessel, and almost three knots faster than previously. Finska withdrew from the route in 1975 and the ILMATAR was used principally as a cruise ship. She was sold to Norwegian owners in 1980, but continued to offer a similar range of cruises encompassing the Baltic and Norway in summer and the Mediterranean and Atlantic Isles in winter. Her new owners were less than successful and she was laid up in 1982. Two years later she was sold to Grundstad Maritime Overseas to run gambling cruises from California, as the VIKING PRINCESS. She later moved to Florida where she continues to operate in a similar role as the PALM BEACH PRINCESS.

PEACEBOAT ORGANISATION

The Company Peace Boat is a Japan-based non-government and non-profit organisation, founded in 1983, that works to promote peace, human rights, equality, sustainable development and environmental protection.

Address 2F 3-14-3 Takadanobaba, Shinjuku, Tokyo 169-0075 Japan

Telephone +81 3 33638047 **Fax** +81 3 33637562

Website www.peaceboat.org

Area operated Three world cruises plus shorter Asian voyages annually

THE TOPAZ	32327t	1956	20.0k	ST2	1600p	1600p	500c	195.1m	25.9m	8.8m	PA

THE TOPAZ was built by the Fairfield Shipbuilding and Engineering Company Ltd (yard number 731) at Govan on the River Clyde in Scotland as the EMPRESS OF BRITAIN for Canadian Pacific Steamships' services from Liverpool to Montreal, and Greenock to Quebec. She was launched by Her Majesty Queen Elizabeth II on 22 June 1955 and sailed on her maiden voyage in April 1956. In 1964 she was sold to Greek Line and became the QUEEN ANNA MARIA, and following a major refit at the Mariotti Shipyard in Genoa she entered service between the

Mediterranean and New York. She was later used exclusively for cruising and in 1975 Carnival Cruise Lines acquired her, when she became that company's second ship, the CARNIVALE. Displaced by new tonnage in 1993 she was renamed FIESTA MARINA for service with Fiestamarina Cruises of Nassau, The Bahamas, but the following year was transferred to Epirotiki Lines as the OLYMPIC for Mediterranean cruising for the short-lived joint venture with Carnival. In 1998 she became THE TOPAZ for Topaz International Shipping of Piraeus and was chartered to the then British tour operator, Thomson Holidays. At the end of her service with Thomson, she was chartered by the Peaceboat Organization in June 2003 without a change of name.

PT PELNI

The Company PT PELNI (PT Pelayaran Nasional Indonesia) was established in 1952 as a direct competitor to the Dutch Koninklijke Paketvaart Maatshaappij, and eventually as the sole operator of passenger liner services within Indonesia. The company is state owned and serves more than 100 ports in 24 provinces of this 17,000-island nation. The company also operates some smaller vessels without overnight berths, and a number of ro-ro ferries. The relationship with the Meyer shipyard began in 1959, when five traditional passenger/cargo vessels were constructed for the company. That relationship was substantially strengthened following a shipping disaster off the Indonesian coast in 1981, after which the Government began a major modernisation programme for the PT PELNI fleet.

President M Husseyn Umar

Address Jl. Gajah Mada 14, Jakarta 10130, Indonesia

Telephone +62 21 6385 7747 **Fax** +62 21 6386 4837

Website www.pelni.co.id

Area operated Indonesian local passenger services

AWU	6041t	1991	D2	14.0k	54b	915d	84c	99.8m	18.0m	4.2m	IN
BINAIYA	6022t	1994	D2	15.0k	54b	915d	84c	100.0m	18.0m	4.2m	IN
BUKIT RAYA	6041t	1994	D2	14.0k	54b	915d	84c	99.8m	18.0m	4.2m	IN
BUKIT SIGUNTANG	14701t	1996	D2	20.3k	416b	1557d	147c	146.5m	23.4m	5.9m	IN
CIREMAI	14610t	1993	D2	20.0k	416b	1557d	145c	146.5m	23.4m	5.9m	IN
DOBONSOLO	14610t	1993	D2	20.0k	420b	1557d	145c	146.5m	23.4m	5.9m	IN
DORO LONDA	14739t	2001	D2	22.4k	104b	2066d	147c	146.5m	23.4m	5.9m	IN
KAMBUNA	13944t	1984	D2	20.0k	1096b	500d	119c	144.8m	23.4m	5.9m	IN
KELIMUTU	5684t	1986	D2	14.0k	54b	866d	84c	99.8m	18.0m	4.2m	IN
KELUD	14716t	1998	D2	22.4k	416b	1557d	157c	146.5m	23.4m	5.9m	IN
KERINCI	13854t	1983	D2	20.0k	1096b	500d	119c	144.8m	23.4m	5.9m	IN
LABOBAR	15136t	2004	D2	22.4k	66b	3084d	161c	146.5m	23.4m	5.9m	IN
LAMBELU	14701t	1997	D2	20.3k	416b	1557d	147c	146.5m	23.4m	5.9m	IN
LAWIT	5684t	1986	D2	14.0k	54b	866d	84c	99.8m	18.0m	4.2m	IN
LEUSER	6041t	1994	D2	15.0k	54b	915d	84c	99.8m	18.0m	4.2m	IN
NGGAPULU	14800t	2002	D2	22.4k	104b	2102d	155c	145.6m	23.4m	5.9m	IN
RINJANI	13860t	1984	D2	20.0k	1096b	500d	119c	144.8m	23.4m	5.9m	IN
SINABUNG	14716t	1997	D2	20.0k	508b	1398d	147c	146.5m	23.4m	5.9m	IN
SIRIMAU	6041t	1995	D2	15.0k	54b	915d	84c	99.8m	18.0m	4.2m	IN
TATAMAILAU	6041t	1990	D2	15.0k	54b	915d	84c	99.8m	18.0m	4.2m	IN
TIDAR	13888t	1988	D2	20.0k	416b	1488d	145c	144.0m	23.4m	5.9m	IN
TILONGKABILA	6041t	1995	D2	14.0k	54b	915d	84c	99.8m	18.0m	4.2m	IN
UMSINI	13853t	1985	D2	20.0k	1096b	500d	119c	144.0m	23.4m	5.9m	IN

All of the above ships were built by Jos. L Meyer at Papenburg, Germany for PT Pelni.

Key: b = berthed passengers d = deck passengers

RMS QUEEN MARY HOTEL & CONVENTION CENTRE

The Company RMS Foundation is a non-profit foundation, managing the QUEEN MARY. It has been reported recently that the leaseholder, and owner of RMS Foundation, has filed for Chapter 11 protection.

Address 1126 Queens Highway, Long Beach, California 90802, United States of America

Telephone +1 562 435 3511 **Fax** +1 562 437 4531

Website www.queenmary.com

Area operated Static hotel and exhibition centre at Long Beach, California, USA

The **Queen Mary** at Long Beach *(Miles Cowsill)*

The **Rotterdam** in Southampton in the late 1960's *(William Mayes Collection)*

Sea Escape Cruises' *Island Adventure* at Port Everglades *(Andrew Kilk)*

QUEEN MARY	‡81237t	1936	28.5k	ST4			310.7m	36.0m	12.0m	US

QUEEN MARY was first conceived in the late 1920's as Cunard planned its next generation of express Atlantic liners. The order was placed with John Brown & Company, Clydebank, Scotland for what was known as yard number 534 on May 28, 1930. Construction began in December of that year, but within twelve months work had stopped due to the Depression. Eventually, the British Government was prepared to make a loan to allow the completion of the ship, on condition that Cunard and White Star Line were merged. The Government held a 'Golden Share' in order to prevent the company being acquired by foreign interests. Cunard White Star Limited was formed on January 1, 1934 and work on the partially completed ship resumed in April. The QUEEN MARY was launched by Her Majesty Queen Mary on September 26, 1934 and was handed over to Cunard White Star on May 12, 1936. On her sixth round trip she won the coveted Blue Riband from the NORMANDIE, but that ship took it back in 1937. In 1938 the QUEEN MARY regained the title and then held it for fourteen years until she lost it to the UNITED STATES in 1952. She saw impressive war service as a troop transport, carrying up to 10,000 troops at a time. She returned to peacetime transatlantic service in 1946 and continued until September 1967. She was sold to the City of Long Beach for use as a hotel ship and tourist attraction. The City spent a fortune renovating the ship, but her location, some distance from the main waterfront left her somewhat isolated. In 1988 the giant Walt Disney Corporation acquired the company that then held the lease on the ship. Disney disowned the ship in 1991 and her management moved into other hands. The current leaseholder, Queen's Seaport Development, filed for Chapter 11 protection in early 2005 due to falling income.

ROGALAND SJOASPIRANTSKOLE

The Company Rogaland Sjoaspirantskole is a maritime training institution.

Address Tommerodden, 4085 Hundvag, Norway

Telephone +47 5154 7558 **Fax** +47 5186 1885

Website www.gann.no

Area operated Norway

GANN	2191t	1956	14.0k	D1		81.3m	12.6m	4.5m	NO

GANN was built as the Hurtigruten ship RAGNVALD JARL by Blohm & Voss (yard number 789) in Hamburg, Germany for NFDS. That business was absorbed into TFDS in 1989 and the ship was sold six years later to become the maritime training ship GANN.

SEA ESCAPE CRUISES

The Company Sea Escape Cruises is a Florida based operator of gambling cruises.

Address 3045 N Federal Highway, Fort Lauderdale, Florida 33306, United States of America

Telephone +1 954 453 2200 **Fax** +1 954 453 6555

Website www.seaescape.com

Area operated Gambling cruises from Fort Lauderdale, Florida, USA

ISLAND ADVENTURE	15409t	1976	20.0k	D2	585p	p	c	156.3m	21.8m	5.9m	BA

ISLAND ADVENTURE was built by Wartsila (yard number 1222) at Helsinki, Finland as the KAZAKHSTAN, the fourth in a series of five ships for the Black Sea Shipping Company of the Soviet Union. She was renamed UKRAINA in 1994 for Blasco UK as her owners were then styled. In 1996 she became the ROYAL SEAS for Chastnaya Kompaniya Globus of Odessa and was chartered to Royal Seas Cruise Line of Florida. She reverted to the name UKRAINA in 1997 and was subsequently chartered to Sea Escape Cruises, taking the name ISLAND ADVENTURE.

SEA WORLD LTD

The Company Sea World Ltd is a Hong Kong-Chinese joint venture operating this ship as a static hotel in Shekou, China.

Area operated Static hotel ship at Shekou, near Shenzhen, China

MINGHUA	14225t	1962		500p		168.8m	21.8m	6.6m	CH

MINGHUA was built by Chantiers de l'Atlantique (yard number M21) at St Nazaire, France as the four-class passenger liner ANCERVILLE for Paquet Lines and operated between Marseilles and ports in French West Africa. In 1970 she was transferred to Nouvelle Compagnie de Paquebots of Marseilles. She was sold to the China Ocean Shipping Company of Guangzhou in 1973 and used on a trade between China and East Africa, as the MINGHUA, carrying mainly railway construction workers and technicians. She was laid up in 1977, but returned to service in 1979 on charters to several Australian interests, who used her for South Pacific cruises out of Sydney. This lasted until February 1983, when she returned to China for lay-up. In 1984 she was sold to a newly formed Hong Kong-Chinese joint venture company called Sea World Ltd, which converted her into a floating hotel in Shekou, near Shenzhen. Nearby land reclamation projects resulted in the sea surrounding the ship being filled in, leaving the ship marooned in the middle of a park, several hundred metres from the sea. The ship was recently given an extensive renovation and continues to serve as a restaurant, entertainment and banqueting facility.

SEMESTER AT SEA

The Company The Institute for Shipboard Education or Semester at Sea began operating in 1977 aboard the UNIVERSE in conjunction with the University of Colorado. In 1981, the present relationship with the University of Pittsburgh began, using the same ship. She was scrapped in India in 1996 and replaced by the UNIVERSE EXPLORER, built in 1958 as Moore McCormack Lines' BRASIL. When she was sold for scrap in 2004 a fast modern ship, the EXPLORER, was acquired to continue the tradition of the 'university at sea'. These voyages are only available to students that can meet the entry requirements. Meals are served cafeteria style and the students are responsible for most of the housekeeping, leading to a requirement for fewer crew than might be expected on a ship of this size.

Address 811 William Pitt Union, Pittsburgh, Philadelphia 15620 United States of America

Website www.semesteratsea.com

Area operated Three annual round the world voyages

EXPLORER	24318t	2001	28.0k	D2	630s	630s	196c	180.4m	25.5m	7.3m	BA

EXPLORER was built by Blohm & Voss (yard number 962) in Hamburg, Germany, as the OLYMPIC EXPLORER for Royal Olympic Cruises. She was designed with a high speed to operate the company's new 'Three Continents in Seven Days' itinerary. Political unrest and worse in the Middle East caused the abandonment of that programme and the ship was used on more mundane itineraries in the Mediterranean and Caribbean Seas. Ludicrously, after pressure from the Olympic organisation in the run-up to the Athens Olympic Games, the company re-styled itself as Royal Olympia Cruises and the ship was renamed OLYMPIA EXPLORER. The company within ROC that owned the ship filed for bankruptcy in 2003, later bringing down the whole group. She was laid up and later auctioned, being purchased by Stella Maritime and becoming the EXPLORER for Semester at Sea.

SEVASTOPOL PORT AUTHORITY

The Company Sevastopol Port Authority is a Government of Ukraine controlled organisation.

Address Prospekt Nakhimova 5, 335031 Sevastopol, Krym, Ukraine

Area operated Black Sea

KIYEV	7510t	1982		D1	72p	72p	c	110.0m	17.3m	7.2m	UR

KIYEV was built by Sudostroitelnyy Zavod Okean (yard number 201) at Nikolaev, Ukraine as the AKADEMIK ALEKSEY KRYLOV for the Russian Government Ministry of Shipbuilding. She became the KIYEV in 1992 when she was transferred to the Black Sea Institute. She was acquired by her current owner in 2004 and her current use is not known.

SHIPPING CORPORATION OF INDIA

The Company The Shipping Corporation of India, an Indian Government controlled company, was formed in 1961 with the merger of the Eastern Steamship Corporation and the Western Steamship Corporation. The company currently controls about 100 ships including a number of smaller passenger vessels and some ro-ro ferries.

Managing Director P K Srivastava

Address Shipping House, 245 Madam Cama Road, Mumbai 400-021, India

Telephone +91 22 202 6666 **Fax** +91 22 202 6905

Website www.shipindia.com

Area operated Indian Ocean, Andaman and Nicobar Islands

HARSHA VARDHANA	‡8871t	1974	17.0k	D1	753b	d	c	132.6m	21.5m	7.0m	ID
NANCOWRY	14176t	1992	15.5k	D2	300b	900d	119c	157.0m	20.1m	6.7m	ID
NICOBAR	14195t	1991	15.5k	D2	300b	900d	119c	157.0m	20.1m	6.7m	ID

HARSHA VARDHANA was built at the Magazon Dock (yard number 272) in Mumbai, India.

NANCOWRY was built in Szczecin, Poland by Stocznia Szczecinska (yard number B561/02).

NICOBAR was built by Stocznia Szczecinska (yard number B561/01) in Szczecin, Poland.

SINOKOR MERCHANT MARINE

The Company Sinokor Merchant Marine is a Korean container ship operator established in 1989, predominant in the trades between Korea, China and other countries of South East Asia. It operates a large fleet of container ships, including the GOLDEN TRADE, which previously carried passengers.

Address 3Fl Dongsung Building, 17-7 4ka Namdaemun-Ro, Chung-ko, Seoul, Korea

Telephone +82 2 772 8494 **Fax** +82 2 774 8483

Website www.sinokor.co.kr

Area operated South East Asia – but may not be carrying passengers

GOLDEN TRADE	19203t	1988	18.3k	D1	104p	110p	44c	176.7m	26.0m	9.5m	BA

GOLDEN TRADE was built by Hyundai Heavy Industries (yard number 464) at Ulsa, Korea as the AMERICANA for Ivaran Lines service between New York and South America. She has passed through a number of owners before arriving with Sinokor in 2004 and taking the new name GOLDEN TRADE.

SORLANDETS SEILENDE SKOLESKIBS

The Company Sorlandets Seilende Skoleskibs is the Norwegian operator of the training ship SJOKURS.

Address Tollbodgata 2, 4611 Kristiansand S, Norway

Area operated Norway

SJOKURS	1432t	1950	14.0k	D1				67.6m	11.0m	4.8m	NO

SJOKURS was built by Nylands Verksted (yard number 374) at Oslo, Norway as the passenger vessel SANDNES. She was renamed VIKINGFJORD in 1974 and was acquired by the Rogaland Sjoaspirantskole who renamed her GANN. Her current owner acquired her in 1995 and renamed her SJOKURS.

SS ROTTERDAM

The Company The SS ROTTERDAM is owned by the Dutch company SS Rembrandt BV, itself now owned by the City of Rotterdam. Negotiations are underway with commercial organisations with a view to acquiring and operating the ship in Rotterdam. The front-runner appears to be Hotel Cruiseship Operations 2 BV.

Area operated Static hotel and conference centre in Rotterdam eventually, but currently in Gibraltar

ROTTERDAM	39674t	1959	21.5k	ST2				228.2m	28.7m	9.0m	BA

ROTTERDAM was built by the Rotterdam Dry Dock Company (yard number 300) in Rotterdam, The Netherlands as the flagship for Holland America Line's transatlantic service. In later years she was used exclusively as a cruise ship. Carnival acquired Holland America Line in 1988, and the ROTTERDAM continued to serve her new owners, developing a very loyal following. In 1997, she no longer met SOLAS requirements and was withdrawn from service, but quickly snapped-up by Premier Cruise Lines, upgraded and renamed REMBRANDT. She was later going to be renamed BIG RED BOAT IV, but the outcry led to her keeping her name. Premier Cruise Lines failed in 2000 and the REMBRANDT was laid up. She was eventually acquired by Dutch interests with a view to returning her to Rotterdam as a static exhibit and hotel ship. The REMBRANDT was towed to Gibraltar in 2004 for some preliminary work, including asbestos removal, to be carried out. She is expected to return to her birthplace in spring 2005, again named ROTTERDAM.

Peaceboat's **The Topaz** at Dover *(John Hendy)*

St Helena Shipping's **St Helena** at Cardiff *(William Mayes)*

ST HELENA SHIPPING COMPANY

The Company The St Helena Shipping Company was managed from the outset by the Cornish business, Curnow Shipping. The St Helena Shipping Company was formed in 1977 to fill the gap left when the Union Castle Mail Steamship Company ceased to operate passenger ships between the United Kingdom and South Africa (with regular calls at the island of St Helena). The first ST HELENA was a small former Canadian coastal passenger/cargo ship previously named the NORTHLAND PRINCE. She entered service in 1977 and continued until the new ST HELENA was delivered in 1990. During the Falklands War, the first ST HELENA was requisitioned for use as a mother ship for the minesweepers of the Royal Navy. Her temporary replacement was the former Blue Funnel passenger and cargo ship CENTAUR. In 2001 Curnow Shipping lost the contract to manage the ST HELENA and the current managers are Andrew Weir Shipping. The island of St Helena, one of 13 remaining United Kingdom Overseas Territories, will have an airport built by 2010.

Address Andrew Weir Shipping Ltd, Dexter House, 2 Royal Mint Court, London, EC3N 4XX, England

Telephone +44 207 575 6480 **Fax** +44 207 575 6200

Website www.rms-st-helena.com

Area operated South African ports to St Helena, Ascension Island and Tristan da Cunha, with occasional voyages to the UK

ST HELENA	6767t	1990	14.5k	D2	98p	128p	58c	105.0m	19.2m	6.0m	UK

ST HELENA is the last British example of a true working passenger and cargo ship, ordered from the Aberdeen shipyard of Hall Russell in 1987, but completed by A&P Appledore in October 1990 after the collapse of the Scottish builder. She was built as a replacement for the former (smaller) ship of the same name to provide the lifeline service to the island of St Helena, once the staging post for the ships of the British East India Company. Following initial mechanical problems, she has served the Island well for the past 15 years. From 2005 her UK calls are limited to two each year with most voyages linking Cape Town to the island. The ST HELENA is the sole remaining true Royal Mail Ship.

ST TROPEZ CASINO CRUISES

The Company St Tropez Casino Cruises is a Florida based casino ship operator.

Website www.sttropezcasinocruises.com

Area operated Gambling cruises from Port Everglades, Florida

ST TROPEZ	9511t	1974	17.0k	D2				132.0m	19.8m	5.3m	BA

ST TROPEZ was built by the Kynossoura Dockyard Company at Salamis, Greece as the CASTALIA for Hellenic Mediterranean Lines, a larger version of the elegant little AQUARIUS. In 1988 she became the PRIDE OF SAN DIEGO for Sea Escape Cruises, and she later sailed as the TROPIC STAR II. In 1995 she was renamed STENA ARCADIA for Stena America Line and subsequently carried the names EMERALD EMPRESS, SOFIA, ENCHANTED SUN, TALISMAN and MANISTAL before taking her current name in 2003.

STERLING CASINO LINES

The Company Sterling Casino Lines is a Florida based casino operator.

Address 101 George King Boulevard, Suite 3, Cape Canaveral, Florida 32920, United States of America

Telephone +1 800 765 5711 **Fax** +1 321 783 2243

Website www.sterlingcasinolines.com

Area operated Cape Canaveral, Florida, USA

AMBASSADOR II	11940t	1970	20.0k	D2				134.0m	20.8m	4.9m	BA

AMBASSADOR II had her first incarnation as the PRINS OBERON. Built for Sweden's Lion Ferry by Nobiskrug Werft (yard number 663) at Rendsburg, Germany, she entered service on charter to Prinzenlinien on its Bremerhaven, Germany to Harwich, England service. She was sold to her operator in 1978 and continued to serve her North Sea route. Following the closure of the service she undertook a number of charters before becoming Transnordic Line's NORDIC SUN. In 1986 she was renamed CRUISE MUHIBAH for cruising service from Malaysia. She came back to Europe three years later and joined B & I Line in Dublin as the MUNSTER for Irish Sea ferry service. She was sold to New Olympic Ferries of Greece and renamed AMBASSADOR in 1993, but was re-sold within a year to EPA Invest of Limassol, renamed AMBASSADOR II, and put onto the charter market. Over the next three years she undertook a number of charters in the Mediterranean and Baltic Seas. In 1997 she passed to International Shipping Partners of Monrovia and spent almost two years being converted for use as a casino ship by A&P Appledore in England. She began what is likely to be the last phase of her career as a casino ship for Sterling Casino Lines in June 1999.

STF A F CHAPMAN

The Company STF A F Chapman is a hostel ship in Stockholm.

Address Flaggmansvagen 8, 11149 Stockholm, Sweden

Telephone +46 8 463 2266 **Fax** +46 8 611 7155

Website stfchapman.com

Area operated Hostel ship in Stockholm

A F CHAPMAN	‡1425t	1888		136p		71.1m	11.4m	3.7m	SW

A F CHAPMAN was built by the Whitehaven Shipbuilding Company (yard number 65) in Whitehaven, England as the DUNBOYNE for Charles E Martin & Co of Dublin, Ireland. In 1915 she was renamed G D KENNEDY by Norwegian owners and took her current name in 1923 when she was acquired by Swedish owners. During the Second World War she served as a barracks in Stockholm and was acquired by the City of Stockholm in 1947. She served as a youth hostel in Stockholm from about 1949. The ship will be closed for renovation from autumn 2005.

STRATSRAAD LEHMKUHL

The Company Stratsraad Lehmkuhl is a Norwegian sail training ship operator.

Address Slottsgaten 1, 5003 Bergen, Norway

Telephone +47 55 30 17 00 **Fax** +47 55 30 17 01

Area operated Norway

STRATSRAAD LEHMKUHL	1516t	1914	10.0k	SD2		84.6m	12.6m	5.2m	NO

STRATSRAAD LEHMKUHL was built by Schiffswerke u Maschin Joh. C Tecklenborg (yard number 263) at Bremerhaven, Germany as the GROSSHERZOG FRIEDRICH AUGUST.

SULPICIO LINES

The Company Sulpicio Lines was established in 1973 by Mr Go Guioc So, commonly known as Don Sulpicio Go. The company currently also operates a number of smaller passenger ferries, ro-ro ferries and cargo ships.

Chairman Enrique S Go

Address Don Sulpicio Go Building, Sulpicio Go Street, Reclamation Area, Cebu City, Philippines

Telephone +63 32 232 5361

Website www.sulpiciolines.com

Area operated Inter island services within the Philippines

DIPOLOG PRINCESS	‡3786t	1969	18.5k	D1	b		d	c	111.2m	15.2m	5.5m	PH
PRINCESS OF THE CARIBBEAN	‡3552t	1979	20.8k	D2	1041b		d	c	110.5m	15.2m	4.8m	PH

DIPOLOG PRINCESS was built by Onomichi Zosen KK (yard number 210) at Onomichi, Japan as the TOKYO MARU. She became the DON EUSEBIO in 1978 and passed to her current owner in 1989, when she was renamed DIPOLOG PRINCESS. She is used in the domestic trades around the Philippine Archipelago.

PRINCESS OF THE CARIBBEAN was built by Mitsubishi Heavy Industries (yard number 802) at Shimonoseki, Japan as the OGASAWA MARU for Ogasawa Kaiun of Japan. She was acquired by Sulpicio Lines and renamed in 1997.

TECHNICAL UNIVERSITY OF ISTANBUL

AKDENIZ	7864t	1955	17.0k	D2	444p		144.3m	18.6m	6.2m	TU

AKDENIZ is the last surviving member of a series of beautifully proportioned coastal passenger cargo ships built for Turkish Maritime Lines in 1955/56 by A G Weser at Bremen (yard number 1293) in Germany. Her initial employment took her from Istanbul to Piraeus, Naples, Genoa, Marseilles and Barcelona. In later years she operated Turkish coastal services and cruises in the Mediterranean Sea and beyond. She was withdrawn from service in 1997 and transferred to the Technical University of Istanbul for use as a cadet ship for the Turkish Maritime Academy.

St Tropez Casino Line's **St Tropez** at Port Everglades *(Andrew Kilk)*

Sterling Casino Line's **Ambassador II** at Port Canaveral *(Theodore W Scull)*

Technical University of Istanbul's **Akdeniz** at Izmir when in service with Turkish Maritime Lines *(Theodore W Scull)*

Turkish Maritime Lines' **Mavi Marmara** in the Bosphorus *(William Mayes)*

TEXAS TREASURE CRUISES

The Company Texas Treasure Cruises is a trading name for Corpus Christi Day Cruises.

Address 229 Highway 361 South, Port Aransas, Texas 78373, United States of America

Telephone +1 866 468 5825

Website www.txtreasure.com

Area operated Gambling cruises from Port Aransas, Texas

TEXAS TREASURE	9337t	1968	18.0k	D2	1170p		294c	128.0m	20.0m	5.0m	BA

TEXAS TREASURE was built by Swan Hunter & Tyne Shipbuilders (yard number 2029) at Wallsend on Tyne in England as the ST GEORGE for the Harwich to Hook of Holland service of British Rail Sealink. Following the arrival of the ST NICHOLAS in 1983, she was laid up and in the following year was sold to the Greek Ventouris Group and became the PATRA EXPRESS. Later, she was the intended ship for new operator British Iberian Line and was to have been renamed as the MAIDEN CASTLE, but in the event she was sold by her owner to Sea Escape Cruises instead and renamed SCANDINAVIA SKY II, and later SCANDINAVIAN DAWN. In 1996 she was renamed as the DISCOVERY DAWN, becoming the ISLAND DAWN in 1998. Her current name first appeared in 2003 when her current owner acquired her.

TITAN CRUISE LINES

The Company Titan Cruise Lines began operating the gambling ship OCEAN JEWEL OF ST PETERSBURG in July 2004.

President Howard Steffes

Address 100 1st Avenue South, Box 2006, St Petersburg, Florida 33701, United States of America

Telephone +1 727 287 1600

Website www.oceanjewel.com

Area operated Gambling cruises from St Petersburg, Florida, USA

OCEAN JEWEL OF ST PETERSBURG	12602t	1982	18.0k	D2	1010p			136.6m	21.0m	5.6m	SV

OCEAN JEWEL OF ST PETERSBURG was built as the MIKHAIL SUZLOV by Stocznia Szczecinska (yard number B492/04) at Szczecin, one of a series of ships built for the Black Sea Shipping Company. She was laid down as the VASILIY SOLOVYEV SEDOY. In 1989 she was renamed PYOTR PERVVY for conversion for use as an eye hospital. In 1997 she was renamed as the PETR PERVVY. In 2001 she became the OCEAN EMPRESS for Oasis Shipmanagement. She was acquired by her current owner in 2003 and renamed OCEAN JEWEL OF ST PETERSBURG.

TURKISH MARITIME LINES

The Company Turkiye Denizcilik Isletmeleri (Turkish Navigation Management), a company whose origins, through its constituent companies, can be traced as far back as 1843, generally referred to as Turkish Maritime Lines is the Turkish State passenger shipping company controlling around 120 ships, most of which are ferries operating on local services within Turkey, but with some Turkish coastal services and, until recently, international voyages. The MAVI MARMARA and two car ferries the TEKIRDAG and the BANDIRMA are the last remaining middle distance passenger vessels of this once mighty Mediterranean operator, whose routes have now dwindled to almost nothing. The operating company for these three ships is TDI Deniz Yollari Isletmesi (TDI Maritime Lines Management) and it is likely that these vessels and routes will be sold off in the near future.

Address Istanbul Acentesi, Rihtim Caddesi, 80120 Karakoy, Istanbul, Turkey

Telephone +90 212 1515000 **Fax** +90 212 2495391

Website www.tdi.com.tr

Area operated Passenger services within the Black Sea and the Sea of Marmara

MAVI MARMARA	4142t	1994	15.0k	D2	1500p	1500p	c	93.0m	15.8m	5.5m	TU

MAVI MARMARA was built by Turkiye Gemi Sanayii A.S. (yard number 302) at the Halic (Golden Horn) shipyard in Istanbul, Turkey for the Turkish Maritime Lines Group and launched as the BEYDAGI. Her current name translates as Blue Marmara, a reference to one of the seas through which she operates.

UKRAINE MARINE ECOLOGY RESEARCH CENTRE

The Company The Ukraine Marine Ecology Research Centre is a Government of the Republic of Ukraine owned organisation, established in 1994.

Address Frantsuzskiy Bulvar 89, 270009 Odessa, Ukraine

Telephone +380 482 636622 **Fax** +380 482 636741

Area operated Ukraine ports to Istanbul

SEVASTOPOL-I	2996t	1968	16.0k	D2	100p	100p	c	97.1m	13.8m	5.2m	UR

SEVASTOPOL-I was built by Stocznia Szczecinska (yard number B88/02) at Szczecin, Poland as the MUSSON for the Government of Russia's Hydrometeorological Research Institute. She passed to Ukraine Marine Ecology and appears to operate a passenger and cargo service between Ukraine and Istanbul, Turkey. Her sister ship, the PASSAT may or may not carry passengers, but appears to operate cargo sailings from time to time around the Black Sea. A third ship of this type is the BRIZ.

UNIVERSAL ENTERPRISES

The Company Universal Enterprises is a Maldives registered hotel and leisure group.

Address Male, Republic of Maldives

Telephone +960 323080

Area operated Moored as a static live-aboard diving ship off Kandholhudhoo Island, Maldives

ISLAND EXPLORER	2623t	1964	14.0k	D1	132p	132p	58c	87.4m	13.3m	4.6m	MV

ISLAND EXPLORER was built by Akers Mek. Verksted (yard number 550) in Oslo, Norway as the Hurtigruten ship NORDNORGE for OVDS. She was sold in 1996 and briefly became the WORLD LINK before joining her current owner as the ISLAND EXPLORER later that year. Initially she operated 7-day cruises in the Maldives, but has recently been used as a static diving ship.

UNKNOWN OPERATOR – CHINA

Area operated Static in Tianjin, China

ORIENT PRINCESS	10298t	1967	21.5k	D2	301p	488p	240c	150.3m	21.0m	6.6m	PA

ORIENT PRINCESS was built by Chantiers de l'Atlantique (yard number N23) at St Nazaire, France as the passenger cargo ship YAO HUA for the China Ocean Shipping Co of Guangzhou. Initially used on the trade between China and East Africa, she was converted into a cruise ship in the late 1970s and often chartered to US-based cruise operators. In 1986 she was sold to Hong Kong-based buyers, Main Fortune Ltd, and used for overnight casino cruises out of Hong Kong as the ORIENT PRINCESS. These continued until 2002, when the vessel was auctioned in Guangzhou for unpaid crew wages. The ship was then sold to Chinese interests who plan to use her as a static attraction in Tianjin

UNKNOWN OPERATOR – FAR EAST

Area operated Gambling cruises from Hong Kong or Taiwan

ODYSSEUS	9821t	1962	17.0k	D2	448p	486p	190c	145.7m	18.5m	5.5m	GR

ODYSSEUS, completed in 1962 for Companhia Nacional De Navegacao Costeira of Brazil by Soc. Espanola de Construccion Naval (yard number 104) at Bilbao, Spain, the PRINCESA ISABEL entered service as a two-class vessel on the Brazilian coast. By 1969, following the financial difficulties of her owner and the subsequent merger of that company with Lloyd Brasiliero she was sold to the Dominion Far East Line of Hong Kong and towed to the River Clyde in Scotland for refitting by Barclay, Curle & Company. As the MARCO POLO she began cruising to the Far East from Australia in June 1970. In 1978 she was sold to a company associated with the Greek Kavounides family and as the AQUAMARINE proceeded to Greece for a further refit, following which she returned to the Far East to offer cruises from Hong Kong to China and Japan. This proved unsuccessful and she was eventually auctioned, with her mortgage holder, the Commercial Bank of Greece acquiring her. After seven years of lay up, during which auctions and charter attempts had failed, she was acquired by Epirotiki Lines and renamed as the ODYSSEUS. On the merger of that company with Sun Line Cruises she passed into the new Royal Olympic Cruises fleet. A subsequent charter to Legend Cruises as the JOY WAVE proved to be unsuccessful, and so she remained in the ROC fleet. She was sold at auction in April 2005 following the collapse of Royal Olympic Cruises. In Greek Mythology Odysseus was the son of Laertes and was ruler of the Kingdom of Ithaca. Homer's Odyssey recounts the wanderings of Odysseus after the Trojan War.

UNKNOWN OPERATOR – GEORGIA

Area operated Voyages from Georgian ports to Istanbul

VICTORIA		3435t	1962	14.5k	D2	140p	230p		c	101.5m	14.6m	3.8m	GE

VICTORIA was built by Sudostroitelnyy Zavod im A Zhdanov (yard number 691) in Leningrad, Russia as the BUKOVINA, one of a series of ten attractive little ships built for various Russian owners between 1959 and 1963. The series created the first Soviet-built sea-going passenger ships since 1932. The BUKOVINA began service with the Northern Shipping Company of Archangel, although many of her sisters operated in what is now her home territory of the Black Sea. In later life she moved through a variety of owners and managers before changing her name to CROWN in 2001 while in the ownership of UTA Shipping and Trading and moving to the somewhat unlikely flag of Cambodia. In recent years she has operated as the VICTORIA in the Black Sea and currently flies the Georgian flag.

UNKNOWN OPERATOR – NORWAY

Area operated Previously a static restaurant ship in Oslo

HAKON JARL		2173t	1952							80.8m	12.2m	4.5m	NO

HAKON JARL was built by Aalborg Vaerft (yard number 93) at Aalborg in Denmark as the Hurtigruten ship HAKON JARL. In 1983 she was briefly renamed HAKON GAMLE, but then reverted to her original name. She was renamed CHRISTIAN V in 1992, then DIAMOND PRINCESS in 1997 before reverting to her original name in 2004. She was last known operating as a static restaurant ship.

WIDE ASIA

The Company Wide Asia Ltd is a Hong Kong company managing gambling cruise ships operating from Hong Kong.

Address Unit 1101 11/F Office Tower, The Harbour Front, 18-22 Tak Fung Street, Hunghom, Kowloon, Hong Kong

Telephone +852 2739 1346 **Fax** +852 2311 7400

Website www.neptune.com.hk

Area operated Gambling cruises from Hong Kong

CT NEPTUNE		15791t	1976	21.0k	D2	650p	775p	200c	156.3m	21.8m	5.9m	PA

CT NEPTUNE was built by Wartsila (yard number 1223) at Turku, Finland as the Russian cruise ferry KARELIYA. She was one of a class of five similar vessels and operated for many years under charter to London-based CTC cruises, also under the name LEONID BREZHNEV. After the break up of the Soviet Union she was renamed as the KARELIYA by the Black Sea Shipping Company. In 1998 she was sold to Kaalbye Shipping and renamed OLVIA. She was chartered to various cruise operators, and later operated for Peaceboat. She was sold to Wide Asia in early 2005, and entered the Hong Kong casino cruise trade in April as the CT NEPTUNE.

WONINGSTICHTING ROCHDALE

The Company Woningstichting Rochdale operates a floating student hostel in Amsterdam, The Netherlands.

Address Bos en Lommerplein 303, 1055 RW Amsterdam, The Netherlands

Website www.rochdale.nl

Area operated Hostel in Amsterdam

ROCHDALE 1		7662t	1977	18.9k	D2				121.5m	17.5m	4.5m	CY

ROCHDALE 1 was built by Dubigeon-Normandie (yard number 144) at Nantes, France as the AYVAZOVSKIY for the Soviet Danube Shipping Company of Ismail, for service in the Black Sea between Ismail and Istanbul, and as a cruise ship. In 1992 her owners were re-styled as the Ukraina Danube Shipping Company. In 1996 she was renamed the KARINA for charter to the German tour operator Phoenix Reisen. She became the PRIMEXPRESS ISLAND, a Cyprus based casino ship in 2000 and was renamed ROCHDALE 1 in 2003 when acquired by her current owner.

China Sea Discovery (Paul Mason)

Mabuhay Sunshine (Jonathan Boonzaier)

the **leading** *guide to the cruise industry*

section 3

Passenger Ships not currently in service

CAPE COD LIGHT (4,954 gross tons/ 2005) was built by Atlantic Marine (yard number 4243) at Jacksonville, Florida, USA for American Classic Voyages. That group declared bankruptcy in 2001 and the ship may never have actually been completed.

CAPE MAY LIGHT (4,954 gross tons/ 2001) was built by Atlantic Marine (yard number 4242) at Jacksonville, Florida, USA for American Classic Voyages. That group declared bankruptcy in 2001 and the ship was not delivered.

CARIB VACATIONER (‡2,430 gross tons/ 1971) was built by De Merwede (yard number 601) at Hardinxveld in The Netherlands as the KIELER FORDE. She became the NASSAU in 1972, being slightly renamed as NASSAU I in 1978. Two years later she became NASSAU again. From 1982 to 1986 she operated as the very budget cruise ship VACATIONER. She was sold in 1986 and renamed CARIBIC VACATIONER. It appears that she may have been laid up since 1987.

CARIBIC STAR (5,113 gross tons/ 1968) was built as the Spanish car and passenger ferry VICENTE PUCHOL by Union Naval de Levante at Valencia, Spain. She was delivered to Compania Trasmediterranea in December 1968. In 1987 she was sold to Attica Shipping of Greece and renamed ARCADIA. She appears to have been renamed ANGELINA LAURO for a single season in 1990, but reverted to ARCADIA during the following year. In 1997 she passed to Golden Sun Cruises of Greece without a change of name, but was re-acquired by Attica Shipping in 2000. In 2001 she was chartered to Great Lakes Cruises, and following a voyage to the Great Lakes from Europe, her charterers encountered difficulties and were forced to abandon their programme of cruises in the lakes. She was laid up in Montreal for 15 months before being sold at auction to Anaconda Maritime. She was renamed CARIBIC STAR and was to have been chartered to Megawest Cruises of Australia in 2004 for Pacific cruising as the TROPICAL ISLANDER, but that transaction failed to materialise. It appears that she may be destined for World Yacht Club as a condominium ship, but this is still unconfirmed, as was the suggestion that she would go to Royal African Cruises.

CHINA SEA DISCOVERY (24,799 gross tons/ 1956) was built by John Brown & Co (yard number 699) in Glasgow, Scotland as the Cunard transatlantic liner CARINTHIA. In 1968 she was sold to Sitmar Lines and renamed FAIRLAND. She was later rebuilt as the cruise ship FAIRSEA and used on US-based cruises. In 1988 the ship renamed FAIR PRINCESS when Sitmar was sold to Princess Cruises. After a brief spell with P&O Cruises in Australia, the ship was sold to Hong Kong-based China Sea Cruises in 2000. Renamed CHINA SEA DISCOVERY, the ship attempted to operate gambling cruises out of China, Hong Kong and Taiwan, but none of these attempts proved successful. The ship has been laid up under arrest in Kaoshiung for the past two years and is likely soon to be sold for scrap.

GENERAL EDWIN D PATRICK (19,969 gross tons/ 1945) was built by the Bethlehem Alameda shipyard (yard number 9505) at Alameda, USA as the troopship ADMIRAL C F HUGHES. She was renamed GENERAL EDWIN D PATRICK in 1946. She has been laid up since 1968.

GENERAL JOHN POPE (17,833 gross tons/ 1943) was built by the Federal Shipbuilding & Drydock Company (yard number 268) at Kearny, New Jersey, USA as a troopship, one of a series of nine similar vessels. She was designed to carry up to 5,000 troops. She was laid up in 1969.

GREEN COAST (4,992 gross tons/ 1960) was built by VEB Mathias Thesen Werft (yard number 107) at Wismar in Germany as the LITVA for the Black Sea Shipping Company of the USSR. She was one of a series of about 18 well-proportioned small passenger liners that saw service throughout the Soviet sphere of influence and beyond. In 1988 she passed to Brave Commander SA of San Lorenzo and was renamed BOGUCHAR. In 1994 she was acquired by Fu Jian Shipping Company of China, and renamed FU JIAN. She was registered under her current name for Green Coast Shipping in 2000. It is thought that she is laid up in Angola.

LINNEA (2,127 gross tons/ 1964) was built by Frederikshavn Vaerft og Tordok (yard number 238) at Frederikshavn, Denmark as the KUNUNGUAK for the Royal Greenland Trade Department in Copenhagen. She became the OVIK SAGA in 1991 and took her current name in 1995. She is thought to be laid up in Thailand.

MABUHAY SUNSHINE (7,762 gross tons/ 1983) was built for Oshima Unyu KK by Mitsubishi Heavy Industries (yard number 858) at Shimonoseki in Japan as the cruise ship SUNSHINE FUJI for domestic Japanese cruises. She was sold to Mabuhay Holiday Cruises of the Philippines in 1995 and rebuilt as the MABUHAY SUNSHINE, re-entering service on cruises out of Manila in 1996. The venture did not prove successful and the ship has been laid up for sale in Cebu since 1998.

MARIA KOSMAS (3,344 gross tons/ 1977) was built by the Williamstown Naval Dockyard, Williamstown, Victoria, Australia as the oceanographic research vessel HMAS COOK. Following grounding in 1990 she was withdrawn from service. In 1993 she was sold to Greek interests and renamed MARIA KOSMAS for conversion to a cruise ship. She was laid up again in 1996 and in 2002 towed to Dubai. Her current use and whereabouts are unknown.

ODESSA (11,889 gross tons/ 1974) was laid down in 1970 by Vickers Shipbuilding (yard number 1085) at Barrow-in-Furness in England's Lake District as the COPENHAGEN for K/S Nordline of Copenhagen. She was advertised for sale partway through her construction following a disagreement between her builders and her future owner over the escalating costs. That matter was resolved and the building work continued. It was now planned to name her PRINS HENRIK AF DANMARK. The ship was launched without being named, and then towed to Newcastle upon Tyne for completion by Swan Hunter Shipbuilders. She was put up for sale before delivery in 1974, and during the following year she was acquired by the Black Sea Shipping Company and named ODESSA. She cruised for Blasco under the Russian and later the Ukrainian flag, but when her owners fell into financial difficulties the ship was arrested in 1995 and remained laid up in Naples until recently. She is now owned by Bowline Maritime and is undergoing refurbishment in Ukraine for a return to service in the near future.

OLYMPIA I (5,119 gross tons/ 1953) was built by Ansaldo at Livorno, Italy (yard number 1475) as the ACHILLEUS for the Greek ship owner Nomikos Lines. In 1968 she was acquired by Kavounides (Hellenic Cruises) and renamed as the ORION. Following the failure of that company she was laid up in 1987, and remained in that state for eight years. She was partially converted for use as a day cruise ship in 1995 and renamed THOMAS II. She came under the control of Royal Olympic Cruises in 1997 and was renamed OLYMPIA I. She remains in lay up in Eleusis Bay, Greece. Olympia was the site of the original Olympic Games, begun in 776 BC and dedicated to the Olympian Gods.

PATRIOT STATE (11,188 gross tons/ 1964) was built by Bethlehem Steel Company (yard number 4602) at Sparrows Point, USA as the SANTA MERCEDES for Grace Line of New York. She operated on the service from New York around South America. In 1983 she passed to the US Maritime Commission and was converted for use as a training ship for the Massachusetts Marine Academy. She is currently laid up in the James River.

PHILIPPINE DREAM (9,318 gross tons/ 1966) was built by Uraga Heavy Industries (yard number 885) at Yokosuka in Japan for the Japan National Railways as the train ferry TOWADA MARU. She was sold to the Japan Sea Passenger Co in 1989 and extensively rebuilt as the cruise ship JAPANESE DREAM for overnight cruises between Kobe and Yokohama. The ship proved unsuccessful and was laid up in January 1992. She was then sold to Philippine owners who used her as a hotel and casino in Cebu under the name PHILIPPINE DREAM. The hotel closed down several years ago and the ship remains laid up in a quagmire of legal problems. It is expected she will be sold for scrap as soon as these problems are solved.

REGENT SKY (c50,000 gross tons/ not completed) was laid down in 1979 by Stocznia in Komuny Paryskiej (yard number B494/04) in Gdynia, Poland as the STENA BALTICA, the final member of a class of four large overnight ferries for Stena Line of Gothenburg. Ten years later she was still incomplete and the order for the final two ships was cancelled. The hull was taken to the Avlis Shipyard at Chalkis in Greece for completion as the REGENT SKY for Regency Cruises. Regency Cruises later collapsed and the shipyard now owns what there is of the ship. It is unlikely that this vessel will ever be completed.

SAVANNAH (13,599 gross tons/ 1961) was built for the United States Department of Commerce by the New York Shipbuilding Corporation (yard number 529) at Camden, New Jersey, USA as the world's first nuclear powered merchant ship. Following a series of demonstration and experimental voyages she entered commercial service in 1964 mainly between US ports and the Mediterranean. From 1965 she ceased to carry passengers. In 1972 she was laid up at Savannah. From 1981 to 1994 she was a museum ship at Charleston, South Carolina but has subsequently been laid up in the James River.

SCANDINAVIA (5,209 gross tons/ 1927) was built by Gotaverken in Gothenburg as the cruise ship STELLA POLARIS for the Bergen Line. Following war use by the Germans as an officers' accommodation ship, she passed to Sweden's Clipper Line in 1949. She was sold in 1969 to Japanese interests, renamed SCANDINAVIA and converted for use as a Hotel at Izu, Japan. It appears that the ship is no longer in use and may be for sale.

STATE (13,319 gross tons/ 1952) was built by the New York Shipbuilding Corporation (yard number 485) at Camden, New Jersey, USA. She was laid down for American President Lines as the PRESIDENT JACKSON, but was completed as the troopship BARRETT. In 1973 she was renamed EMPIRE STATE V when she became a training ship for the New York Maritime Academy. In 1978 her name was shortened to EMPIRE STATE, and it was further shortened in 1990 when she became the STATE. She is laid up in the James River.

WALRUS (15,343 gross tons/ 1990) was built by Union Naval de Levante (yard number 185) at Valencia, Spain for Crown Cruise Lines, a subsidiary of Effjohn Intl. The ship operated cruises in the Caribbean and South Pacific until being chartered to Singaporean interests for use as the casino cruise ship NAUTICAN in 1995. The Singaporean authorities banished the ship from its waters a few months later, and it moved up to Hong Kong, where it operated as the WALRUS until replaced by the CT NEPTUNE in April 2005. The ship has been returned to Effjohn, and is laid up awaiting new employment.

Odessa *(Douglas Cromby)*

Walrus *(Andrew Kilk)*

WORLD DISCOVERER (6,072 gross tons/ 1989) was built by Rauma Repola (yard number 304) at Rauma, Finland as the DELFIN CLIPPER for Delfin Cruises. Following the failure of Delfin she was repossessed by her builder and later renamed SALLY CLIPPER in 1990 for a charter to Sally Line for Baltic cruising. In 1992 she became the BALTIC CLIPPER and later that year was renamed again, becoming the DELFIN STAR for gambling cruises from Hong Kong and Singapore. She was sold to the Samsung Shipyard in South Korea in 1997 and renamed DREAM 21. She was subsequently renamed WORLD DISCOVERER in 2002 when sold to Discoverer Reederie (the owner of Society Expeditions). Society Expeditions ceased trading in June 2004. She was subsequently repossessed by the Sembawang Shipyard, which was owed substantial sums in respect of her conversion, and remains laid up in Singapore.

XANADU 2 (2,496 gross tons/ 1955) was built by Blohm & Voss (yard number 786) in Hamburg, Germany as the WAPPEN VON HAMBURG for the day cruise business from Hamburg and Cuxhaven to Helgoland and Hornum. She carried 1600 passengers as built. In 1960 she was sold to Nomikos Lines of Greece, who had her refitted to carry 186 cruise passengers. She was renamed as the DELOS for cruising in the Greek Islands. In 1967 Westours acquired her for use as the Alaskan cruise ship POLAR STAR. In 1970 she passed to subsidiary company West Lines as the PACIFIC STAR. Only two years later she was sold to Xanadu Cruises and renamed as the XANADU. Eventually unable to compete, she was laid up in Vancouver in 1977. She was sold in the mid 1980's to become the exhibition and trade fair ship EXPEX. She moved to lay up off Los Angeles, but little was done to convert her for her new role. In 1991 she was acquired by Friendships, and renamed FAITHFUL for conversion to a mission ship. That never materialised and she was eventually seized and sold to James Mitchell, who intended to use her as a hospital ship, for which she was renamed XANADU 2. She remains laid up.

The following vessels, all former Russian passenger ships have remained elusive as this book went to press and it is possible that some or all of them have now been scrapped.

BAYKAL (5230 gross tons/ 1962) built for the Far East Shipping Company and last reported in Vladivostok.

BETA (3219 gross tons/ 1962) built as the AFGHANISTAN and last reported laid up in Novorossiysk.

NIKOLAYEVSK (5230 gross tons/ 1962) last reported laid up in Sochi.

SOUNDS OF ORIENTS (5230 gross tons/ 1961) built as the KHABAROVSK and last reported at Vladivostok.

WANG FU (3219 gross tons/ 1961) built as the TADZHIKISTAN and last reported laid up in China.

the **leading** guide to the cruise industry

section 4 - late news

Coco Explorer Cruises' COCO EXPLORER 1 was withdrawn from service towards the end of July 2005 and offered for sale. She will be replaced by the COCO EXPLORER 2, which is currently listed in the 'Ships not currently in service' section as the CARIBIC STAR.

Ocean Five's ROYAL PACIFIC caught fire and capsized while refitting in Taiwan.

Mediterranean Shipping Cruises is reported to have signed a letter of intent for Alstom Chantiers de l'Atlantique to build two 100,000-ton+ ships.

Celebrity Cruises has signed a letter of intent for Jos. L Meyer to build one 100,000- ton+ ship, with an option on a second.

Pullmanturs has purchased the R SIX and renamed her BLUE DREAM. She had previously been marketed as the BLUE STAR, while her sister, the R FIVE (now Oceania Cruises NAUTICA) was previously marketed as the BLUE DREAM.

Costa Line's COSTA MARINA will switch from the German Market to the French Market, being replaced by the slightly larger COSTA ALLEGRA.

Louis Cruise Lines' is reported to have acquired the AEGEAN 1 from Golden Star Cruises. No new name has been announced.

The ODYSSEUS, listed in 'Passenger Ships in other roles' under Unknown Operator – Far East is owned by Mantovana Holding Limited, a British Virgin Islands company, and has been renamed LUCKY STAR.

The ORIANA (page 180) never recovered from her partial sinking and was sold to Chinese shipbreakers.

The VICTORIA, listed in 'Passenger Ships in other roles' under Unknown Operator – Georgia is now owned by Victoria Ship Management, a Ukraine registered company. The ship is now registered in St Kitts & Nevis and is operated by Poseidon Limited.

Siam Cruise Line ceased trading at the end of July and the ANDAMAN PRINCESS was laid up.

the **leading** *guide to the cruise industry*
section 5 - some recent departures

The **Albatros** was built for Cunard Line as the **Sylvania** (*William Mayes*)

Costa Line's **Eugenio C** saw final service as **The Big Red Boat II** (*William Mayes*)

Canadian Pacific's **Empress of Canada** saw final service as the **Apollon** *(William Mayes Collection)*

The **Stella Solaris** was built as the **Cambodge** *(William Mayes)*

Epirotiki's **Orpheus** was built as the Irish Sea ferry **Munster** *(William Mayes Collection)*

The **Windsor Castle** spent many years laid up in Greece as the **Margarita L** *(William Mayes)*

Holland America's **Volendam** saw final service as the **Universe** (*William Mayes Collection*)

The **Wind Song** was scuttled after an engine room fire *(Andrew Kilk)*

Shaw Savill's **Southern Cross** survived for almost 50 years in a variety of roles *(William Mayes Collection)*

The **Taras Shevchenko** kept her original name until her final voyage *(Theodore W Scull)*

The *La Palma* was built as the *Ferdinand de Lesseps* *(Andrew Kilk)*

The *Fedor Shalyapin* was built for Cunard Line as the *Ivernia* *(William Mayes)*

The **Sunward** saw final service as **The Empress** *(William Mayes Collection)*

The **Meridian** was built for Lloyd Triestino as the **Galileo Galilei** *(Theodore W Scull)*

the **leading** *guide to the cruise industry*
section 6 -bibliography

Books

Bent, Mike *Coastal Express* Conway Maritime Press 1987

Brogen, Klas (ed) *Guide 05*, Shippax Information 2005

Brogen, Klas (ed) *Statistics 05* Shippax Information 2005

Brogen, Klas (ed) *Designs (various editions)* Shippax Information

Cartwright, Roger and Harvey, Clive *Cruise Britannia* Tempus Publishing 2004

Cooke, Anthony *Emigrant Ships* Carmania Press

Cooke, Anthony *Liners and Cruise Ships- Some notable smaller vessels* Carmania Press 1996

Cooke, Anthony *Liners and Cruise Ships 2- Some notable smaller vessels* Carmania Press 2000

Cooke, Anthony *Liners and Cruise Ships 3- Further notable smaller vessels* Carmania Press 2003

Cowsill, Miles, Hendy, John and Mayes, William *P&O The Fleet* Ferry Publications 2000

Dickinson, Bob and Vladimir, Andy *Selling the Sea* John Wiley & Sons 1997

Dunn, Laurence *Mediterranean Shipping* Carmania Press 1999

Dunn, Laurence *Passenger Liners* Adlard Coles 1965

Elisio, Maurizio and Piccione, Paolo *The Costa Liners* Carmania Press 1997

Hackmann, Peter (ed) *Passenger Ships for Indonesia* Meyer Werft 2002

Harvey, William J *Stena 1939-1989* Stena 1989

Haws, Duncan *Merchant Fleets 25* TCL Publications 1993

Hornsby, David *Ocean Ships 13th Edition*, Ian Allan 2004

Kludas, Arnold *Great Passenger Ships of the World Today*, Patrick Stephens 1992

Kludas, Arnold, Heine, Frank and Lose, Frank *Die Grossen Passagierschiffe der Welt* Koehler 2002

Latimer, David W *Passenger Ships of the 20th Century – An illustrated Encyclopaedia* Colourpoint 2002

Lloyds Cruise Yearbook, Informa Publishing 2004

May, John and Mayes, William *Ferries 2004 Southern Europe* Overview Press 2004

McCart, Neil *Passenger Ships of the Orient Line* Patrick Stephen 1987

Miller, William H *The Cruise Ships* Conway Maritime Press 1988

Miller, William H *The Chandris Liners* Carmania Press 1993

Miller, William H *Passenger Liners Italian Style* Carmania Press 1996

Miller, William H *Going Dutch, The Holland America Line Story* Carmania Press 1998

Miller, William H *Passenger Liners French Style* Carmania Press 2001

Peter, Bruce *Passenger Liners Scandinavian Style* Carmania Press 2003

Rabson, Stephen and O'Donoghue, Kevin *P&O A Fleet History* The World Ship Society 1987

Rothe, Claus *Die Deutschen Traumschiffe* Koehler 1997

Rothe, Claus *Welt der Passagierschiffe unter Hammer und Sichel* DSV-Verlag 1994

de Schipper, A and Janse, J *Mediterranean Shipping Company-Over 30 years of success* MSC 2003

Scull, Theodore W *100 Best Cruise Vacations* Globe Perquot 2004

Vapalahti, Hannu *Finnish Passenger Ships 1960-1996 Volumes 1 & 2* Judicor 1996

Ward, Douglas *Ocean Cruising & Cruise Ships 2005* Berlitz 2005

Widdows, Nick *Ferries 2003 British Isles and Northern Europe* Ferry Publications 2003

Williams, David *Cruise Ships* Ian Allan 2001

Wilson, E A *Soviet Passenger Ships 1917-1977* The World Ship Society 1978

Worker, Colin *The World's Passenger Ships* Ian Allan 1967

Periodicals

Cruise & Ferry Info Shippax Information

Fairplay Lloyds Register-Fairplay

Lloyds Cruise International, Informa Publishing

Lloyds List Informa Publishing

Marine News, The World Ship Society

Sea Lines, The Ocean Liner Society

Ships in Focus Record Ships in Focus Publications

Steamboat Bill The Steamship Historical Society of America

Other sources

Company brochures

Company websites

Linerslist, a membership site on Yahoo Groups

Sea Web – the Internet Ships Register from Lloyds Register-Fairplay

Among the titles listed above there are a surprising number of conflicts in what ought to be factual information. It is therefore possible that some errors have crept into this book. I would appreciate notification of any information that might be suspect, so that the next edition will be an even more accurate portrayal of the cruise ships of the world. william.mayes@overviewpress.co.uk

the **leading** *guide to the cruise industry*

section 7 -index of companies

the **leading** *guide to the cruise industry*

section 8 -index of former names

Former Name	Current Name
ACHILLEUS	OLYMPIA I
ADMIRAL C F HUGHES	GENERAL EDWIN D PATRICK
ADMIRAL LAZAREV	IGOR FARKHUTDINOV
ADONIA	SEA PRINCESS
AEGEAN DOLPHIN	AEGEAN 1
AFGHANISTAN	BETA
AIDA	AIDACARA
AKADEMIK ALEKSEY KRYLOV	KIYEV
AKADEMIK NICOLAY PILYU	SEVEN SEAS NAVIGATOR
AKADEMIK SHULEYKIN	POLYARNYY PIONER
AKADEMIK VERNADSKIY	GLORIYA
AKROTIRI EXPRESS	OCEAN MONARCH
ALEKSANDR PUSHKIN	MARCO POLO
ALEXANDRA	COSTA ALLEGRA
ALKYON	AEGEAN 1
ALLA TARASOVA	CLIPPER ADVENTURER
AMBASSADOR	AMBASSADOR II
AMERICA	SEA VOYAGER
AMERICANA	GOLDEN TRADE
AMETISTA	JI MEI
ANAR	PRINCESS DANAE
ANCERVILLE	MINGHUA
ANGELINA LAURO	CARIBIC STAR
ANGELITA	SEA CLOUD
ANNA NERY	SALAMIS GLORY
ANNIE JOHNSON	COSTA ALLEGRA
ANTARNA	SEA CLOUD
ANTONIO LAZARO	LOGOS II
APOLLO	ANDAMAN PRINCESS
APOLLON	GOLDEN PRINCE
AQUAMARINE	ODYSSEUS
AQUARIUS	ADRIANA
ARCADIA	CARIBIC STAR
ARCADIA	OCEAN VILLAGE
ARGO	LOGOS II
ARGUS	POLYNESIA
ARKADIYA	ENCHANTED CAPRI
ARKONA	ASTORIA
A'ROSA BLU	AIDABLU
ASEAN WORLD	LEISURE WORLD
ASIAN PRINCESS	PHILIPPINES
ASTOR	ASTORIA
ASTRA	ARION
ASTRA I	ARION
ASTRA II	MACAU SUCCESS
ASUKA	AMADEA
ATLANTIC	MELODY
AUGUSTUS	PHILIPPINES
AURORA I	MEGASTAR TAURUS
AURORA II	MEGASTAR ARIES
AWANI DREAM	GRAND VICTORIA

EMPIRE STATE V	STATE	HMAS COOK	MARIA KOSMAS
EMPRESS OF BRITAIN	THE TOPAZ	HMS KILCHERNAN	KRISTINA BRAHE
ENCHANTED SUN	ST TROPEZ	HOMERIC	COSTA EUROPA
ERNEST HEMINGWAY	TURAMA	HOMERIC	OCEAN MAJESTY
EROS	IASON	HOMERIC RENAISSANCE	GRAND VICTORIA
ESTRELLA DO MAR	COCO EXPLORER I	HORIZON	ISLAND STAR
EUROPA	HOLIDAY DREAM	HOTU MATUA	ANTARCTIC DREAM
EUROPEAN STARS	MSC SINFONIA	HUMBER GUARDIAN	TROPIC SUN
EUROPEAN VISION	MSC ARMONIA	HUSSAR	MANDALAY
EUROSUN	WASA QUEEN	HUSSAR	SEA CLOUD
EXPEX	XANADU 2	HYUNDAI KUMGANG	BOUDICCA
EXPLORER II ALEXANDER VON HUMBOLDT		HYUNDAI PONGNAE	OMAR III
EXPLORER STARSHIP	LE DIAMANT	HYUNDAI PUNGAK	DISCOVERY
FABIOLAVILLE	HAI HUA	IBEROSTAR MISTRAL	MISTRAL
FAIR PRINCESS	CHINA SEA DISCOVERY	ILLYRIA II	CALLISTO
FAIRLAND	CHINA SEA DISCOVERY	ILMATAR	PALM BEACH PRINCESS
FAIRSEA	CHINA SEA DISCOVERY	INGRID	AFRICA MERCY
FAIRSKY	PACIFIC SKY	IONIAN HARMONY	CALYPSO
FAITHFUL	XANADU 2	IRENE	COCO EXPLORER I
FANTASY WORLD	LEISURE WORLD	ISLAND ADVENTURE	DISCOVERY
FIESTA MARINA	THE TOPAZ	ISLAND DAWN	TEXAS TREASURE
FINLANDIA	GOLDEN PRINCESS	ISLAND HOLIDAY	ENCHANTED CAPRI
FINNHANSA	PRINCESA MARISSA	ISLAND PRINCESS	DISCOVERY
FINNSTAR	GOLDEN PRINCESS	ISLAND SUN	CORINTHIAN II
FIRDA	DARLI	ISTRA	ARION
FLAMENCO	NEW FLAMENCO	ITALIA	COSTA MARINA
FORCE TIDE	PACIFIC EXPLORER	ITALIA	SAPPHIRE
FRANCA C	DOULOS	ITALIA 1	ATHENA
FRANCE	NORWAY	ITALIA PRIMA	ATHENA
FRANCE II	LEGACY	JALINA	JI MEI
FRANCESCA	THE IRIS	JAPANESE DREAM	PHILIPPINE DREAM
FRANKFURT	ALEXANDER	JASON	IASON
FREE STATE MARINER	MONTEREY	JEAN MERMOZ	SERENADE
FRIDTJOF NANSEN	ATHENA	JIN JIANG	JI MEI
FRONTIER SPIRIT	BREMEN	JOURNEY OF THE SEAS	NAVIGATOR OF THE
FU JIAN	GREEN COAST		SEAS
FUTURE SEAS	EMPRESS OF THE SEAS	JOY WAVE	GOLDEN PRINCESS
FYODOR DOSTOEVSKIY	ASTOR	JOY WAVE	ODYSSEUS
G D KENNEDY	A F CHAPMAN	JUAN MARCH	OCEAN MAJESTY
GANN	SJOKURS	JUBILEE	PACIFIC SUN
GOLDEN ODYSSEY	MACAU SUCCESS	JUGOSLAVIA	HERMES
GOLDEN PRINCESS	BOUDICCA	JUPITER	MIRAGE I
GRAND LATINO	BOUDICCA	KALYPSO	STAR PISCES
GRAND VOYAGER	VOYAGER	KARELIYA	CT NEPTUNE
GREAT SEA	PHILIPPINES	KARINA	ROCHDALE I
GRIPSHOLM	SAGA ROSE	KAZAKHSTAN	ISLAND ADVENTURE
GROSSHERZOG FRIEDRICH AUGUST		KAZAKHSTAN II	DELPHIN
	STRATSRAAD LEHMKUHL	KHABAROVSK	SOUNDS OF ORIENTS
GRUZIA	VAN GOGH	KIELER FORDE	CARIB VACATIONER
GUNES DIL	SAVARONA	KIMA	OMEGA
GUSTAV VASA	LOGOS HOPE	KONSTANTIN SIMONOV	THE IRIS
GWAREK	ROYAL CLIPPER	KOSTER	KRONPRINSESSE MARTHA
HAKON GAMLE	HAKON JARL	KUNGSHOLM	MONA LISA
HAMBURG	MAXIM GORKIY	KUNUNGUAK	LINNEA
HANSEATIC	MAXIM GORKIY	KYPROS STAR	OCEAN MAJESTY
HARALD JARL	ANDREA	LADY DI	MEGASTAR TAURUS
HARDANGERFJORD	DARLI	LADY DIANA	MEGASTAR TAURUS
HARDANGERFJORD I	DARLI	LADY SARAH	MEGASTAR ARIES
HELGOLAND	GALAPAGOS LEGEND	LARVIKSPILEN	GALAPAGOS LEGEND

PEARL	GOLDEN PRINCESS	RENAISSANCE TWO	EASYCRUISEONE
PEARL OF SCANDINAVIA	GOLDEN PRINCESS	RENAISSANCE THREE	GALAPAGOS
PEARL OF SEYCHELLES	FIJI PRINCESS		EXPLORER II
PEREGRINE MARINER	AKADEMIK IOFFE	RENAISSANCE FOUR	CLELIA II
PEREGRINE VOYAGER	AKADEMIK SERGEI	RENAISSANCE FIVE	SPIRIT OF OCEANUS
	VAVILOV	RENAISSANCE SIX	HEBRIDEAN SPIRIT
PETR PERVVY	OCEAN JEWEL OF ST	RENAISSANCE SEVEN	CORINTHIAN II
	PETERSBURG	RENAISSANCE EIGHT	ISLAND SKY
PHAROS	AMAZING GRACE	RESEARCHER	USHUAIA
PILGRIM BELLE	SPIRIT OF 98	RIVAGE MARTINIQUE	FIJI PRINCESS
PILOTO PARDO	ANTARCTIC DREAM	RIVAGES GUADELOUPE	ISLANDER
PIONEER	YANKEE CLIPPER	RIVIERA I	ROYAL PACIFIC
PLATINUM	DISCOVERY	ROMA	DOULOS
POLAR STAR	XANADU 2	ROYAL DREAM	OCEAN PRINCESS
POLARLYS	CARIBBEAN MERCY	ROYAL MAJESTY	NORWEGIAN MAJESTY
PONGNAE	OMAR III	ROYAL ODYSSEY	ALBATROS
PORT MELBOURNE	PRINCESS DANAE	ROYAL PRINCESS	ARTEMIS
PORT SYDNEY	OCEAN MONARCH	ROYAL SEAS	ISLAND ADVENTURE
PRESIDENT	PHILIPPINES	ROYAL VIKING QUEEN	SEABOURN LEGEND
PRIDE OF SAN DIEGO	ST TROPEZ	ROYAL VIKING SEA	ALBATROS
PRIMEXPRESS ISLAND	ROCHDALE I	ROYAL VIKING SKY	BOUDICCA
PRINCE	GOLDEN PRINCE	ROYAL VIKING STAR	BLACK WATCH
PRINCESA ISABEL	ODYSSEUS	ROYAL VIKING SUN	PRINSENDAM
PRINCESA OCEANICA	SAPPHIRE	ROYALE OCEANIC	OCEANIC
PRINCESS ITALIA	SAPPHIRE	RYFYLKE	KRONPRINSESSE MARTHA
PRINCESS MAHSURI	ORANGE MELODY	SAGA PEARL	ALEXANDER VON HUMBOLDT
PRINCESS MAHSURI	SPIRIT OF ADVENTURE	SAGA PEARL	EXPLORER II
PRINCESSAN	PRINCESA MARISSA	SAGAFJORD	SAGA ROSE
PRINS OBERON	AMBASSADOR II	SAGGIT ITTUK	DISKO II
PRINSESSE RAGNHILD	JI MEI	SALLY ALBATROSS	SILJA OPERA
PUTRI BINTANG	AMUSEMENT WORLD	SALLY CARAVELLE	TURAMA
PYOTR PERVVY	OCEAN JEWEL OF ST	SALLY CLIPPER	WORLD DISCOVERER
	PETERSBURG	SAN GIORGIO	ROYAL STAR
QUEEN ANNA MARIA	THE TOPAZ	SANDNES	SJOKURS
QUEEN ODYSSEY	SEABOURN LEGEND	SANTA MARIA DE LA CARIDAD	COCO
QUEEN VICTORIA	ARCADIA		EXPLORER I
R ONE	INSIGNIA	SANTA MERCEDES	PATRIOT STATE
R TWO	REGATTA	SANTA ROSA	THE EMERALD
R THREE	PACIFIC PRINCESS	SAPPHIRE PRINCESS	DIAMOND PRINCESS
R FOUR	TAHITIAN PRINCESS	SCANDINAVIA	ISLAND ESCAPE
R FIVE	NAUTICA	SCANDINAVIA SKY II	TEXAS TREASURE
R SIX	R6 BLUE STAR	SCANDINAVIAN DAWN	TEXAS TREASURE
R SEVEN	DELPHIN RENAISSANCE	SCANDINAVICA	MIRAGE I
R EIGHT	MINERVA II	SEA GODDESS I	SEADREAM I
RADISSON DIAMOND	OMAR STAR	SEA GODDESS II	SEADREAM II
RAGNVALD JARL	GANN	SEA LUCK I	INDEPENDENCE
RAINBOW	THE EMERALD	SEA PRINCE	SAPPHIRE
REGENT JEWEL	CALYPSO	SEA PRINCE V	SAPPHIRE
REGENT MOON	COSTA ALLEGRA	SEA PRINCESS	MONA LISA
REGENT RAINBOW	THE EMERALD	SEA VENTURE	PACIFIC
REGENT SPIRIT	SALAMIS GLORY	SEABOURN GODDESS I	SEADREAM I
REGENT SUN	COSTA MARINA	SEABOURN GODDESS II	SEADREAM II
REGINA MARIS	ALEXANDER	SEABOURN SUN	PRINSENDAM
REGINA RENAISSANCE	CORINTHIAN II	SEASPIRIT	SPIRIT OF ENDEAVOUR
REMBRANDT	ROTTERDAM	SEAWARD	SUPERSTAR LIBRA
RENAI I	CORINTHIAN II	SEAWING	PERLA
RENAI II	ISLAND SKY	SEMINOLE EXPRESS	MIRAGE I
RENAISSANCE	GRAND VICTORIA	SHANGRI-LA WORLD	LEISURE WORLD
RENAISSANCE	LEISURE WORLD I	SHEARWATER	POLARIS

the **leading** *guide to the cruise industry*
section 9 -index